BUSINESS AND PRODUCTION FOR GAMES: A GAMEDEV.NET COLLECTION

DREW SIKORA AND JOHN HATTAN

SERIES EDITORS

Course Technology PTR

A part of Cengage Learning

COURSE TECHNOLOGY
CENGAGE Learning

Australia • Brazil • Japan • Korea • Mexico • Singapore • Spain • United Kingdom • United States

COURSE TECHNOLOGY
CENGAGE Learning™

**Business and Production for Games:
A GameDev.net Collection**
Drew Sikora and John Hattan

**Publisher and General Manager, Course
Technology PTR:** Stacy L. Hiquet

Associate Director of Marketing: Sarah Panella

Manager of Editorial Services: Heather Talbot

Marketing Manager: Jordan Casey

Acquisitions Editor: Heather Hurley

Project Editor and Copy Editor: Kim Benbow

Technical Reviewers: Drew Sikora and
John Hattan

Editorial Services Coordinator: Jen Blaney

Interior Layout Tech: Macmillan Publishing
Solutions

Cover Designer: Mike Tanamachi

Indexer: Sharon Hilgenberg

Proofreader: Melba Hopper

For product information and technology assistance, contact us at
Cengage Learning Customer & Sales Support, 1-800-354-9706

For permission to use material from this text or product, submit all
requests online at **www.cengage.com/permissions**
Further permissions questions can be emailed to
permissionrequest@cengage.com

Microsoft, Windows, and Internet Explorer are either registered
trademarks or trademarks of Microsoft Corporation in the United States
and/or other countries.
All other trademarks are the property of their respective owners.

Library of Congress Control Number: 2008930426

ISBN-13: 978-1-59863-809-7

ISBN-10: 1-59863-809-2

Course Technology, a part of Cengage Learning
20 Channel Center Street
Boston, MA 02210
USA

Cengage Learning is a leading provider of customized learning solutions
with office locations around the globe, including Singapore, the United
Kingdom, Australia, Mexico, Brazil, and Japan. Locate your local office at:
international.cengage.com/region

Cengage Learning products are represented in Canada by Nelson
Education, Ltd.

For your lifelong learning solutions, visit **courseptr.com**

Visit our corporate website at **cengage.com**

Printed in Canada
1 2 3 4 5 6 7 11 10 09

To all the members of the GDNet community,
from which this book was ultimately born.

ACKNOWLEDGMENTS

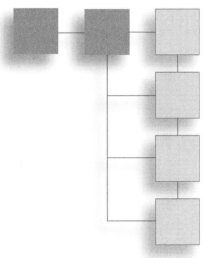

All the contributors listed in the table of contents deserve to be recognized for agreeing to let their works be included in this book. I'd like to extend additional thanks to Otamere, Joshua, Mason, Richard, and Joe (twice over) for taking the time to dust off their old works and take to them with hammer and chisel to produce updated chapters for this book. My undying gratitude goes out to Mona, Dylan, Raymond, Rick, and John for creating completely original works—sometimes under tight deadlines with me constantly hassling them for final drafts. This book would not have been the same without both the updated and original chapters included herein.

I'd like to also thank my co-editor John Hattan, who no doubt took great joy (and pain) in picking apart all my written pieces for this book. While I like to write things as they sound in my head, he definitely has the better grasp of "proper" grammar in regard to words on the page.

Last but not least, this book would never even have been possible without the support of Heather Hurley, Kim Benbow, and the rest of the fine people over at Cengage Learning. Many thanks for making this, my first editing gig, a painless endeavor and leaving me wanting to do more in the future rather than leaving me with clumps of hair in my hands and veins popping out of my forehead.

Drew Sikora

ABOUT THE SERIES EDITORS

Drew Sikora has been active in the games industry since 2001, when he co-founded the NJ North IGDA chapter with Darrell Porcher, which has since grown to become one of the leading IGDA chapters in the world. He's been involved with GameDev.net since 2000, becoming executive producer in 2006 and working hard with his team of awesome people to make GameDev.net a valuable resource for game developers of all trades. Drew has also worked with Game Institute since its conception in 2001, supporting the growing community, managing live seminars on game development topics by experienced industry members and judging the Institute's regular game programming challenges. His past writing credits include three chapters in *Game Design Perspectives* (Charles River Media, 2002) and well over 100 articles and interviews published on GameDev.net covering industry events and game development topics. Since 2008, he's been mentoring students attending the GDC as part of the IGDA's scholarship program. In whatever spare time he has, he likes to program small game projects whenever he gets the urge.

When Drew isn't doing anything industry related, he can be found practicing martial arts, bouncing high on a trampoline or tumbling, doing stunt work, playing his PlayStation3, driving really fast in his car or on his motorcycle, hanging with friends, or musing about something on his blog at www.blade-edge.com.

John Hattan has been working steadily in the casual game space since the TRS-80 days and professionally since 1990. After seeing his small-format games turned down for what ended up being Radio Shack's last store-brand PC, he took them independent, eventually releasing them as a set of discount game packs through a couple of shelf publishers. Following the demise of discount game shelf publishing, he sold his games on the Internet, both as pay-for-play and ad-supported. He continues to work in the casual game space as an independent developer, writing viral games for web portals and widget platforms. The games are always available on his web site, The Code Zone (www.thecodezone.com).

In addition to games, John writes weekly product reviews and blog entries for GameDev.net from his home office in Texas. When not working on games in one way or another, he manages his wife's civil engineering firm and helps raise their daughter.

Contents

FOREWORD

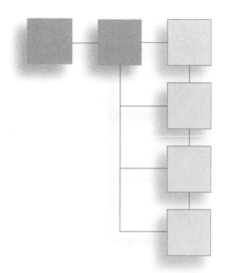

Back when we launched GameDev.net, the world was a different place. There were only a handful of books covering game development, and many of those were rapidly becoming outdated. There were a lot of game development web sites, but the content they offered was sparse and intended primarily for hobbyists. Whether you were someone trying to break into the games industry, a developer trying to create a game in your spare time, or someone making games for a living, finding information or like-minded individuals was no easy task. Even your friend Google was still in diapers and not a lot of help yet!

Our goal in founding GameDev.net was simple: provide a place where game developers of all walks of life could come together, freely exchange information and ideas, and network. In the nearly 10 years since then, we've seen the site and community grow to reach hundreds of thousands of game developers all over the world. We've seen an increasing number of professional game developers join the community, and we've even seen people go from being complete newbies to joining the ranks of EA, Ubisoft, and many others.

Many people have given back to the community, sharing their time and knowledge through the over 4 million posts to our forums, and also by contributing articles.

Over the past decade, we've received literally thousands of articles covering a wide range of topics. The best of these have withstood the test of time, becoming staples in their respective topics. Working closely with our good friends at

Cengage Learning, Drew and John have assembled these articles here, in printed form for the first time. They've also solicited new articles that will be exclusively available in these books.

This book features articles that will be invaluable to anyone running or thinking about running their own game company, especially small independents. As *Business and Production for Games: A GameDev.net Collection* demonstrates, there is more to game development than programming, art, and game design.

You'll learn how to approach your business as a professional from the wildly successful former Association of Shareware Professionals president Steve Pavlina. You'll receive expert marketing advice from Matrix Games founder Joe Lieberman (no, not the U.S. senator). Numerous authors will advise you on how to make the most of limited resources, and others will guide you in developing efficient production processes. And if that's not enough, other authors will remind you of the importance of intellectual property, sales, and team leadership.

Continuing in our tradition of bringing a variety of topics together from a variety of sources, this book captures the best of GameDev.net's community in the business and production world. We hope you find the information invaluable in your pursuit of game development success.

Dave Astle
Kevin Hawkins
Founders, GameDev.net

PART 1

BUSINESS

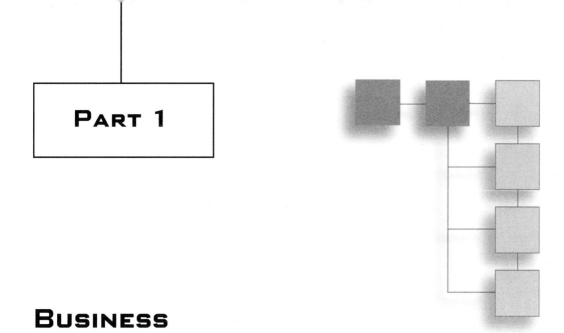

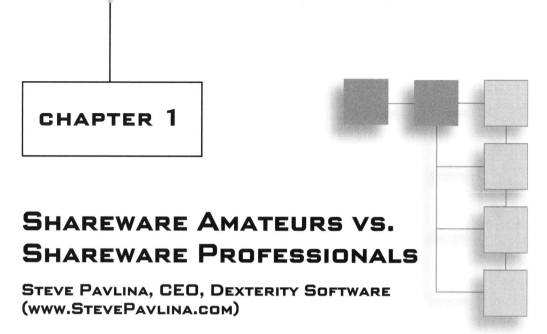

CHAPTER 1

SHAREWARE AMATEURS VS. SHAREWARE PROFESSIONALS

STEVE PAVLINA, CEO, DEXTERITY SOFTWARE (WWW.STEVEPAVLINA.COM)

Why is it that some shareware developers seem to be hugely successful in financial terms, growing their sales from scratch to generate tens of thousands of dollars in income, while the vast majority struggle to generate even a handful of sales? The answer can be found by exploring the difference in mindsets between both groups. For convenience, I'll label them as the *professional* and the *amateur*.

Product Development Cycle

Amateur	Professional
1. Get inspired by an idea for a product.	1. Do basic market research to determine the best opportunities for new products.
2. Create the product, regardless of whether there's a market for it.	2. Design a product that inspires you and that can exploit the market opportunities you identified.
3. Release the product.	3. Create the product along with the system for selling the product and the marketing plan.
4. Promote the product sporadically until bored with marketing.	4. Release the product.
5. Note dismal results.	5. Promote the product systematically according to the marketing plan.
6. Ask disempowering questions like, "Why do my sales suck?"	6. Measure results and gather feedback.
7. Sulk for a while.	7. Study and learn from the top industry performers (companies and products).
8. Network mostly with others who are also getting dismal results, taking comfort in the fact that you aren't alone.	8. Ask empowering questions like, "How can I increase sales by 20% or more?"
9. Make a few sporadic changes to product or web site (maybe).	

10. Abandon the product (aside from continuing   9. Update the product, the sales system, and
     to process orders and handle support), and   the marketing plan based on lessons learned.
     move on to the next product with step 1.   10. Repeat from step 5.

After the first pass through this cycle, the initial results for the amateur and the professional may be virtually identical. But, whereas the amateur typically stops after the first pass, the professional understands that this is just the beginning. Let's say they each release products that initially generate $100 per month in sales. The amateur will often conclude that the product is a failure, perhaps make a few minor revisions that don't help much, and then move on to the next product. But the professional asks, "How can I get to $200 per month?" By iterating through this cycle of refinement and rerelease many times (often more than 10 times over a period of several years), the professional may ultimately end up with a hit that generates thousands of dollars in monthly income. To the amateur, that initial $100 per month is seen as a flop. To the professional, however, it is seen as a seed. The professional understands that the initial launch is only the first step in a long stream of future updates and refinements, not just to the product but also to the sales system and the marketing plan. Following is a discussion of why this works.

In order to make a single shareware sale, an enormous number of factors must all come together synergistically. The chance of getting all these factors correct on the initial release is slim to none. Let's say there are only 10 critical factors in making a shareware sale (the quality of the product, the market demand for the product, the effectiveness of your registration incentives, the effectiveness of your ordering system, the file size of your shareware demo, and so on). And let's say that for each factor there is a range of effectiveness from 0% to 100%. *Understand this*: these factors don't add—they multiply! If all of your critical factors are at 100%, but just one is at 0%, that means you could be getting zero sales, even though you did most things perfectly. For instance, you could have a truly brilliant product, but if people don't feel secure using your order form, that single flaw could cost you most of your potential sales.

What if each of these 10 factors was at 60% effectiveness? Do you realize that this means you're only getting $0.6^{10} = 0.6\%$ of the sales you could be getting? Even if each factor is at 90% effectiveness, that's still only 35% of optimal. Obviously this model is oversimplified. My goal is to dispel the prevailing myth that if each part of your ordering pathway is "good but not great," your final sales will be good too—the reality is that lots of good factors multiply together to create "utterly dismal." Here's the formula:

$$(\text{Good but not great})^N = \text{Utterly dismal (for a sufficiently large N).}$$

If everything about your product is just good (say 60% of optimal), this doesn't mean you'll be getting 60% of the potential sales. It means you're more likely getting less than 1% of the sales you could be getting. Refining the critical success factors and making each part of your product, your sales system, and your marketing just a little bit better with each consecutive release is how you grow your sales massively over time. It isn't out of the question that you can double or triple your sales in a day by doing this.

Now the truth of the matter is that most initial releases are nowhere near averaging 60% effectiveness for all critical success factors. Especially for first-time developers, there are probably many factors that are at 10% or less. The headline on your product web page, for instance, may be nonexistent or poorly written. Your product may have bugs or compatibility problems that prevent many people from running it. Your web site may look unprofessional and scare potential customers away. You may not have even scratched the surface of all the marketing you should be doing. Perhaps you only have one product and aren't experiencing the benefits of cross-selling other products. It's entirely possible that when all these factors come together, you may be generating something like 0.01% of the potential results that your product is capable of, if you were to continue to nurture its development.

Selling software through shareware channels is very different than selling software at retail. With "try before you buy," each potential customer can go through a huge number of steps before buying, any one of which can kill the sale. Just one suboptimal factor can cost you most of your potential sales, and when combined, multiple suboptimal factors may be tossing out potential customers left and right. Picture a ball rolling down a pipe with 10 holes. If the ball passes all the way through the pipe without falling through any holes, you make a sale. But if the ball falls through even one of those 10 holes, the sale is lost. The way you get your product from dismal sales to outstanding sales is by systematically identifying and plugging those holes.

Having been in this industry for many years, I've seen this cycle repeat itself again and again. You would be absolutely amazed at how many of the greatest shareware hits experienced dismal sales after their initial release—sometimes even no sales at all in the entire first year. But the developers turned them into hits by continuously improving those critical success factors over a period of years.

So which is the better approach? To release five products in five years, each at 0.01% effectiveness, or to raise a single product from 0.01% to 2%? If 0.01% makes you an average of $100 per month, the first scenario will get you to $500 per month, and this is exactly what amateur developers do. But the second scenario will get you to $20,000 per month with just one product, and it requires less work too.

There are three good reasons why experienced professional shareware developers are often able to release more consistent hits than less experienced amateurs. First, the pros have already plugged many of the holes in their system that are shared by all products, such as optimizing their web sites to sell, refining the ordering process, implementing a money-back guarantee, crafting a solid marketing plan, gaining excellent search engine placement, and so on. So when a new product is released, it inherits the benefits of prior system-wide optimization work. Secondly, the pros can apply the wisdom gained from refining each previous product to any new release, so when they release a new product, they've already eliminated all the obvious sale killers that still plague amateur developers. And thirdly, the pros have already internalized the attitude that the first release is just the beginning; thus they expect to continue to refine the product and immediately start listening to user feedback to help them locate new holes that need to be plugged.

It is rare in the extreme that a developer's initial release will be anywhere near its full potential, even if the developer has vast experience. If you release a new shareware product, I guarantee it's going to be riddled with flaws, and it's probably earning less than 1% of its potential. If you raise each of 10 critical success factors by just 5%, you'll increase your sales by 60%. And if you do this over and over again, you'll see your monthly sales gradually climb: $100, $160, $250, $400, $650, $1000, $1700, $2700, $4300, $6900, $11,000, $18,000, and so on. Note that you don't even reach $1000 per month until the fifth iteration!!!

In order to improve these critical success factors, you have to confront the brutal, objective facts. Invite others to evaluate your product, your web site, and your ordering system. This requires putting your ego aside and being as open-minded as possible. Find out how others are marketing their products. Listen to what others have to say; don't delude yourself by trying to persuade them you're right and they're wrong. Don't worry about trying to make everything perfect all at once. But see if you can increase several critical success factors by a small amount with each successive release. For instance, you might try to make your product page just 20% more effective, your registration incentives 10% more enticing, your product interface 30% more intuitive, and so on.

As a personal example, shortly after I released *Dweep* in mid-1999, I began getting requests for an expansion pack of more levels. So I released an expansion pack. Players also complained that *Dweep* moved too slowly and needed a speed control. So I added a speed control. Then players wanted another expansion pack, so I released that. Then players wanted a level editor, so I added that. Then players wanted to be able to post their own levels, so I added a free levels archive. That turned out to be too much work to maintain, so I eventually took it down and replaced it with a forum where players can post their own levels, which worked out wonderfully. During that time, I also made major revisions to the web site, the marketing process, the ordering system, cross-promotions with others games, and the price (raising it from $9.95 to $24.95 while increasing the number of levels from 30 to 152). Most of *Dweep*'s sales were a result of these later refinements, not the initial release.

The amateur mindset leaves most of the potential rewards forever untapped, wallowing below 1% of the true potential. But professionals keep going, treating that shareware product as a tree that must be patiently watered before it bears a full harvest of fruit. I suppose you could say that the amateur sees the glass as 99.99% empty, while the professional sees it at 0.01% full.

Personal Development

Now let's explore the differences between shareware amateurs and professionals in terms of personal development.

Amateur	Professional
1. Myopically focus personal development efforts on the areas you enjoy most (such as design or programming) as opposed to the areas where improvement would yield the greatest results (such as marketing or self-discipline).	1. Take personal inventory of strengths as well as weaknesses that specifically detract from those strengths (e.g., poor goal setting habits result in unfocused marketing plan).
	2. Identify key knowledge/skills that must be mastered (marketing, selling, programming, etc.) as well as key character traits that need improvement

2. Gain knowledge sporadically through just one or two primary sources (i.e., reading books and articles, but not live seminars or audio programs).
3. Apply your new knowledge to making your strengths even stronger (i.e., product development), while falling further behind in your weakest areas (i.e., marketing and sales).
4. Guard the best of what you've learned as a treasured secret. Maintain a competitive scarcity mentality.
5. Repeat from step 1.

(organization, self-discipline, focus, motivation, etc.).
3. Identify multiple sources where knowledge/skills/traits can be improved (mentors, business associates, books to read, organizations to join, conferences/seminars to attend, etc.).
4. Take action by diving into these sources. Read the books, join and become active in the organizations, attend the conferences/seminars, and learn from the key individuals.
5. Patiently apply the new knowledge to your business and life, realizing that even small gains will compound exponentially as you continue running this cycle year after year.
6. Pass on your new wisdom to others by sharing advice, writing, volunteering, mentoring others, etc. Maintain a noncompetitive abundance mentality.
7. Repeat from step 1.

The amateur sees personal development in narrow, mono-dimensional terms (i.e., becoming a better developer). Efforts are focused on acquiring more knowledge within this limited field. A shareware amateur's bookshelf will be dominated by books within a narrow field, such as software development, virtually ignoring other crucial parts of the business like marketing and sales.

By contrast, the professional takes a holistic approach. The professional understands that all areas of one's life are intertwined, and that a weakness in one area (such as financial management) can detract from strengths in other areas (such as programming). The professional's bookshelf will likely be filled with a varied mix of books on topics such as business, marketing, sales, finance, technology, psychology, philosophy, health, and relationships. The professional keeps an open mind to acquiring knowledge through a variety of media, perhaps reading a book on software development, having a discussion with peers about marketing, listening to an audio program on time management, and attending a seminar on sales techniques. The professional seeks to advance on multiple fronts, understanding that a 10% improvement in five different areas will yield better results than a 50% improvement in just one.

The amateur guards knowledge as a scarce resource—a competitive edge. Thus the amateur rarely becomes known in professional circles, missing out on scores of lucrative opportunities that professionals frequently share with each other.

This attitude constricts the flow of new knowledge back to the amateur, and the result is that the amateur is cut off and isolated from the "inner circle" of the highly successful within his or her industry. Few bother to help the amateur directly because the amateur has never done anything for them and is relatively unknown. The amateur is stuck in a downward spiral of scarcity where growing the business feels like climbing a mountain.

Conversely, the professional understands the importance of information flow and that passing on knowledge to others only deepens his or her understanding. This sharing of knowledge plants seeds of abundance that benefit the professional for years to come. By giving openly and generously, the professional develops a positive reputation that attracts other professionals. An abundance of new opportunities flow to the professional through this network, seemingly without effort. This creates an upward spiral where the professional is able to leverage this network to grow his or her business with relative ease.

Psychological Factors

Finally, let's dive into the psychological factors.

Amateur	Professional
1. Nonexistent or foggy goals ("make more money").	1. Crystal-clear goals, committed to writing ("Increase sales by 20% within 3 months").[1]
2. Sporadic motivation coming from irregular outside influences (inspiring book/movie, great conversation, flash of insight, etc.).	2. Deliberate cultivation of burning desire.[2]
3. Focus on making money and getting customers to buy.	3. Focus on filling customer needs and providing value.
4. Seeks to blame poor results on outside factors (poor economy, competition, lack of luck, unfairness, shortcomings of shareware model, etc.).	4. Accepts responsibility for poor results, seeks to understand causes and learn from them (registration incentives need improvement, product descriptions need rewriting, etc.).
5. Expends effort on the most enjoyable actions.	5. Seeks to understand causes of poor results and learn from them.
6. Scarcity mentality based on zero-sum thinking ("I'm not going to give anything away unless I get something in return").	6. Expends efforts on the most important actions (in terms of achieving goals) and finds ways to enjoy the process.
7. Short-range time perspective used in planning, often limited to the timeline of a single product cycle.	7. Abundance mentality based on law of sowing and reaping ("givers get").
8. Sees problems as obstacles.	8. Long-range time perspective used in planning, often thinking 5+ years ahead.
9. Persistent self-doubt ("success is elusive").	9. Sees problems as opportunities.
	10. Persistent confidence and faith ("success is inevitable").

10. Unbalanced approach improving major strengths while letting other areas slide.

11. Believes that success comes from doing (work), then having (results), then being (successful).

12. "Once I achieve this (foggy) goal, then I'll be successful."

13. Weak commitment ("I'll try this and see what happens").

14. Avoids facing brutal facts, stays within comfort zone ("I don't enjoy/understand marketing, so I'll just keep programming for now").

15. Believes that risk-taking and luck are necessary for big breakthroughs ("Releasing a new product is like betting on a spin of the roulette wheel").

16. Success stories from others increase feelings of anxiety, inadequacy, or resentment.

17. Associates most frequently with other amateurs who are equally confused, having less frequent contact with professionals (group griping and pity parties outweigh true learning experiences).

18. Negative attitude rips many new ideas to shreds before they pass the incubation stage.

19. Negative associations to building business (customers are headaches, too many responsibilities, being overextended, burning out, a risky gamble, can't make money *and* do what I love).

11. Balanced approach to improving multiple weak areas that detract from strengths.

12. Understands that success comes from first being (successful in one's thoughts), then doing (actions consistent with those thoughts), then having (results consistent with those actions).

13. "Once I believe I'm successful, the external results will naturally follow."

14. Strong commitment ("I will find a way or make one").

15. Confronts brutal facts head on ("Marketing is crucial to my business, so I must become a master marketer").

16. Avoids unnecessary risks and bets on opportunities with the strongest chance of success while seeking to minimize the potential downside ("Releasing a new product isn't a gamble; I'll just keep refining it over time until it ultimately becomes a hit").

17. Success stories from others are mined for new ideas and insights.

18. Networks with focused and successful professionals, learning by osmosis.

19. Associates most frequently with other focused and successful professionals, less frequent contact with amateurs (continuous flow of knowledge and ideas).

20. Positive attitude lets new ideas incubate in imagination before putting them to the test in the real world.

21. Positive associations to building business (financial abundance, good life for family, early retirement, freedom, making people happy, fulfilling one's dreams, giving to charity, creating jobs, etc.).

[1]http://www.stevepavlina.com/articles/power-of-clarity.htm.
[2]http://www.stevepavlina.com/articles/cultivating-burning-desire.htm.

When results are weak, the amateur seeks security, comfort, and consolation. Amateurs want to know they aren't alone, so they find safety in numbers by holding group griping sessions in forums that attract other amateurs. Their inner insecurity makes it very hard for them to accept failure, so they're looking to put the blame elsewhere—on the failure of the shareware system, on the economy, and so on. Amateurs look for validation of their position, seeking out "experts" who agree that success in their field is hopeless and that only the really lucky can succeed. When hearing of dismal sales from others, they feel more secure. Success stories are unnerving to the amateur, often making them feel anxious, envious, or resentful.

The professional, on the other hand, is emotionally secure. The professional seeks understanding and knowledge. The professional accepts personal responsibility for his or her results and is always looking to improve. When the professional suffers a setback, he or she wants to understand the causes, assuming that the reason for failure was a lack of understanding or skill that led to mistakes. The professional will suffer failures at least as big as the amateur, if not bigger, but the professional will learn from each experience and move forward with an even stronger plan.

You can't tell an early professional from an amateur purely by looking at a one-time snapshot of their results. The key differences are internal. Professionals and amateurs who start from scratch may begin on the same footing. After the first year their initial results may appear similar. But fast forward 10 years—most likely the amateur will have given up and left the business or is still barely eking out a living. Meanwhile the professional has become an established leader with a strong, sustainable income.

So what is the essential difference between the shareware amateur and the shareware professional? It can be summarized in just one word: fear. The amateur feels vulnerable, believing that certain things might happen that he or she will be unable to handle. The amateur doesn't want to deal with products that aren't selling well, avoids facing his or her deepest inadequacies, and seeks to manage fear by clinging to the familiar and the comfortable. Instead of pursuing the greatest opportunities, the amateur pursues the safest and most comfortable paths. For instance, an amateur who feels more comfortable programming than marketing will heavily favor programming projects, whether or not that's what the business needs most. The amateur ties much of his or her sense of self-worth to external factors, and when those factors are threatened, the amateur feels a strong urge to return to the safety of the comfort zone.

The professional, on the other hand, has internalized thoughts of security and abundance. The professional believes that no matter what happens, he or she will be able to handle it. The professional doesn't cling to a comfort zone. When faced with change, he or she embraces it, seeks out the hidden opportunities, and charges boldly ahead. This isn't to say that professionals never feel fear; they do.

The difference is that professionals turn and face their fears instead of shrinking from them.

Amateurs will normally not be consciously aware of their fears. Such fears will be hidden behind rationalizations such as, "I simply don't like marketing," "I'm genetically disadvantaged when it comes to planning," or "I feel like a scam artist when I write sales copy." Thinking about such tasks and projects will typically make the amateur feel a sense of discomfort, anxiety, or even dread, but they often won't consciously know why. When confronted with these shortcomings, the amateur will often become emotional, sarcastic, and defensive. But, whereas the amateur addresses this problem by getting defensive and shrinking back into the comfort zone, the professional lets go of his or her ego and strives to become consciously aware of his or her fears, driving them into the open where they readily dissolve. A professional says, "I probably feel uncomfortable marketing right now because of my lack of experience, but I know other people who happen to love marketing. I'll talk to them to see what they like about it, get some book recommendations, and within a few years, I'll be outstanding at marketing as well." Alternatively, a professional might hire or partner with someone else who has the skills he or she lacks, but the decision will be made out of awareness of this deficiency, not from fear and denial.

These models of the amateur and the professional are abstractions of course. Between them lies a continuum where real people can be found. Hopefully, you'll find the contrasts between these two poles helpful in continuing your own professional development.

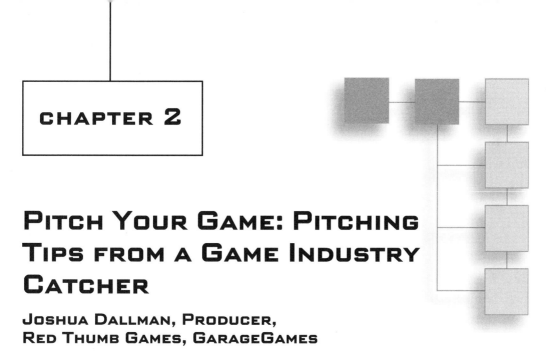

CHAPTER 2

PITCH YOUR GAME: PITCHING TIPS FROM A GAME INDUSTRY CATCHER

JOSHUA DALLMAN, PRODUCER,
RED THUMB GAMES, GARAGEGAMES

In the past few years as a producer for GarageGames, I've reviewed hundreds of video game pitches from developers and studios. Having seen the good and the bad, I offer practical tips to help developers successfully pitch themselves or their game to any publisher without boring the publisher or losing their interest.

The range of pitches I've reviewed is huge, from literally two-word e-mails ("you like?" with an attached movie) to 30-page design docs complete with an appendix detailing every mouse click. Everything from casual puzzle games to WOW clones, from someone who's never shipped a game requesting a third of a million dollars to start their business to experienced developers delivering sober and intriguing proposals. Here's my industry experience advice.

Research the Publisher

First things first—*do your homework*. This is true for any type of publishing, be it books or film. If the publisher is Popcap, don't pitch them the next *Half-Life*. If the only casual game a company has made was five years ago, chances are they won't fund your match three clone. Target publishers in your genre for a greater response rate. Look at each publisher's portfolio to see what they are interested in. If you do not do this work, you are wasting their time and yours. That is time you could spend targeting more likely publishers.

A Picture Is Worth a Thousand Words

If your pitch contains only text, it will be scanned over, and crucial details may be missed. While it takes time to process words, visual scenes are processed quickly by the brain. And game industry people, especially creatives, are visual communicators. A quickly mocked up in-game screen will tell more about the game than a page worth of text. The more clearly you can communicate your idea, the better it can be weighed, and the more likely it is to be of interest. A picture draws a viewer into its scene—it says, "imagine this interactive, animated, and brought to life." It captures the viewer's imagination in ways that the best placed words cannot. Photoshop mock-ups, programmer art, MS Paint, it doesn't matter—any sketch is better than none. If you have a real concept artist and include preproduction art in the pitch, it is that much stronger and shows you put that much more thought into all aspects of the pitch.

"No" Can Happen in One Sentence

Present your high-level concept first, with one sentence. If the high concept is accepted, the publisher will continue to read for greater detail. If the high concept is rejected, the publisher stops right there, and any work you did on further details for the pitch are irrelevant. For example, your high-level concept may be a genre the publisher does not work with, may be something considered too risky (an MMO), or the publisher may already have a title in the works that is too similar to consider a second. Don't assume or expect the publisher to read the whole pitch—it can end at the first sentence—which brings us straight to the next point.

Have Many Things to Pitch

Don't put all your eggs in one basket. If the publisher rejects one pitch, that doesn't mean the end of the relationship—if you have more pitches up your sleeve. Be prepared to pitch multiple different projects, as well as a diverse range of projects (though not all across the board and too diverse). I know one developer whose game a publisher loved. He pitched them an idea for his next game. The publisher wasn't impressed and was having second thoughts about the developer. Luckily he had a backup pitch for another game, which was an instant hit, making the publisher forget all about the weak first pitch. *He got signed.* One game was RPG-like, the other arcade-like. The second pitch was not a trivial variation of the first, but not as widely divergent as MMO/match-3 either. By that token, don't have so many games to pitch that you're just firing in the dark and seeing what sticks. Anyone can do that, and it shows no commitment on your part.

Be Professional

Your pitch should be a professional presentation, not informal. You are, after all, formally requesting publishing services and/or funding. A conversational style is indirect and meandering. *If you want to be seriously considered, be serious.*

Be Passionate about What You Pitch

This is harder with a paper pitch than an in-person one, but despite being professional in a pitch, passion comes through nonetheless. It's simple: if a developer is passionate about a project, they are more likely to make sure they create a fantastic product and follow through on deadlines. If a developer seems ambivalent, then guess what, so will the publisher, and they'll find a passionate studio elsewhere.

Know What You Are Making

Know what your core game concept is. Know what elements support that. Know your design inside and out. Publishers will not pay you to experiment or prototype. Granted, your design may change through the course of development, but you are not pitching a direction, you are pitching a specific game. Make sure you know what that is and can communicate it simply and clearly. Be able to answer why you are making the game that you are beyond just "I think I will like it."

Know Budgets

I've been pitched by developers who, upon asked what their proposed budget is, said they had no idea. I've seen budgets whose only line item is "the game," with the total amount listed and no further details. Make sure you know what you are asking payment for. How much will be needed for art? For code? For administrative overhead? Are you familiar with contractor costs for these things? Do you have ballparks of man hours required for various features? How much of your budget could be saved by cutting feature X? By adding feature X? As much of this should be known up front, not discovered later on. What's the commercially reasonable quality level that the publisher contractually expects, and how much will that cost to produce?

You Can Be Greedy or Stupid, but Not Both

If you have a great proposal, but are asking for too much money and too many "deal points" (no exclusivity, no right to sequel, no alternate format publishing), you can still be negotiated with. If you have a great proposal at the right price, but are missing a big piece of the picture (neglecting customer service costs for an MMO or neglecting the true difficulty of implementing a certain feature, for example), you are still potentially in business. But *if you are both greedy and stupid* there is no reason for a publisher to work with you, no matter how great your game is. There are simply far too many intelligent, humble, capable developers out there for the publisher to work with in your place. This industry has a surplus of people wanting to be in it, not a shortage. Avoid these pitfalls.

Be Almost Greedy

I am showing my indie developer colors here, but it's good advice and bears passing along. It's true not just in the video game industry but for any business deal. We have a tendency to shortchange ourselves or to expect the execution to be perfect with no bumps and fail to account for the unforeseeable. Rule of thumb: ask for slightly more than you're comfortable with. At the same time, be prepared for slightly less than you're comfortable with. Somewhere in that zone your game will get made.

License and Registration, Please

In a publisher's eyes, the team you have is as important as the game or concept itself. Ask yourself the following questions and be prepared to answer them. What have you shipped? What is your industry experience? What contract work have you successfully completed? *Be honest with yourself.* Now ask, do the answers to these match up with what you're proposing and asking for? *Make sure they do.* Publishers do not see just the project but the faces behind them. They need a reliable team behind the game to minimize the risk that they will not get a return on their investment. In sales, it is cheaper to get repeat customers than to find new ones. Publishing is no different—it is more effective to work with existing partners than to identify and orient new ones. More often than not, publishers are looking for long-term developers to trust. If all you see is the one game, or all you're showing is one game, and not the value of the team behind it, your vision is too narrow.

When's It Shipping?

Have a timeline and associated costs for dates. Milestones can be feature-based (prototype/campaign/multiplayer/final art/bugs) or stage-based (alpha/beta/RC/gold) or both. There is no absolute standard except that without this information, the publisher is going to be left wondering how long your project will take. Moreover, the publisher needs to know how much you need at each of these stages so they can project their internal budget accordingly. You're not going to get paid entirely up front, or entirely upon completion, so set your needs and expectations here and be ready to negotiate.

Competitors

Capably discuss your game's position in the marketplace. More is better than not enough. How have other games in the genre performed? What was the last succeeding similar product? How is your game similar to and unique from competing products? Who are your competitors, and why is your game better? These are all important questions to answer. A pitch that is weak but that deeply understands its competitors is as likely to succeed as a pitch that is strong and dismisses or misses the mark on its competitors. Showing that you know who else has your same idea and who has executed it well (or who has failed) tells the publisher you are that much more likely to succeed yourself. It shows that you deeply understand your genre and have done your homework.

Now with 8-Way Joystick and Second Button!

Platform matters! If it's an arcade cabinet game, how will you leverage that? If it's a cellphone game, a web game, or a LAN party game, how will you leverage those? Miss this, and nobody will notice. But include it and get it right, and it's that much more firepower to ignite the flame of a green light.

"It's for Hardcore Gamers...*and* My Little Sister!"

Know who your target consumer is. "Everyone" or "people who like racing games" does nothing but tell the publisher that you didn't do your homework or don't really understand the game industry. There is no one right answer to this or right way to do it, but it should be some blend of age/gender/hobby/lifestyle/game preferences, and the range should not be too broad. If "9 to 90" is your "target," that's not really a target, is it? You can't help but hit it. Find something and aim for it. Then find ways to strengthen the pitch for that particular market.

What You Do—Do That

Stay within your limits. A publisher is not going to pay for you to shoot for never-before-attempted feats to see if you can. Where there is money, there is by necessity certainty. Staying within limits reduces the risk of failure for both parties. If you've never done networked games, don't pitch a networked racing game. If you've never worked with physics, don't pitch a game that relies on physics as a key component.

To the Point

Stay to the point. You do need to share the plan for how you will produce the game. You don't need to detail what source control methods and what team management techniques you will use. You do need to state clearly what the game content will be. You don't need to share the plan of how you will run the details of your business and which HMO you will be choosing for your employees. Stay relevant to the publisher. If you need an affirmative pat on the back for the details of your other plans, get that from a fellow developer or a friend, not from the publisher. They have neither the time nor the interest.

Business Is Business

Don't get personal or take things personally. The games industry is a business. The people reviewing your game are not there to make you feel good about yourself; they are there to further mutual and legitimate business interests. They are in that business because it satisfies personal interests they have, including creative and social ones, but that does not make things personal. You will make friends, and business relationships blur into social relationships, but at the end of the day, and especially with a new potential partner, business is business.

Don't Ramble (Like Me)

Less is more. Publishers get dozens of pitches a day. Your pitch is not an essay or book. The more text you have, the less likely they will read it. If your "killer feature" is buried on page 28 in section 3 subsection B, they will never get to it.

Make bulleted lists and summarize things until more detail is requested. Your first pitch should be three pages: an introduction letter, a one-page overview, and some mock-ups or concept art (ideally with a link to a demo) with an invitation to see more if there is interest. You have all day to write up the most detailed proposal on earth. Publishers do not have all day to read dozens of them. And they get only dozens a day if they're lucky. I've heard of publishers that field hundreds every day.

Tie In

The more relevant you can be to the publisher's history, the better. Do your homework. For example if they made a hit FPS game, acknowledge it or try to tie your game to it ("like your game X, my game has an emphasis on team co-op"). But don't go to absurd lengths ("like your game X, my game also has graphics!"). Yes, this is partly ego stroking. And yes, it does work (but will only get you so far).

Originality

Your pitch should be original. As soon as you say "it's X but with Y," most publishers will no longer look at what you're doing but will instead focus on who you are. Anyone can come up with "X but with Y," but only a very talented team that knows what it's doing could pull it off. If the best you have is a rip-off of an old game with some different features, or a mash-up of some popular games, don't bother unless you've successfully done it before.

Orson Welles Syndrome

Be flexible with your features. This isn't about the publisher trying to creatively control your project. They don't have the time or desire to do that. If a publisher is interested in your game but wants to scale up or down, react accordingly. If they don't like a certain feature and you're not married to it, let it go. Don't be too defensive or worried about "the publisher designing your game for you" until you actually feel like it's happening. Asking to drop a certain feature or set is not a slippery slope and is common practice. This does not mean the publisher is designing your game.

I Am Error

Don't try to impress the publisher with your knowledge of games or the gaming history. It's irrelevant to the pitch. If you have a good pitch or idea, your knowledge of games will be self-evident.

"Zzzz . . ." Is Not the Sound of Approval

This is not an insider industry tip. If you bore the publisher, your proposal will not be looked at, and you will be passed over. Keep this in mind as a general rule of thumb when preparing any part of your pitch.

Who What Where When How Why

Make sure to go back and ask yourself if you've covered all the basics: who, what, where, when, how, and why. *Who* are you making the game for, and who will be working on it? *What* is the game itself? *Where* will the game live (what platform is it ideal for—certain platforms cater better to certain markets than others, PC/ strategy, for example)? *When* can you start? *How* long will it take? *What* are your milestones? *How* will you develop the game—with *what* tools and tech and with *what* kind of team (in-house or contractors)? *Why* do you believe the game will be a success and is worth looking at? (And none of these should be a three-page impassioned essay about how you've been playing games since you were five and know everything about them.)

Let Me Play!!!

A playable prototype or demo is golden. No graphics, no sound, no building out of the game—just core game proof of concept. A pitch with pictures will get 10 times further than a pitch without. *A pitch with a prototype will get a HUNDRED times further than a pitch without.* Don't apologize for the demo; they've heard "this isn't the final game art or gameplay" as many times as I've heard "please excuse the mess" when walking into a perfectly nice home. Even if a pitch is rejected, if you resubmitted it with a playable demo, it could be reconsidered. Many publishers will not accept unsolicited pitches without a playable demo.

Mess Up

You'll make mistakes and it's okay. If you think there are people in the industry who know everything and never make mistakes, you're wrong. You don't need to be that person because that person doesn't exist. If the publisher raises an issue that you hadn't yet considered, don't front—the publisher is smarter than that. Fess up to it, and tell them you'll discuss it with your team and follow up—then actually do it. But be humble.

This article is by no means a step-by-step guide on how to pitch. This is general advice for studios of all sizes or individuals, professional or not, on how to pitch publishers, solicited or not. I've worked with some great developers and studios over the years, and I hope to work with plenty more.

Happy game-making!

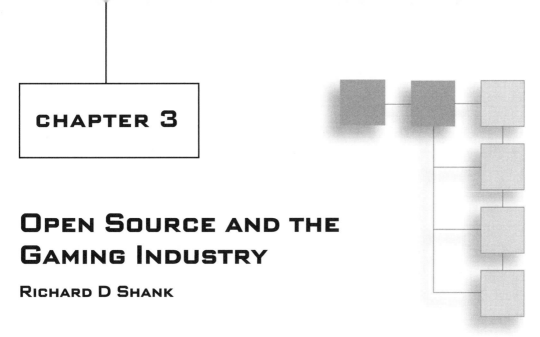

CHAPTER 3

OPEN SOURCE AND THE GAMING INDUSTRY

RICHARD D SHANK

Wait! Don't skip this chapter. I know you think this doesn't apply to you—after all you don't program for Linux. But there is a lot more to open source than just the penguin. Many companies are taking advantage of open source software, much in part to the increasing popularity of Linux. Open source has become a big buzzword, with many people not really understanding what it is. In fact, most people are using open source software and don't even realize it. When you are looking at a web site or checking your e-mail, chances are the inner workings (the mail transports and web servers) are open source.

So where do you begin? Let's start with a little history behind open source.

Sharing source goes back as early as the 1950s when the SHARE group was formed to exchange code for IBM mainframes. IBM released the source to the software for their mainframes, allowing changes for specific needs. This updated code was passed around the SHARE group, creating the earliest form of open source.

In 1985, the Free Software Foundation was formed by Richard Stallman, to promote the freedom to distribute and modify computer software without restriction. Stallman had been working in the AI department at MIT and left in 1984 to began writing GNU free software. (GNU is pronounced "guh-NEW" and it stands for "GNU's Not UNIX").

The Free Software Foundation (www.fsf.org) defines free software as a matter of liberty, not price. To understand the concept, you should think of "free" as in "free speech," not as in "free beer." Free software is a matter of users' freedom to run, copy, distribute, study, change, and improve the software.

In 1997, a paper written by Eric S. Raymond, "The Cathedral and the Bazaar" (www.catb.org/~esr/writings/cathedral-bazaar/) triggered a series of events that led to the forming of the Open Source Institute (OSI). One of the more significant events at the time was Netscape releasing the source to their browser. That project is still alive and well with various projects like the Firefox browser and the NVU (www.nvu.com) HTML editor. The OSI was jointly founded by Eric Raymond and Bruce Perens in late February 1998 as a general educational and advocacy organization.

Next, it is necessary to understand what open source software is and what it is not. Open source in its purist sense is software that has the source code available to anyone who desires it. That individual is free to use the code as he sees fit; however, any modifications to the code must be made available for everyone to use and modify, under the same conditions. According to www.opensource.org, "Open source promotes software reliability and quality by supporting independent peer review and rapid evolution of source code."

It's not source code that you download from a web site with permission to redistribute and modify and also to add additional restrictions to it. It's not a free program like Artweaver (www.artweaver.de) that's made available to the public for free without the source code. It's not source code released into the public domain where the rights to the code are forfeited. It is also not source code that's distributed freely with a clause saying it has to be non-profit. Open source creates a system of free access of information for the greater good of the project.

Types of Licenses

There are two categories of open source licenses, copyleft and permissive. A *copyleft* license is primarily concerned with preserving open software rights in forked versions of the project. It requires that any subsequent code be released and any finished products release the source code for the product. A *permissive* license places minimum restrictions on the source code. It can be modified without releasing the modifications. A permissive license can work hand in hand with closed, proprietary code.

Of the copyleft licenses, the most widely used is the general public license (GPL) from the Free Software Foundation. It has a couple of variations, the LGPL and the AGPL. The LGPL (Lesser General Public License) makes a specific piece of code open source, but other parts of the project can be proprietary source code. The AGPL (Affero General Public License) focuses on software as a service and relaxes some restrictions on releasing the source to network clients. You can find out more about these licenses at www.gnu.org/licenses.

The BSD (Berkeley Software Distribution) is a popular permissive license; in fact, often a permissive license will be referred to as a "BSD type" license. There are a number of variations on each of these licenses. If you go to www.opensource.org/ licenses, you can find a number of licenses approved by the OSI.

There is great debate about the various types of licenses and the impact of each. Some game developers shy away from a restrictive copyleft license. There are parts of games that sometimes need to be kept away from view. Sometimes to stop cheating, sometimes to create an edge in the market. Also, there is the perspective that a copyleft license doesn't provide true freedom. There is a great blog post on copyleft (GPL) licenses for games at www.gamedev.net/community/forums/mod/ journal/journal.asp?jn=348262&cmonth=6&cyear=2008&cday=20.

Really, the choice in license is about what is best for your project. It may make more sense to have closed source, or it may make sense to use open source and open your own source. There is a great overview of the legal aspects of open source licenses at www.softwarefreedom.org/resources/2008/foss-primer.html.

Open Source Games

There are several open source games available. Some games have been released as open source, some have become open after a commercial release. On Wikipedia is a list of open source games, but I'll highlight a few here.

- **Parallel Realities** has a number of open source games, including *Blob Wars: Metal Blob Solid* (www.parallelrealities.co.uk/blobWars.php), a 2D arcade game. A cool thing that Parallel Realties does is release the making-of for several games (www.parallelrealities.co.uk/makingOfMBS.php).

- **Alien Trap** has released a 3D shooter called *Nexuiz* (www.alientrap.org/ nexuiz/), a game that is built on the *Darkplaces* engine, a fork of the *Quake 1* engine. There is a *Super Mario Cart* clone called *SuperTuxKart* (www .supertuxkart.sourceforge.net). The site has a good bit of information about the workings of the game and how to create additional levels.

- **Vega Strike** (www.vegastrike.sourceforge.net) is a 3D Action-Space-Sim. The web site has a great deal of documentation and a developers blog. *Warzone 2100* (www.wz2100.net) is a real-time strategy game that was released commercially in 1999, then released as open source in 2004. All of these games (and there are many others) provide a good starting point for developing your own game and for seeing various ways to organize an open source game project.

There is also an open source game that is a joint venture between Blender and Crystal Space teams. The name for the project is Apricot (www.apricot .blender.org) and is worth checking out. Speaking of Crystal Space, there are a few commercially released games that were made from the CS engine, including *Ice Land* (www.play-publishing.com/?id=38).

How Open Source Helps the Gaming Industry

Funding

There are a few options for getting some funding for open source games. Right now Google has the Summer of Code (www.code.google.com/soc) that pays college students to develop open source software over the summer. There are a couple of other groups that provide funding to open source projects: one is Linux Fund (www.linuxfund.org) and another is SPI (www.spi-inc.org). There is not a lot of funding money to go around, but every little bit helps. Another idea is to do as the Apricot project did and pre-sell your final product. Some vendors may also donate hardware to an open source project.

Tools

A great number of tools are available for about anything you need to do in creating a game. Using open source software can greatly reduce the cost of development. For example, you can use Eclipse (www.eclipse.org) for your IDE, Open Office (www.openoffice.org) for document writing, GIMP (www.gimp.org) for editing raster graphics, Inkscape (www.inkscape.org) for vector editing, Blender (www.blender.org) for 3D modeling, and Audacity (www.audacity.sourceforge .net) for sound editing.

When using open source tools, at the very least, provide feedback. It will give you and the rest of the world a better product. If you have time to spare, write some code or documentation. It would still save money from buying the commercially available products.

Information Sharing

Many think that the single greatest element in the rapid advancement of the gaming industry is the wide open exchange of knowledge. There are many web sites with gaming information, source code for games being released to be examined and studied, and magazines and books giving anyone the ability to understand game-making techniques. Open source also encourages and promotes this same information sharing.

Back in 2004, I started using the Mojavi framework for web development. I was able to get quite an education on the Model View Controller pattern from Sean Kerr, the developer of the framework, just by hitting the forums, IMing, and volunteering to help out when possible. In return, I wrote documentation and tutorials for the project. We both benefited (and so did the community), and as a bonus, I had the opportunity to get to know a great person. Unfortunately, Sean was unable to maintain Mojavi, but the project forked and now lives on in Agavi (www.agavi.org).

Reduced Overhead

Using open source libraries is a great way to reduce time in a project, save money, and have more developers working on making the best library possible. The many eyes on a project are one of the greatest strengths of open source software.

There are a number of open source libraries available; doing a search for your need with the phrase "open source" opens a world of possibilities. A few libraries to consider are the Simple and Fast Multimedia Layer (www.sfml-dev.org), a cross-platform multimedia library designed to provide low-level access to audio, keyboard, mouse, joystick, and networking. You could use the SQLite (www.sqlite.org) database in your game for data storage.

Do you need a game engine? You could use the Crystal Space engine (www.crystalspace3D.org). Is there a need to write a scripting language when you could use Python (www.python.org)? If you need an audio library, then you could use OpenAL (www.openal.org). Is it completely necessary to write a physics library when the Bullet library (www.bulletphysics.com) might work for you?

Development Speed

Imagine the ego trip for a hard-core gamer to be able to say that he beta tested the newest RPG on the market. This alone will draw a number of contributors to an open source game project, especially if there is some credit in the finished game.

Having additional coders for fixing or improving code after an alpha or beta stage can be a great benefit to the project. Often times, as the project comes to a close, there is great pressure to hurry up and get the product finished. This is an area where open source can also be a benefit. The additional coders working on your project will be anxious to see the project finish and potentially increase their productivity.

I did an informal survey of developers on a couple of open source projects. I found, on average, the programmers that responded to the survey spent 87 hours a month writing code for various open source projects; the time spent ranged from 10 hours a month to about 350 hours a month. Look at it this way: if you have four outside developers (which is very realistic) spending an average of 87 hours a month on your project, you have picked up the equivalent of a full-time programmer for the project without the added cost.

Additionally, just over half of those who responded said they made sure the code compiles and cleans up minor errors on a daily or bi-daily basis. Also, many developers spent time on documentations and product support.

Reduced Redundancy

A few years back, in writing a 3ds importer for the Crystal Space library, I felt like there could be a lot of time saved if I could find someone who had already done the dirty work of translating the 3ds information. I found lib3ds (www.lib3ds.sourceforge.net), which suited my needs; however, I found that the I/O interface was specifically for disk access. Crystal Space uses a virtual file system, making it incompatible with lib3ds.

I sent an e-mail to JE Hoffman, project leader of lib3ds and told him my dilemma. He gladly rewrote the interface to use any data format, and it was integrated into Crystal Space. However, the story doesn't end there. Lib3ds was known to work only on Windows and Linux. Crystal Space covers many more platforms. I sent an e-mail to the Crystal Space list asking for help to get lib3ds to work on other platforms. A Crystal Space developer, Eric Sunshine, responded and helped out on making lib3ds available for more platforms.

This was a win-win situation. Crystal Space got an importer, and lib3ds was made available on more platforms. The programming community also benefits with having a more versatile library.

While this may not seem like the greatest example, how many trivial programming tasks consume parts of your day? Do you really need to write a compression library or will zlib (www.gzip.org/zlib/) work just as well for you?

Project Stability

Project stability could be the greatest case for using open source software. Open source software has been peer reviewed every step of the way. It has been tried in a number of environments and under a number of conditions. Just think of the number of machines with the wide variety of configurations that will be testing the product.

Mature open source code is as bulletproof as software ever gets. Why? It's always being looked over and compiled and tested. In my survey of open source developers, a number of developers spent a sizable percentage of their time making sure the code was in tip-top shape.

Broader Market

Why do game companies limit the number of platforms for which the product is available? Is it because they don't want that market share? Of course not. The reason is, that market share doesn't cover the costs of developing for that platform.

Would that platform be profitable if it could be added for next to nothing? Absolutely. This is another added benefit of open source; end users are often more than willing to do the necessary work to make a game work on their platform. Each added port is an added market for the game.

The additional exposure for the game generated by being an open source project can also help the project gain a greater market share. Anyone contributing code to the project would have an additional incentive to purchase the finished game.

Opportunity for Lone Gunmen

There have been many lamentations lately for the solo game developer. Oh, the good ol' days of the past when you could write a game yourself, put it in a zip-lock bag, and sell it at a computer show. I don't believe the days of the solo developer have to be a distant memory.

Granted, a single developer will never put together a project with the scope of *Scorched 3D* (www.scorched3d.co.uk/), but a *Zuma*-type game could be developed by a single developer. There are a number of open source tools and libraries available for creating Flash games or Java-based games that can be delivered across a number of platforms. Head on over to www.OSFlash.org to get connected to other Flash developers and find out what open source tools are available.

Making Money with Open Source

The first argument you will hear from businesses concerning open source is that you cannot make money with it. *Au contraire.* There are companies making money with open source; I'll look at a few and look at some ways that you can use open source to make money making games.

The first thing I would recommend is heading over to www.pentaho.org/beekeeper to download and read the brilliant paper called "The Beekeeper." It is a well-thought-out analogy on making money with open source and can provide great insight into how open source fits into a business model.

Creating Titles

If your focus is making games and not creating technology, open source is an excellent way to focus more of your resources on the gameplay and less on the technology involved. A line of titles could be made from open source code, keeping the content of the game protected and making money from that as normal; just the cost of development would go down. I believe this would also help to shift the focus of games from eye candy to content.

Selling Libraries

Dual licensing is the best of both worlds. This can be a working model for companies that make money from selling libraries. You have an open version, licensed with a GPL-like license, that helps with development and finding bugs. With the GPL, any additional work by other developers would go back to the project. However, if a company wanted to use the library as a base to start from, but not give any new development back to the community, then you charge the developer for the same software under a different license.

Selling Support

Much of the money made in selling libraries is actually in the form of selling support. This is included in the initial cost of the library; however, many have an additional fee for each continuing year after the first year. The same could be done with open source software. The support could include initial training for the product, setting up systems for the product, implementing specific changes to the software, and telephone support.

Selling support doesn't have to be limited to software you have developed. Many open source projects fall short in documentation and support. You could step in to offer that service for companies trying to decrease the learning curve.

Peripheral Makers

If you make the drivers for sound cards open source, you increase the potential of your hardware working on a greater number of platforms. With peripherals, there is probably no revenue from the drivers, so the cost of moving to open source is minimal.

Having the drivers readily available and modifiable encourages developers to add support for a product in the game. This increases the number of products and, sub-sequentially, the number of potential end users for their product.

In 2007, when AMD started opening up their graphics drivers, Novell released an alpha version of the ATI Radeon driver in just eight days. It definitely makes more sense for developers who know an operating system to write a driver.

Writing

Who could better give a view of a project than one of its developers? There are many writing opportunities available. A book about using the software could be helpful to developers using the software. Magazine articles about the technology used in the software would help to give greater insight into the project and give back to the community.

While this isn't an option for everyone, there are those who could make money this way. A variation on this theme would be giving speeches about areas of the software.

Downsides

As with any good thing, there are a few downsides as well. This is also true of open source. However, most of the downsides can be dealt with if enough thought and effort is put into it.

Clusters

Often group designing ends up being more talk than action. Or if there weren't a unified direction, the project would end up going nowhere. Either of these could cause the project to go into a serious tailspin.

A cluster could be overcome by having a good design document. Another possible solution to this could be doing all of the engine design internally then opening the project up. It may even be a good idea to delay releasing the code until the alpha release of the project.

Cheaters

This is a serious, legitimate concern. Cheaters take away from the enjoyment of other players. This concern already exists with proprietary source code, having the source wide open would make it easier for cheaters to see how to beat the system. This was a problem when the source for *Quake* was released as open source. Will this be the one area that makes open source difficult to use in the gaming industry?

One solution is to use a license, such as the BSD, that would allow for the non-distribution of sensitive client/server code.

The Competitive Edge

Many companies feel that having the latest and greatest eye candy gives them a competitive edge. Open source would take some of this away. Anyone using your code would have the same features. Even if they weren't using your code, they could see what was being implemented, describe it to another programmer, and legally have the same features without deriving from the original work.

However, real competitive advantages do not come from having "cooler" graphics than the next game; they come from having solid, creative gameplay. If the focus remains on gameplay and not on graphics, then someone getting your newest graphical feature becomes less of a concern.

Conclusion

Unfortunately, many developers are very dogmatic when it comes to open source software. So the flame wars about proprietary verses open source rage on. Then it becomes evil capitalist against dazed and confused socialist. All of this is counterproductive and takes away from making games.

It is best to remember that open source is a tool to make better software. Not everyone wants to use that tool. Some think that proprietary software is the way to go. Of course, everyone has the right to be wrong!

Seriously, determining if open source is right for a project has to be decided on an individual basis. Eric S. Raymond has said that open source is not for everyone. His writings are a good place to start in considering if open source is right for your project (www.catb.org/~esr/writings/magic-cauldron/magic-cauldron.html).

In the end, it's all about writing code and making games; and while healthy debates are good and very much needed, open source shouldn't be treated like a religious experience.

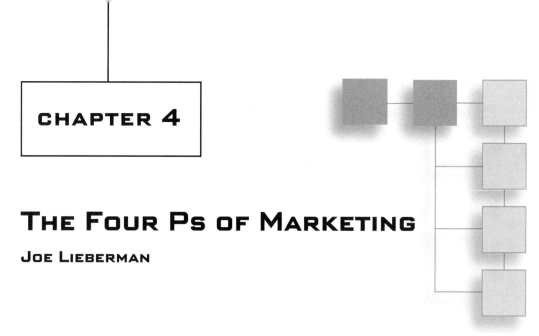

CHAPTER 4

THE FOUR PS OF MARKETING

JOE LIEBERMAN

A preface for this article is that the game market changes extremely quickly. While the foundation of this article is the Four Ps of marketing (and those will never be out of date), the specifics may change fairly rapidly. The original article published to GameDev.net focused on a lot of things that were very specific to the downloadable market. Instead, I will focus this more on the marketing principles, so it won't be out of date by the time you read it.

The most common mistake people make is assuming that if you make it, they will download it. If you create a game, the publishers will find you. If you make the game, the players will find you. That when you are done pounding the code and graphics into the software, you have but to sit and watch the money roll in. . . .

Wake up! It doesn't work that way anywhere in the world. If you are not spending at least 25% of the time it took you to create the game marketing it, then you are doing something wrong. There are a million things to be done, but before you do any of them you have to learn a little bit about what marketing is, keeping these key concepts in mind for each and every decision you make.

The foundation of all marketing, where it all begins, is referred to as the Four Ps. They are *product, price, place,* and *promotion.* In this article, I will go over the Four Ps in the broadest sense and try to relate them to game-specific items. If there is a specific problem with your product that needs overcoming, such as designing a package, I suggest picking up some more detailed texts on each of the Four Ps individually.

Product

In video games, product is probably the thing coders and developers think about most. It is a good thing, because in gaming, product *is* the most important factor. I know, we all remember some really *bad* products that had good marketing and turned out to make a bundle, but that scenario is the exception, not the rule. It is far easier to market a good product than a bad one, and I doubt any indie developer has the assets to market a bad product. The two key words for a product are *want* and *need*. You have to make sure you are giving customers both, and those two things are not always the same!

Okay, so I can't tell you how to make a good product—well, not in a few paragraphs anyway. Long story short here is make the game good, but there are some items in the product that impact your sales that I can talk about in this small space.

Design of a demo product is one. A key concept, for instance, is making your product accessible to a wide audience. This means being compatible with as many systems as you can. Try to design the game and the demo to not require any reading or preferably any help files. You only have a limited amount of time to show your new client your game—you don't want to squander that time having them read help files. That said, if the game is complex enough that some help-file reading needs to be done, make sure you *force* them to read and understand. Remember: The customer *wants* to instantly play but *needs* to learn the basic controls!

A very common question concerning the product is, What is the best way to make a demo? There are three basic demo types:

- **Time Limited:**
  Pro: Gives the user a taste of what the full version is like. Most portals require a 60-minute demo.
  Con: It is very hard to time the demo to end where the person is hungry for more.

- **Feature Limited:**
  Pro: Easy to dangle the additional features right in front of the user.
  Con: Some people may not buy because they didn't experience a feature they wanted or didn't know a feature was there that should have been dangled better.

- **Episodic:**
  Pro: Easy to end the plot or game at a cliff-hanger. Giving away an episode can count as having a "free" game to use to promote your site.

Con: Could give too much of your game away. People may be content to play only your demo and never upgrade.

There is no right answer when it comes down to it. Every demo type has been used successfully by some people. The key to designing a good demo is that the demo ends right when the person is really getting into it. I like to use this motto: Give the customers all that they need and a taste of what they want, and then leave them hanging.

I point out the irony that, to me, time limited is the least effective demo type but the one used by most portals. Why? Uniformity. If every demo was different, portals worry it would confuse users; they frankly don't trust you to do a good job making it any other way. Still, it shouldn't stop you from trying to get them to use what model you think suits your game best.

Product also refers to what is sometimes called the fifth P: *package.* You'd only use that in retail marketing, as online stuff really has no package. Here I'm focusing on online goods, so no box and no package. When you go into retail, know this: A good box sells games!

Price

Possibly the most complicated process in any industry, price is a huge factor in the success of your product. One key concept is that price is not the same as *value.* The main concern you should have is to deliver your product so that its value is greater than its price; otherwise, people won't buy it. In this section, I touch on four different concepts of price. There are *many* more, but these are some of the biggest:

- **Prestige pricing** is a term that basically says, "A more expensive product is a higher quality product." Nine out of 10 people will tell you, when faced with two identical products, the one with the higher price tag is the higher-quality product. Prestige price refers to this effect: A $20 game is a better game than a $10 game. A higher price does raise the value of the product, but not necessarily equal to the increase in price. Sometimes it is possible to use a discount to give a product the volume of a lower cost without loss of prestige.

- **Penetration pricing** is the strategy that says, "A lower price will generate more volume." More volume means more market share. More market share means more future sales. A $10 game generates more sales than a $20 game, but maybe not more profit. Penetration is best used with a product that has strong viral capacity—that is, the more people who buy the game create more potential for future people to buy the game. Read that line as many times as it takes to let it sink in. In penetration pricing, you are often sacrificing profit per unit in order to generate more sales for your next product, or for this product at a much later date.

- **The Hardest Dollar concept**: In online sales, it is common that anyone willing to spend $1 on your game would be willing to spend $10 or $20. This is saying that the hardest part of an online sale is simply getting a user to open his wallet. This is also why subscription sales work so well, as the customer's wallet is automatically open every month, thus neutralizing the largest hurdle. It is quite possible to use this "If they'd spend $1" mentality as justification for a higher price, but it is important to note that the impact of this decreases the farther from $1 you get. At $30, it's likely you'll be back to your normal demand curve.

- **Intangible terms of sale** is often seen in offerings outside of a pure dollar-and-cents value: customer support, support from the developer, or getting 25% off your next purchase. These are just a few of the intangible benefits you can tack onto your product. By offering intangible benefits, you can often increase the value of the product without altering its price.

Place

Luckily for all of you, there are not too many place decisions to make in games. Download, CD, retail, or online publisher—that covers all the main ones you will encounter. Place is the distribution and where people get the product to try it or buy it. Each place decision has its own benefits and pains, and odds are you can put your product in every "place."

Download is what I work most with, though you can offer a CD as a part of the download package from places like Swift CD. In general, getting downloads amounts to putting your game in as many places as possible. To that end, you have places to submit downloadable games like shareware directories, you have places that review and cover games, and you have forums and interest groups that you should approach. Getting downloads is a tough business these days, as there is a lot of competition.

Retail is the most expensive and most difficult. You *will* need a publisher if you want to get into a retail store. In general, putting a retail title on a shelf runs anywhere between $100,000 and $200,000 or more. And that is just to get your title on a shelf! Usually, marketing is not handled by the developer here, so most of this is out of your hands. Sadly this can also mean you are just part of long tail sales, and your individual product is just a meaningless number to them. Yep, expect to get raked over the coals in retail. These days it's a collapsing market, but there is still money to be made there.

Nowadays, the most common form of place is an online publisher. These non-exclusive houses hold most of the downloadable market. The amount you get per sale tends to range between 20% and 40%, and in exchange, you have access to their users. They don't actively market your product, but the exposure you get on their site can be turned and used in your favor. It will get people actively looking for your product, so make sure there is a good way for them to use search engines to find *your* site so you can promote your games directly, hopefully stealing away a few users from the portals.

Promotion

Last but not least is promotion. Ask 10 people on the street what a marketing person does, and all 10 will probably tell you that promotion is what they do. The preceding three Ps are also what we do, but it's not what people think about. Promotion is the combination of advertising, publicity, and buzz (a subset of publicity).

Buzz is the hardest to create and the hardest to control. Most firms actually avoid trying to make buzz because of the havoc it can cause. Buzz items are typically fads, and the problem it most frequently creates is demand exceeding capacity. In the download world, it is not as big of a deal, thankfully. To create buzz, basically you need a viral product and a huge quantity of publicity, advertising, and customer discussion over your product in a very short period of time. I'll go out on a limb and say it should be your goal to achieve as much buzz as possible, but it's not really the focus of your efforts.

Publicity is "free" advertising. Reviews, interviews, and previews are the most common forms of this. Also included are press releases, screenshots, and link exchanges. The downside of publicity is that it usually takes a lot of time and work to get. Remember, if you build it they will *not* come. Reviewers will not bang down your door, and you have to do more than just submit your game to some unknown e-mail address. To get publicity, you must be tenacious. Get people's contact info and talk to them as frequently as you can, both before and after your game is released. Even after they review it, stay in touch and keep them informed of what you're up to. You never know when someone will write an article and mention upcoming games or ideas.

Advertising is a much easier creature; it's also much more expensive. To correctly advertise, you must know your target market and your conversion rate. Conversion rates are how many sales you get for every 100 downloads. Ads must also be targeted. *Target* refers to what group is most likely to buy your game. Lately there has been a lot of emphasis on Google Adwords from sites, and Google is a good advertising source, but part of me thinks it's a copout from doing research and finding better deals. In recent years, Google has become less and less profitable for online games due to increased competition.

The Four (or Five) Ps are pretty much the backbone for everything else in promotion. The simple goal here is to get you to think about each of them. How does your product look, and how well is the demo designed? Where will you be distributing it, and are you guaranteed to get where you want to go? Who is handling the promotion of your product, and what budget do you have for that person and advertising? Does that person have all the contacts in place and ready to go when the product is ready? Will you charge the standard $19.95 for this game, or are you going to try something different? What intangible benefits to the sale can you add?

Think about these things and others that come to your mind. I recommend writing the questions and the answers (if you have them) in a document and bringing it up once in a while to remind yourself of the focus and goals of each of the Four Ps. You'll be glad you did!

CHAPTER 5

ADVERTISING YOUR GAMES

JOE LIEBERMAN

Advertising has always been a rough market. Not only is it extremely competitive, expensive, and risky, but it also changes as fast as any market. If I had written this article a few years ago, let's say in 2005, it would have been all about how to use Google Adwords. Today, while Google can still provide a good outlet, it's not your one-stop shop any longer for advertising glory.

So where do you turn? Well, the sad reality may be nowhere. Games are a low-margin, low-conversion business, and when you are competing with spyware and big business, it's pretty clear who gets the most revenue per user. There are, however, some terms and descriptions that apply to all advertising models and methods. If your game falls into the category where you could benefit from one of these approaches, by all means use it and try to get some positive return on investment (ROI) on your ad spending.

In order of importance, these terms are as follows:

1. Bulls-eye targeting

2. Competitor targeting

3. Horizontal targeting

4. Vertical targeting

Bulls-Eye Targeting

The key to successful advertising is targeting the ads to the users most likely to purchase your product. Seems like a no-brainer, right? Unfortunately, the trouble typically comes from figuring out who the heck your target market really is, and once you do figure it out, how do you go about reaching them? In order to determine the *most* targeted user, you start at the very highest level of user interest and awareness. This is, in fact, people who are interested in your game specifically. Once again, the sad fact is, unless you have a preexisting audience, then this group of people is pretty small. Still, advertising to your own audience tends to be dirt cheap and super effective. Do not fret about your preexisting users not liking a sudden e-mail from the developer. I find that while you will get a few complaints, the impact of such a thing is tremendously positive for sales and growth.

Competitor Targeting

This leads us to the next group—people who are interested in similar games to yours. I'm not talking about people who like *Risk* also liking some board-strategy game; I am talking about the people who have cloned another game in part or in whole. This is where Google and other contextual/search ads come in most handy. Advertising on the keywords of your competitor's products gives you an opportunity to piggyback on their success. Nothing in advertising is easy, though, and what you're going to find is that most of the people looking for a specific product are *not* looking for an alternative. This means you'll be bidding less than everyone else and won't be able to pull big volume even on a popular game. Still, if you have a hidden object game and put an ad on every other hidden object game's name, you'd probably do enough volume to make it worthwhile.

Horizontal vs. Vertical Targeting

Before I dive into the next two approaches, an explanation is necessary to illustrate the difference between them. This applies to all industries, so it's a useful concept you are certain to run into again someday. Vertical and horizontal targeting are both about getting into the mind of the consumer, which makes it a rather tricky thing to define. Vertical refers to drilling down into the subdivisions of human interest. Creepy as it sounds, it is best described by example. A vertical chain looks like this: I like games. I like sports games. I like strategy games. I like sports games. I like sports strategy games. You can move up or down this chain to increase or decrease the targeting. Each level of vertical "down" is a better target, but as you may suspect, a smaller one as well. So far we've been very far down the vertical chain, so next we'll go up the vertical chain a little, making things less targeted but still within the vertical area.

Vertical markets are all the rage these days, probably because they clearly make sense. Horizontal is in reference to the breadth of the interest level of a particular group. This makes a whole lot less sense, and you'll find tons of different definitions of a horizontal market out there. One person I know defines a horizontal market only as a product with near-universal appeal. Spreadsheet software or games as a whole could also qualify. An ad targeting anyone who enjoys games would be a horizontal ad; this ad could appear on any web site, and, because of its universal appeal, attract attention no matter what. I say that's a load of bunk, and I simply call these things universal products/ads.

So how do I define horizontals? Visualize a point-down triangle, and draw three horizontal lines in that triangle. The top and broadest area in the example is "I like games" while the bottom is "I like sports strategy games." Where it says "I like sports games," draw a vertical line and also write "I like strategy games." This is an example of two different horizontals occupying *very* close proximity. Not mentioned is the very high likelihood of this person saying, "I like sports." Here you have a completely separate triangle (vertical). It would appear horizontally across from "I like games." In that triangle, "I like soccer" would be below it, horizontally across from "I like soccer games." This is where I derive the idea of a "horizontal" target. Because games are a universally enjoyed commodity (yeah, okay, let's just say it is), then you can clearly advertise in a vertical market connected to your horizontal chain! Time for a shoddy picture! (See Figure 5.1.)

Horizontal Targeting

So here is the big error people make. The next recommendation I have is to aim at the horizontal niche of your game, assuming you have one. Let's say you made a World War II clone of *Risk*. You've exhausted aiming ads at *Risk* players. The horizontal target after that would be to aim at people interested in World War II. This is where most people make the common mistake of thinking that their next target is a vertical niche, for instance, targeting people interested in board games. The horizontal niche often has so much less competition that it is cheaper and more effective to focus on horizontal positions. So in this example, my next place to go would be World War II web sites. Not all games have a clear horizontal

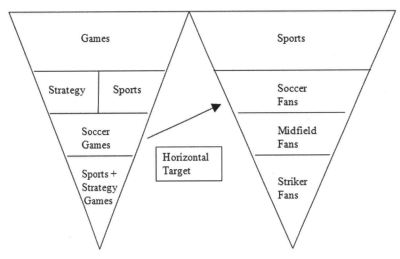

Figure 5.1

niche, however. If your game is about WWII, you're in good shape. If your game is about cute balls of fluff, you're outta luck. If your game is about fairies, you may be able to find some fairy web sites, but odds are you're not going to see much volume.

Vertical Targeting

The place most people want to put their ads for some reason is the vertical niche. If I made a board game, I would want to advertise on board game sites. The fact is, I have almost *never* found this to be an effective method (ROI-wise) for advertising a game. You can still try it—focus on running ads on game sites or sites related to the exact genre of your game. The closer you can get to your game's look, feel, and genre, the better. I wouldn't bet much money on it though. The simple fact is, competition is too high and that drives prices up.

So that is the overall strategy of where to run ads. There are a few items that have common questions and concerns left, though, so I'll focus on a few corner-case questions.

Probably the most common question is, "How does X company turn a profit when they are spending Y dollars on ads!?" The answer may be that they don't. Not all ads are run for a positive ROI. Sometimes it is smart to employ a loss leader strategy. If you can spend $21 to make $20 but attract 1000 people per dollar "lost," then it may be to your advantage to lose a dollar simply to gain the attention, e-mail addresses, and name recognition of those 1000 people. However, in the realm of an indie or small-time development studio, a loss leader strategy is rarely an option. So lets focus on getting a positive ROI.

Another good question is, "What about print advertising (or radio or TV)?" The short answer is "Forget it." Print, TV, and radio all are brand-awareness focused media. You could build up your company reputation with a slick jingle, and on a national campaign that could mean big bucks. For a TV ad, if you are a studio that has made only one game and it is available only online, there is a huge barrier to get people off their lazy butts, walk over to the computer, download that one game, and then make a purchase. It's a heck of a lot easier when their lazy butts are already parked in front of the PC, and your banner ad is slapping them in the face. The only exception to this is if you can somehow negotiate some huge perk to your ads, such as being the featured game on a demo CD or getting a three-day, three-article front page feature on a game magazine's web site. Basically, in this case, you are getting something large enough that the print ad is no longer really what you're buying, merely the means to an end. Web-based ads will always have a better ROI, and I can't think of a single case where a single product site has seen otherwise.

Here's another interesting question: "what is the most effective form of online ads?" The answer to this varies widely with how good you are at creating ad copy (good text, good graphics, interesting sales pitch, and so on). However, if I had to pick one, I would actually say e-mail newsletters have the best bang for your buck; just be careful that you aren't working with a spam company. If, for instance, your WWII *Risk* clone found a WWII web site with a newsletter that offered an ad spot (advertorial preferably), I would be on that like white on rice. Don't be put off by the fact the CPM is going to be high ($5 to $25 is not unheard of for a newsletter).

Finally let's define some terms/acronyms you're bound to run into—in case you're a total noob at this:

- **CTR (click-through rate)**: The percentage of people who click on an ad. A standard banner ad should range between .5 and 2%, depending on position, quality, targeting, etc.

- **CPM (cost per mille)**: How much 1,000 displays of your ad costs. An ad that costs $1.00 CPM and has a 1% CTR means you are paying 10 cents per click.

- **CPC (cost per click)**: How much you are paying per click.

- **CPA (cost per action)**: Payment is made only when the user performs an action, such as signing up for an account, newsletter, or making a purchase. Also known as PPA, PFP, and CPL.

- **ROI (return on investment)**: Mentioned previously, but also keep in mind that ROI factors in future value of visitors as well. If the average purchasing user buys 1.2 games, all of that value should be factored into the ad buy. Keep in mind, however, that ad-based visitors are *not* equal to the average visitor and should be tracked separately. An ad-based visitor may convert half as likely and make only 1.1 sales per purchase.

- **RPM (revenue per mille)**: This typically refers to a single page view and all the ads on that page. So if you had three ads paying 1.00 CPM, you'd say your page RPM is 3.00.

- **IAB (interactive advertising bureau) ad sizes:** This bureau defined the "standard" ad sizes that we see. If someone asks for IAB-sized ads, they probably mean 728 x 90 (superbanner/leaderboard), 160 or 120 x 600 (sky and wide sky), and/or 300 x 250 (box) sized ads. Other very common IAB sizes include 468 x 60 (banner), 88 x 31 (button), and 125 x 125 (square). In games, we also see a fair number of 100 x 100 ads, but those are not IAB standard.

- **RON/ROS (run of network/site)**: This refers to buying or selling an ad across an entire network or site with no special targeting.

And so what can you take away from this? Hopefully, it is this: advertising is really freakin' hard! If you've planned your success around an ad budget rather than a stellar product, you're in deep doodoo. Also, other than giving you a good dose of pessimism, there are a lot of terms and concepts flung around the ad world. The reality is that people will be impressed if you can fling terms and concepts back at them. Finally, if you do decide to advertise using the targeting models I discussed, it will give you the best fighting chance for success.

CHAPTER 6

SUBMITTING YOUR GAME TO RETAILERS

RICK CAREY (RICK@BRILLIANTGAMES.NET)

Everybody loves to hate the Big Retailers. We hate them for all of their big corporate attitudes, for having no regard for the little guy, and for the big Evil Empire vibe that they put out. At the same time, most of us would be willing to perform many sundry acts and even sell a portion of our souls to be able to get a product on their shelves. Unfortunately, in order to do this, we must deal with the corporate bureaucracy that exists within the bowels of the Big Retailer.

While this article is written primarily with the brick-and-mortar retailer in mind, many of the items discussed here are equally applicable for sending submissions to a publisher or an online retailer. Each company is going to have its own internal practices and machinations to contend with, so you may very well find more similarities between one retailer and a publisher than one retailer and another retailer.

Choosing a Retailer

The first stage after developing the product is to decide which company or companies get the opportunity to sell your item. If you are sending out submissions to many retailers, it's very important that you don't prejudge them to try to determine whether they are likely to carry your product or not. For example, if your product is geared toward a more casual user, you may think it's a waste of time to send a submission to a retailer that only carries top-shelf titles. However, retailers are constantly reinventing themselves and trying to expand their market share, and your submission may hit them at the very moment when they are looking to expand their line into exactly your product's niche.

Prototypes

Next, you will need to create your first prototypes. Retailers are generally looking for a finished or nearly finished product (some won't want to even look at your product until it is shelf ready), and they will want a lot of them. If you have the means to produce your own CDs, gift boxes, manuals, registration cards, and other materials in large quantities, then you may be able to deal directly with the retailer. However, if this production is beyond your means, then you're better off seeking out a publisher to get your product made and presented to the retailer. Be aware that even when you get the sale, you're not likely to get any payment up front. Retailers like to pay on credit just like everyone else. Some will want to pay 30 to 90 days after the product is delivered. And don't be surprised if that time goes by and you have to call to remind them that they owe you money. Keep this in mind when you're creating your publishing budget.

If you're going to self-publish, don't make a big run of your product before showing it to the prospective retailers. The number of retailers to whom you submit the product will help you determine how many units should be in the first product run. Make a few mockups for each retailer, based on their guidelines (if any). It's entirely possible that the retailer will ask for some changes to the product before they purchase it for their shelves. If you've already printed thousands of units, you'll either have to eat that cost or find someplace else to sell them as is. Additionally, if the retailer knows that you've already printed a large volume, they will consider their options limited to "go" or "no go." On the plus side, if you already have a large production run, having many units preprinted will allow the retailer to take delivery more quickly; many retailers are supremely concerned with how fast they can get new products to the market. However, this should only be considered an option if you're dealing with new technology or you have experience with producing your own product and are reasonably certain that you can cover all of your bases.

Product Requirements

The retailer may provide you with a set of guidelines or requirements for submitting a new product to them. Between retailers, this document can vary from a single page with general guidelines up to a 1,000-page document that details everything down to the font size you must use in your help files and which shoe you must tie first on the day you mail them the submission. Additionally, you may encounter some retailers that provide no guidance at all. The jury is still out on which of these is the better scenario.

The guideline documents will likely use three different words to dictate the level of compliance that is required for each guideline or requirement. They are "may," "should," and "must." The counters to these are also used: "may not," "should not," and "must not." These words take on very specific meanings in this context:

- **May:** This is an allowance. These items are permissible but by no means are requirements. This is typically used with items in which there could be confusion. Sometimes this is used as a clarification of a "should" or a "must."

- **Should:** This is a preference. These are items that the retailer would like to see included in a product to the degree that they could give preferential treatment to any products that include them. However, failure to provide the "should" item is not considered a show-stopper.

- **Must:** This is a requirement. Typically, this word *is* reserved for show-stoppers. Products that do not meet this requirement are generally rejected if the product cannot be altered to comply. This may also be an item that is dictated by law.

Example: "Software products MUST be compatible with Windows XP and Windows Vista, SHOULD be compatible with Windows 98 and Windows 2000, and MAY be compatible with Macintosh operating systems."

You should take any requirements supplied by the retailer seriously. If they've gone to all the trouble of actually creating them and supplying them to you, then you can be sure that *they* will take the requirements seriously. That being said, you should also note that these requirements could be subject to interpretation or even be waived entirely if you provide a compelling enough argument. Often, the requirements are written by one department, but the final decision on acceptability is in the hands of another department.

If you are lucky enough to work with a company that provides clear guidelines, then I can conclude with "do it how they want," as the primary focus of this article is on submissions to a retailer that provides no guidance at all. This article, based on personal experience and research, will try to give you an idea of the sorts of things that a retailer will expect of you and what you can expect from the retailer. Note, however, that this information cannot be considered all-inclusive—your mileage may vary.

The Process

In every large retail establishment, there is a process for getting products to the shelves. Beyond the obvious logistical problems of warehousing and shipping, each retailer has a process for reviewing products from a vendor to determine if their product is worthy of the retailer's highly valuable shelf space (real or virtual). It may not always be a good, or even logical, process, but it's the one you must deal with if you want your product distributed. The first step in this process is to get your product in front of the right person.

If you're sending in your product without any prior introductions or requests from the retailer for a sample, it's important to send it to someone specific. You should be sending it addressed to an actual person if at all possible or, at the very least, to a specific department within the company. It's always best to try to get in contact with someone at the retailer *and* get at least a verbal agreement from him or her to look at your product. This will give you the beginnings of a relationship with someone at the company and also a contact point for following up on the progress of your submission.

Finding a Contact

The best way to go about getting in touch with an actual person is to start calling the company's corporate headquarters. Making blind calls like this can be intimidating and can often lead to dead-ends. First, be sure to call the corporate headquarters number and not the customer service line. These two numbers lead to very different places in the corporation. Once you have the corporate operator on the line, ask for the software buyer. This can prove difficult if you don't know who the buyer is, so you can ask instead for a department. Asking for a department will often get you to an administrative assistant for that department, and he or she may be more willing to help you find the right person. Different companies will have different names for the buying department, so you may need to try several before finding the right one. Some department names that you can try are Software Procurement (though this might send you to the IT department), Buying, Product Development, Quality Control, Quality Assurance, Product Engineering, and Software Development. If you are still unable to get a name, don't let that keep you from sending your submission. At the very least, your research should have helped you determine the correct department.

Initial Submission

Once you know who gets your product, the initial submission should be as final as you are able to make it. That's not to say that you still don't have some changes to make to the product, documentation, or packaging, but what you send in should be the latest and greatest that you can produce. Right now, the biggest emphasis should be on the product and the accompanying documentation.

Even if you're sending the product sample in for a "first look," you need to anticipate that someone is going to take a serious and in-depth look at your product. That may not actually happen until much later (or even after a subsequent sample submission), but you should be ready for it if it happens early in the process.

Specific Requirements

Retailers will expect you to follow standard user interface (UI) conventions where appropriate. For example, in game design, you can be very liberal with the UI for the game itself; however, you'll be expected to follow standard UI conventions for installation screens as well as configuration and setting screens. If your product emulates the operation of any well-known convention (such as an embedded calculator or spreadsheet), it is in your best interest to make your UI behave according to established expectations.

You can also expect the retailer to have specific requirements as to which OS platforms the software must be compatible with. Unfortunately, there are so many variations of different operating systems, with all the different patches and service packs that can be installed, that unless the retailer tells you exactly what configurations they are going to test with, it'll be virtually impossible for you to anticipate and test on exactly the same configurations. However, you must perform your due diligence to try to make sure that your product is as compatible with the expected operating systems as is reasonably possible.

Documentation

At this stage, comprehensive documentation is just as important as the product. When submitting your product, it is vital that you supply separate printed documentation with your submission. Even if you have created a nice, in-depth help system within your product, send along a printed version of the user's manual as well. If you haven't written all of that yet, then you need to take the time to bang something out that will at least tell the buyer or the evaluator how to install and operate your product. If for some reason you cannot detail the functionality of all features, then you must at least list all of the features so that the evaluator will know about them and can try them out. A lack of documentation can result in your submission being rejected with a comment like, "We couldn't make it work. . . no docs."

Installation instructions need to be substantially more detailed than "Run setup and follow the onscreen prompts." Even if you've designed the installation to be nearly foolproof and idiot-proof, you have no idea what class of fools and idiots the retailer may have hired to evaluate your product. An excellent approach is to take screen shots of each step of the installation procedure and put them all in a document with detailed instructions on each screen. These installation instructions may end up as part of the final user documentation at the retailer's discretion.

A similar method should be followed for help screens, setup screens, and perhaps even the main operation of the product. Remember that it's always better to err on the side of too much documentation rather than not enough.

The final two pieces of documentation that you need to have are the deviation list and the text list. A deviation list highlights all items in your submitted product version that still need work before final release. These may be items that you need to do, or items that require input or work from other parties, including the retailer, translators, copy editors, or other people. Never make any assumptions. If you know of something that still must be changed, include it on the deviation list! Otherwise, the evaluator may assume that your product is broken and that you have no clue.

The text list is needed in case the retailer also wants to have your product available in multiple languages. To be ready for this, you should have a file prepared that contains all of the text in your product.

Note

This means ALL OF THE TEXT. Not just the help files, not just the manual—*all of the text.*

The retailer may require you to get the translations and include them in your product, documentation, and packaging, or they may have their own translators provide the translation for you to include. Either way, be prepared to supply them with everything they will need to be translated up front.

Now that you have your docs in a row, be sure you pay attention to any documentation, guidelines, comments, or other communication that you receive from the retailer regarding the terminology they use. Large organizations create their own processes and requirements as well as their own language. Learn this language as best as you can, and use it in your correspondence with them.

Product Development

When the retailer accepts your product submission, the company will likely create a timeline for getting your product onto their shelves, which they may do with or without your input. Once they have communicated the schedule with you, it's vitally important that you give serious consideration to your ability to meet the schedule. If the schedule seems outside of your capabilities or unrealistic in any way, communicate that to the retailer immediately so the schedule may be adjusted. Adherence to the schedule can be an important part of your agreement with the retailer, and failure to meet the schedule can result in monetary consequences on your part.

Evaluation

Once you've sent the product in, someone is going to test your product for the retailer. This may be a buyer or a dedicated evaluator. A buyer will likely not give your product the in-depth scrutiny that an evaluator might. The buyer is usually just checking to see that your product functions (if he loads it at all). An evaluator is usually trained to run your product through a battery of tests and will actually attempt to break it. It's their job.

Evaluators receive a great deal of their job satisfaction from being able to break your product. If you get back comments along the lines of, "The shade of pink in level 1 does not match the shade of pink in level 3," then you should be very proud of yourself as you have forced the evaluator to hunt for the tiniest little nit that he can pick in order to justify his existence and his paycheck (and you should also fix your pinks). Just because you may think that an evaluator's comments seem insignificant and maybe even petty, this person may hold a great deal of influence over whether your product gets any farther with the retailer.

Comments and Communication

Once the evaluator has looked at your product and provided comments and requested changes to the product, documentation, and/or packaging, it is important that you respond in a timely and professional manner. And when you do respond, be sure to address each of the comments individually.

For example, if you get back a number of seemingly trivial comments that can all be addressed in short order, don't simply say "all comments noted." Individually address each comment, acknowledge the comment, and state what action will be taken. You may end up with several items that say something along the lines of, "Noted—the help text is in the wrong shade of gray. It will be changed to #CCC gray in the next sample. Please recheck then."

For more serious issues, take the same approach but do not feel that you need to go into too much detail. If the evaluator finds a bug in your program, acknowledge the error and advise what actions you'll take to remedy the problem. You don't need to detail exactly what you're changing in your code, only that you are making changes to fix the problem and when the retailer can see the improved samples.

There is also the possibility that the evaluator may find problems you cannot reproduce. If this happens, you need to shift into high gear and figure out what's going on. If you simply tell the retailer that you cannot duplicate the problem, your product may get dropped. If you cannot duplicate the error, immediately ask for any log files that your software may generate. You might also request a video from the evaluator so that you can see exactly what is happening to create the error. You should try to get as much information as possible about the setup that they are using, including hardware, software, peripherals, Internet connection, and anything else that may or may not seem relevant.

If after all of this you still cannot duplicate the problem, you may have to resort to a trip to the retailer's testing facility to see the problem firsthand. However, this will only happen if the retailer is willing to put up with your visit. A vendor visit is a big hassle for the retailer and a serious disruption to the workflow. Be sure to take along your own development hardware and software so that you can try to make changes on the spot (or at least in your hotel room that night).

After you have addressed the evaluator's comments and each issue has been resolved (either by acceptance of the issue as is or promises from you to fix the issue), a subsequent sample will probably be required to verify that requested changes have been made and that the product is ready for production.

The Contract

At this point, if the retailer agrees to buy your product, their lawyers will probably hand you a large document that details your responsibilities and the retailer's obligations. This is a good time to get your lawyer involved (you do have a lawyer, right?). While you may not be likely to get any of the provisions in the document changed in your favor, having someone decipher the legalese and detail exactly what it is that you're agreeing to can save you a great deal of trouble and headache down the road. Remember—*their* lawyers wrote the agreement, and it's designed to work in *their* best interest, not yours.

After the Sale

Even if the retailer is supposedly handling all customer support for your product, you should expect to receive some calls and/or e-mails if your name, company name, or web site is anywhere in or on the product. Consequently, the retailer may expect you to handle all of the customer support for your product. No matter how simple, intuitive, or trivial you think your product is, there will always be some amount of customer support involved.

It is also possible that the retailer may ask for a "running change" on subsequent orders due to returns, customer comments, and/or complaints on the initial version. In anticipation of these changes, do not overproduce in expectation of future orders; compliance with the running-change requests may be a prerequisite for the retailer accepting delivery of additional orders.

As you can see, there are a lot of areas that you must cover in getting your product onto the shelves of the Big Retailers. If you manage to navigate the maze of corporate bureaucracy and make the sale, you just might get your product in front of millions of potential customers and reap the benefits of entrenched emplacement in the landscape of our consumer-driven marketplace.

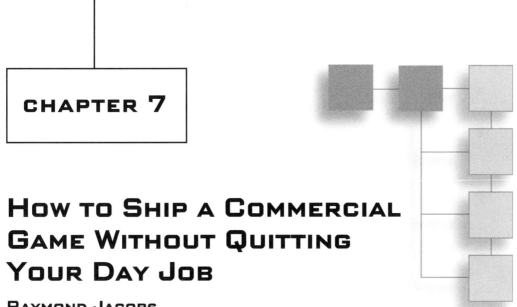

CHAPTER 7

How to Ship a Commercial Game Without Quitting Your Day Job

Raymond Jacobs

Anyone who has played games has at one point or another thought "If I made a game it would have this and be like that." This is mostly done in passing from one gamer to another. A select few decide to carry out their plans to create a game. Some find jobs in the industry, and others strike out on their own. Here I'll be talking about the passionate and elusive indie game developer. So, you've been dreaming about game development for years now, and perhaps you've picked up some programming, art, and writing skills along the way. You're ready to do something big and maybe acquire some fame and fortune. The first rule of indie game development is that it is difficult; very often you have low-to-no budget, and most of the work is done by one or two people in their spare time. Unless you are independently wealthy, you're going to need a day job; it doesn't matter what it is as long as it pays the bills and gives you enough time to work on your game. But before you start slinging code and drawing pretty pictures, you need to take a higher-level look at the business aspect of your game if ever you hope to sell it.

Financial Target

When deciding your financial target, you need to decide what kind of typical business model your game will follow. Let's compare two common avenues: freeware and retail.

Freeware

If you're a new face to the indie scene, a freeware game might be your ticket to greatness. Freeware is just that—a game that is free—and there are some major benefits to this.

Freeware games:

- Are likely to reach a large portion of your target market; the more eyes on your product, the more people know about you, and building a fan base is key to sales of future titles.

- Are inherently sold as is, and you avoid the issues of a financial transaction and the liabilities that can come with it; in short, if the game turns out to be a flop, you don't *need* to support it.

- Can generate indirect revenue via web site advertising or even, potentially, donations.

- Get a bit of slack; if it's your first game, it's likely not going to be the greatest thing since sliced bread, and people generally understand that something they got for free is allowed to be a bit under quality.

However it's not all good. Freeware games can also:

- Give the impression of a lack of quality or prestige; people generally expect good things to cost money, so a free game can give the impression that it is less than worthy.

- Not generate any direct revenue! No cash means no change of your current double-duty day/night job scenario.

In short, if you're just testing the waters and seeking fame more than fortune, a freeware game is probably what you want to develop.

Retail

The heavyweight of the games industry, retail games (sold either online or in stores) are commercial items and typically sport demos to allow users to "try before they buy." Typical prices per unit usually range from $9.95 to $59.95, depending on the title and its prestige. As an indie, you'll likely be in the $9.95 to $29.95 range, as it seems this is what the current market tends to bear. Retail games, like everything else, have their pros and cons as well.

Retail games:

- Give a psychological feeling of prestige; if a company is asking money for a product, then subconsciously that product is worth money and therefore has implied value.

- Provide potentially large amounts of direct revenue, assuming you manage to sell enough copies.

- Are the typical mode of PC game sales; people are generally comfortable with purchasing a computer game off a shelf.

The downsides are:

- People expect retail games to be similar to AAA quality games, so you may find yourself up against stiff competition and unable to get shelf space.

- The additional overhead of selling a retail game and associated advertising and support can be daunting for a first-time indie.

Division of Labor

When getting ready to develop an indie game, you must decide how many people will be involved with the development. Let's compare the two styles of indie game development: lone wolf and team.

Lone Wolf

A lone wolf "team" is actually the lack of a team; it is a single developer who does all the writing, programming, scripting, graphics, sound—you name it. However, some indies consider themselves lone wolves even when they outsource some or most of their work (such as graphics, sound effects, music, or even programming). So to be a lone wolf usually means to be only a single person directly dedicated to the project's success. If you're highly self-motivated and have a broad skill set, then you might be happier as a lone wolf (with some potential outsourcing if you have the capital).

Pros in a lone wolf team:

- You have all the say.

- You reap all the reward.

Cons in a lone wolf team:

- It is hard to stay motivated, as you are the only driving force. (Generally having others working with you can stimulate motivation.)

- The "idea pool" is a little shallow; you may have some great ideas, but almost all ideas can be better through refinement from others.

- You do all the work; creating a game is a lot of work, so unless you plan to outsource some things, be prepared for a long development cycle.

Team

A team atmosphere can be very beneficial to an indie game project; the diversity of its members can help to create unique elements that a single person likely could not. Dividing the work load among multiple people can make the development cycle shorter and make work easier for each member. Teams, however, are not without their problems. As most of us know, even under the best circumstances, personalities can grate on one another and tempers can flare. If you are a social person and/or don't have all the skills needed to write an entire game yourself (and don't have the capital to outsource), then chances are you're going to need a team.

Pros in a team:

- Work is divided to achieve parallelism and avoid burnout.

- Ideas from different individuals can create interesting game designs.

Cons in a team:

- Less potential profit gain per team member; in a team of three (assuming equal division), a net profit of $100,000 becomes only $33,000 per person. That's a big difference!

- People are people; people get tired, irritable, and bored. People can also be unreliable, so if you introduce others into the scenario, be ready to deal with drama in addition to development.

Financial Needs

The financial needs of an indie can vary widely. Some can get by on a case of soda and a pack of gum, and others will need a massive loan. What you need and if you're able/willing to get it can determine a lot about your project.

Human Resources

The first major financial topic is the people who are going to be working with/for you; it is not uncommon to find many indie team members working for nothing. Some people just want the experience and prestige of releasing a game. Most members, however, will want at least a promissory of something, assuming that the title is meant to be a commercial product. Commonly, for small teams, the typical "we'll split the earnings" is done, and it can range from a verbal/written agreement to a more formal contractor agreement. Other teams work on a payment-per-asset type system, where particular tasks are priced and paid out as they are completed. This is very similar to outsourcing.

Workstation

Most indie development takes place on consumer-grade PC hardware with some being above normal in processing power, memory, and graphics hardware. Upgrading an existing computer is usually a much cheaper solution than building an entirely new machine. You will want to make sure your machine can handle the proposed tools required for development in an efficient manner. Time spent waiting for code to compile is time lost to other tasks.

Indie team members are usually responsible for their own tools; however, it is not uncommon for a team leader to purchase a particular hardware upgrade to bring a member's machine up to par. Practices can vary widely, though.

Software

Another sizable expenditure can be the software tools needed for the project and its resource production. Software can range from free to thousands of dollars per license. Indies should try to favor free software in the interest of budget; however, superior pay software benefits should be realized and licenses purchased where needed.

Marketing

Promotion of your project, both in development and after release, can carry heavy costs. At the very least, you will want a web site domain and a web host; avoid free hosting like the plague, as they are usually slow. Ads and restrictions can give a bad impression to your visitors as well. An effective form of free marketing is to discover and join online game communities that fall into your project's genre. Dropping the occasional mention of your project's progress, having a signature link to your web site, and becoming a general asset to the community are good ways to build awareness of your project. Internet advertising (banners, etc.) can be effective but costly for a low conversion rate. Traditional advertising (television, radio, newspapers) isn't usually well suited for indies due to its high cost and wide targeting.

Quality of Life

Developing indie games will put an additional strain on your personal and professional life. Your project will likely demand a large amount of your free time. Less free time for yourself and loved ones can cause issues, so it's important that you and your loved ones understand this up front. If you have a significant other, spouse, and/or children, your free time with them is likely to be reduced; it is important to pre-arrange what is acceptable so that your great indie game project doesn't end up ruining your personal relationships. For yourself, understand that you will need to make your project a priority; as with most things, if you do not focus on your game, it will not get done. Intense personal discipline is required for completing a game project (especially if you're a lone wolf). If every time you sit down to work on your game, and then promptly decide to go to the movies instead or hang out with friends, chances are you don't have enough self-discipline.

You should weigh your own internal motivation level when it comes to getting work done. For most of us, we are sometimes very motivated and most other times not very motivated. You should try to capture times of extreme motivation and use them to make major progress. Use times of low motivation to spend with family and friends.

Just as with people, absence makes the heart grow fonder, and giving your project a day or two or even a week of rest can help remotivate you and give you some added perspective on the project.

Beginning Your First Title

So you've decided on a financial target, settled on a team structure, and weighed the financial and personal sacrifices. You're ready to begin your first indie title. Now it's time to get creative and smart. You're going to do some things wrong the first time around, but experience is the best teacher.

Target Market

Your target market is the group of people you are planning to market your game to. Understanding their general mindset, what they expect, and what they are willing to pay is essential. You will make some wrong assumptions the first time around, but their feedback will help to mold your impression of them. Chances are, if you're reading this, you have an "ideal" game idea in mind, so it's time to ask yourself some questions about the idea to see if it fits your current decisions of financial target, team structure, and financial needs.

- Who are the people currently playing games that are like your idea? (Teens? Kids? Women over 40? Twenty-something men?)

- What is the current state of the market in relation to your game idea's genre? (Hugely popular and flooded? Value-priced games? Niche? Dead genre?)

- Does the current pricing trend for your genre meet your financial target? (Are you hoping to get $40.00 per unit for a genre that usually gets $9.95?)

- What sets your idea apart from the rest of the genre? (If your genre is very saturated, you need to set yourself apart from others in a positive way.)

- Are the variations in your game things that have been widely requested by the market? (If forums all over the Internet are saying "wish this game genre had a save feature," making a game with one might be a good idea.)

- Can I honestly see myself developing this project, or is it a pipe dream? (Be realistic. Fooling yourself in your imagination is easy, but eventually it needs to be developed and *that* you can't fake.)

For each question do your best to qualify your answer by asking, "What data do I have to back up my answer?" (News articles? Observation? Just a guess?)

Design

You've got a basic game idea, and you think there is enough of a market to meet your financial target. It's time to get down to the details. The first rule of designing a game is this: if it's not in the design document, it's not in the game. What this means is that game projects are usually too large to be left to winging it, and "we'll figure it out later" doesn't usually fly either. If you can't design it on paper, you certainly can't develop it. Design is cheap; it uses high-level ideas, paper, and pencils or digital documents. Make your mistakes now, when it's less costly to fix them.

Let's explore some guidelines for designing a game:

- **Start somewhere:** Even if it's an incomplete idea, write it down. It's easier to refine something than to think of a complete idea from nothing.

- **Be realistic:** If you don't know how to do complex high-dynamic rendering or are unlikely to make graphics for 40 character races, then be realistic and don't make it part of the design.

- **Keep it small:** Any project you dream of is likely to take twice as long as you anticipate; a well-done small game is far better than a large unfinished game. Keep it small and get it done.

- **Think it out:** Game ideas tend to have a well-defined beginning, a well-defined end, and an obscure middle; take the time to develop that 10 hours of gameplay that you've been quoting so it doesn't sneak up on you later.

- **Make it fun:** Fun is subjective and genre specific. No one likes a boring game. People play games to experience things and enjoy themselves, so know your target market and deliver that.

Marketing

Starting early on, marketing is important; you need to make people aware of your project if you ever hope to sell it. Using your web site to feed scraps of content and information is a good way to keep people wanting more. Always be sure to use at least one or two images per paragraph of text (humans are visual creatures). Do your best to keep the text amount low so that people are more likely to read it. Now is a good time to form relationships on forums; the relationships you form now become your first round of sales later. A key thing to remember is that news sites love news, and they are always looking for new content. Be sure to send press releases (usually a blurb of text with links to images or videos of content) to big gaming sites. The sites feed off one another, so news of your game will soon be spread all over the Internet, and that's what you want.

Building Your Team

You've got your game design document, and the community has gotten a taste of what's to come, so unless you've decided to go it alone, you're going to need a team. Becoming skilled in indie team recruiting comes with experience. Chances are you'll be working together over the Internet via an instant messenger client and a collaborative development versioning tool, such as Subversion.

When recruiting you will likely need some form of marketing materials, concept images, design document synopsis, etc. Be sure to pick only skilled individuals and avoid overzealous "newbies." It doesn't matter how motivated someone is if they don't have the skills you need. Chances are you will be trying to sell potential members on a percentage of sales from the project. This is best handled in writing, and you may want to consult a lawyer.

After you've recruited a member, you should gauge their motivation and output. If they constantly promise to deliver an asset or be online at a particular time and don't come through, chances are they are hurting the project more than helping. It is for this reason that you should specify a period of evaluation before signing any kind of financial agreement contract.

Development

You've got a plan and a team, and you're ready to start full-on development. This is your long "march to the sea" where your planning and dedication will determine if you're going to make it.

Tooling Up

Based on your needs and the needs of your team, you may need to purchase software licenses; at the very least, you will need to have a stable infrastructure for communication between your team and yourself. From the programming side, depending on the skills of your team and your game design, you will need to decide whether to purchase an existing game engine, use a freeware engine, or roll your own engine/framework. There are various benefits and drawbacks in different engine strategies. Purchasing an existing game engine can be a large upfront cost, but it can also help ensure your success. Be sure that there is well-written documentation and a strong development community so you have somewhere to turn for answers. This same criteria applies to freeware engines as well. As for rolling your own engine/framework, a word of wisdom: depending on your chosen game genre, writing your own game engine can be a project unto itself. You can literally spend years on an engine before you even get into serious game development, and years in the games industry might as well be decades. However, if you have a strong technical lead on your team, writing your own engine can be extremely rewarding if done properly. It can set your game apart from others and incorporate new and innovative features that might not be available in other boilerplate engines.

Workflow

Once you have chosen an engine technology and you've built various proof-of-concepts, it's time to get down to content product and integration—in short, actually building the game. There are various styles of game development, but the one I'll talk about here is known as *iterative development*.

Using an iterative development strategy, the goal is to build the game in several subsequent passes spanning the entire length of the game, from start to finish. Each pass adds more workable elements to the game and the gameplay. The more complex your game is, the more passes you will want to do in order to ensure that each individual aspect of your game is working properly before moving on.

Well-designed passes involve similar kinds of work. One such pass could be the *environmental* pass, where maps/rooms/scenes are created and sparsely decorated with various assets that are outlined by the design document. Scripting and other gameplay-related aspects can be grouped into a pass as well.

After a pass has been completed, there will commonly be one or more *cleanup* passes. Cleanup passes allow you to refine your previous work and focus on smaller details that may have been overlooked during the previous passes. Passes are likely to continue well after beta testing as you continue to tighten up various elements, such as graphics, sound, and gameplay.

Pros:

- Allows changes or issues spotted early to be removed or reworked without a lot of lost work.

- Results in a very refined game; the more times you refine something, the better it gets.

- The extra attention of passes and testing tends to catch bugs.

Cons:

- Can result in longer overall development times due to reworking of things that could have been done together (such as writing a scene, and then adding sound effects later rather than doing it all at once).

- The constant revisiting of scenes and puzzles can make you sick of the game prematurely.

- It takes a long time before you see the game in its pretty and polished state, whereas seeing a finished scene boosts motivation.

Staying Motivated

As an indie, motivation is key. If you're not motivated, you're not going to work on your game, plain and simple. In addition to this, know that no one is motivated 100% of the time. Burnout happens, and when it does, it's the developer who realizes it, manages it, and doesn't give up who finishes the game. Keeping yourself and your team members (if you have any) motivated is a big job and it's essential, so here are some tips:

- When you're not feeling motivated, talk with your teammates about the good work you've done so far.

- If you and your teammates are within a relatively close physical distance, invite them over for dinner or a party for milestones to add more of a human element to the development.

- Reward excellent work with gift cards/certificates.

- Make lists and set milestones (I can quit for the day if I just finish four tasks).

- Play games that helped motivate you to develop indie games in the first place.

- Listen to motivational music to get you pumped up and ready to develop.

- If you're just plain burned out, give yourself (and your developers) a couple of days or a week to relax; chances are the game will be pulling you back before you know it.

Wrapping Up

You've spent months on your project. You estimate it's about 80% done, team members have come and gone, and you've got a really good core team. Now you're ready to put this puppy to bed. It's commonly said that the last 10% of any project can take up to 50% of the overall project time, and while that is usually an exaggeration, it is true that finishing off a project takes a ton of effort.

By now, you're probably sick to death of hearing about your project. You can't remember the last time you weren't thinking about it. Well, the good news is, this is all natural and you're almost there!

Now is the time to buckle down and get it finished. Use lists to log little things that need to get finished and pick these off one by one. Play through the game often, writing down little issues you observe. Around this time, you'll also start to get the itch to change things that don't really need to be changed. Some changes could be potentially devastating, introduce bugs, and set you back months. You need to be practical, and as sad as it is, those issues will just have to wait for a service release or the next game. Learn from your mistakes and carry your knowledge forward.

Release and Promotion

You're done! Hooray! Now that you've got a finished game and a market that wants it, the time has come to release it and promote it.

Getting It Out the Door

There comes a time when good is good enough, and where another brush stroke might just ruin the canvas. The team is tired and the project is looking pretty good. Your task lists are all marked off, and you're building the installer. It's time.

When preparing the release (and potentially demo) packages, be sure to use a quality installer program with a good track record. Test the installer on various platforms with various hardware configurations; this is a good way to catch small, overlooked errors that could leave a bad taste in a customer's mouth. Once you feel comfortable that it installs and plays well on various machines, you're ready to release it to the public; but first you need to revisit the business side of things.

Marketing Revisited

If you're hoping for publisher support, now is the time to talk with them. Be sure that you have a bug-free demo prepared to show them. Business can move very slow at times, so be prepared for months to go by before a contract is signed. It is possible that for your first title you won't get picked up by a publisher; in that case, self-publishing is the way to go.

First, you will need a way to process the payments from all those people waiting to purchase your game. This can usually be done for a percent of sales or a monthly fee via various online processors that supply a shopping-cart type interface.

After you've decided on an online processor, you need to decide on a price point for your game. What are your competitors charging for similar products? How does your game compare to theirs? Chances are you should price your game similar to others in your genre, and as your game ages, you can lower the price point.

Upon the release of your game, make sure to update your web site with current information as well as the ability to download a demo and purchase the full version displayed prominently. Send out a press release to your list of news sources and online game communities to make them aware.

Support

As soon as your game hits the streets, there will be people who are experiencing various issues, and they will want solutions to their problems. A support forum accessible via your web site is a good solution for an indie. There you can post links to patches/updates and general information for game issues. As your community grows, it can also self-help itself sometimes far better than you are able to do. Keep in mind that customer satisfaction is key. A happy customer can potentially provide you a dedicated sale for every game you ever write, and that is very important.

Sales

Increasing sales of your product can be achieved in various ways. A common tactic is to employ holiday sales, dress up the web site in holiday-appropriate colors and themes, and offer a discount during the holiday season. Be sure to send a press release about this sale so that news sources can pick it up.

Lowering prices can increase sales by capturing the segment of the market that was waiting for your prices to drop; however, don't lower your prices rashly or often, as this can be interpreted that your product is having trouble selling and, as such, is not worth buying.

Postmortem

A *postmortem* is a process used to analyze a finished project and learn from the experience. For teams, a postmortem can simply be a group discussion with an agenda. Or for the lone wolf, simply making a formalized list can help to structure your thoughts.

Some things to consider in a postmortem:

- How long did the project take compared to original speculations?

- Who worked on the project, and where was their time spent?

- What went wrong with the project?

- What can be done differently based on observations of problems?

- What worked really well?

- Concrete guidelines for future projects.

It is very important that observations of pitfalls are recorded so that you can learn from the past and not be doomed to repeat it. You will likely have learned a lot from your first game, some of which will make your next game better and some which might not. Experience is the key to building better games and keeping up with the industry. As an indie, it is most important that you enjoy your craft and are able to justify the effort.

CHAPTER 8

LEGAL ISSUES IN GAME DEVELOPMENT

MONA IBRAHIM

As a game developer, you work in an industry that is controlled by, and often complicated by, the law. While you don't need to be a lawyer to program and develop games and software in this industry, it is wise to know enough about the law to know when to ask for help. This article is designed to teach you the basics of two areas of law that you will routinely confront in game development: intellectual property and transactional (contract) law. The first half of this article will cover the basic elements of intellectual property law. The second portion will cover some of the basics of contracts and transactions, as well as specific contracts you will confront in your career. The discussion will primarily concern U.S. law, although some international law is included in certain contexts. While a few cases and controversies may be cited, this discussion will cover the topics with broad strokes.[1] Therefore, it is important to note that this primer should not serve as a substitute for qualified legal counsel if you are engaged in a legal dispute.

Intellectual Property Law Within the Games Industry

Intellectual property law is designed to reward and motivate the contributions of human intellect by making certain rights in those contributions commercially valuable. Stated simply, intellectual property law is the body of rights that enables

---

[1]For further resources concerning cases and codes, visit the FindLaw web site at www.findlaw.com/casecode or the Cornell Law Library at www.law.cornell.edu.

you to make a profit from your ideas. There are three major forms of intellectual property (IP) that are protected under United States law: copyright, patent, and trademark. Copyright law protects creative and original works, such as music, code, and audiovisual displays. Trademark law protects the brand names and other characteristics that identify the source of a product in commerce. Patents protect methods, processes, devices, and other useful inventions. All three will be discussed in this chapter.

Because this is such a dense and complicated body of law, I will frequently provide examples. It is important to note, however, that the examples only approach rules generally. Specific facts and components in a legal issue could easily change the answer. Rules also may differ from jurisdiction to jurisdiction. The Federal District Courts of New York may apply different standards than the Federal District Courts of California. Therefore, examples should *not* be used as something to rely upon if you have specific questions. Any legal questions should be addressed by a legal professional.

Copyrights in the Games Industry

Copyright law plays a major role in the game development industry. Although this discussion focuses primarily on U.S. copyright law, it's important to note that international copyright law and the Berne Convention can have a significant effect on the protections and rights in and to your game product.

What Is a Copyright?

A copyright is a type of intellectual property that gives the owner a bundle of rights in a creative work for a limited time.[2] To protect those rights, the copyright owner must actively pursue those who infringe on their copyright. A valid copyright is automatically created in any original work of authorship that is fixed in a tangible form. In other words, protection begins once an original idea is written down, recorded, or saved to your hard drive. The types of work that are protected include literary works (i.e., both source and binary code and any underlying story or script), music (the musical composition and the sound recording are protected separately), choreography, audiovisual works (film, cinematography, anything that combines audio with visual displays), graphical

---

[2]For individuals, the time frame is the life of the author plus 70 years. For companies and anonymous authors, 95 years after the work's first publication or 120 years after its creation, whichever is earlier.

works (photography, paintings, artwork), and the like. Thanks to various international treaties,[3] basic copyright protections are extended to works published internationally. However, you should consult an attorney to determine your rights in a foreign country if you choose to publish abroad.

It is important to note here that ideas, names, and general concepts in and of themselves are not protected by copyright. Nor is an idea copyrightable without more to it. Only the *tangible* expression of an idea is protected under federal copyright law. The bundle of rights that are protected by copyright include the following:

- The right to reproduce (make copies)

- The right to distribute

- The right to publicly perform

- The right to publicly display

- The right to create derivative works of the original work

- The right to digitally transmit (in the case of sound recordings)

The author is the original owner of the copyright, and the owner is the exclusive rights holder. The owner is, therefore, the only entity authorized to engage in any of the aforementioned activities with regard to the particular work in question. For example, if you write a program, you are the owner of the copyright. You are the only one authorized to perform any of the activities listed in this bundle of rights.

The commercial value in a copyright comes from the ability to license, transfer, or sell any of the rights listed. The rights are severable from one another and may be licensed on an exclusive or non-exclusive basis. The ability to purchase and sell the right to copy, perform, or create derivative works of a protected and lucrative property is the purpose of the copyright system in the United States—by giving works of creativity and intellect commercial value, the laws of copyright give authors an incentive to create new valuable works and share those works with the world.

---

[3]Namely, these are the Berne Convention, Geneva Convention, and WIPO. There are currently 163 signatories to the Berne Convention.

Ownership

When more than one person contributes to a work and no agreement exists, the co-authors are joint owners in the copyright and everyone retains an equal share in the entire work. However, copyright law acknowledges that this isn't practical when a company relies on hundreds of contributions from hundreds of employees or independent contractors. In an employer/employee context, the employer always owns the copyright. If you are hired as an employee programmer by a game developer, the studio owns the rights to any original code you create. In an independent contractor situation, the independent contractor agreement must expressly state that the contribution is a work-for-hire.

Example 1

Alice is a computer programming student. In her free time, she likes to program code for a game she eventually wants to develop. Alice, however, isn't a great artist. She calls her friend Brian, a computer animation student, and asks if Brian would be willing to contribute to the game. Brian agrees. No compensation is discussed and no written agreement exists between Alice and Brian. As to the *game as a whole*, Alice and Brian are joint owners who own an equal, undivided share in the game (if they're the only contributors). This means that neither can do much with the game without permission from the other owner. The exception to this limitation is certain kinds of licensing. Either may license the game on a non-exclusive basis without permission from the other.

Example 2

Same scenario, but instead, Alice agrees to pay Brian for his work. They execute a work-for-hire agreement in writing, where Alice owns all of the rights in the game. In this scenario, Alice owns everything in the game, including the artwork. Brian owns nothing, but he is entitled to his payment. If Alice doesn't pay, the agreement is breached, and they are both joint owners. (For more information, see the section, "Contracts Within the Games Industry," later in this article.)

What Is Copyright Infringement?

Copyright owners have a duty to enforce their rights against infringers or risk losing those rights.[4] You infringe a copyright when you engage in any of the protected copyright activities without permission or license from the copyright owner. Any time you copy, perform or display a copyrighted work without authorization, you are committing copyright infringement. This is called direct

---

[4]*Scenes à faire* (meaning literally "scenes that must be done") is sometimes the result of a failure to enforce a copyright against open and notorious infringement. These are scenes that become defining characteristics of a genre because the subsequent uses were never originally enforced. In other words, the first person who used a young female as a "scream queen" in horror never enforced their rights against subsequent participants in the genre. Because it thereafter became a common feature in the genre, those rights may not be asserted under *scene à faire*. See *Atari, Inc. v. North American Philips Consumer Elecs., Corp.*, 672 F.2d 607, 616 (7th Cir. 1982).

infringement. If you burn software to a CD and the EULA (End User License Agreement) expressly forbids that activity, you are violating the copyright owner's reproduction right. Similarly, if you download a song through Bit-Torrent or another download site without obtaining a license to the sound recording or composition, you are infringing the reproduction right by copying the music to your hard drive. If you later make the folder containing the song available for file sharing, you are infringing on the distribution right of the copyright owner.

There is no such thing as an "innocent infringer" under copyright law, because infringement requires only *access* to the copyrighted work as well as a *substantial similarity* between the copyrighted work and the infringing work. However, the Copyright Act does limit remedies against individuals who could reasonably believe that what they were doing was not copyright infringement (i.e., the infringement wasn't willful, or the infringer reasonably believed that the infringement was protected by fair use). The law of copyright acknowledges that two distinct copyrights can exist in two identical tangible forms of expression if they are independently created from one another. In other words, if two people write stories that are identical to one another without knowledge of each other's works, both may claim a valid copyright so long as neither had access to the other's work.

It should also be noted that multiple components of a work may be protected independently of one another. For instance, the audiovisual display of your game (i.e., the graphics and animation in conjunction with sound effects and music) is protected as an audiovisual work, and your source and binary code are protected as literary works. Not all components need to be infringed upon for copyright infringement to occur. This is particularly relevant in video game law, where under copyright law, copying for the purpose of reverse engineering is not considered copyright infringement.[5]

There are two other forms of copyright infringement: contributory and vicarious infringement. Contributory infringement is attributed to those who induce or materially contribute the infringement. Grokster and Napster were both accused of contributory infringement because their programs materially contributed to their users' direct copyright infringement.[6] Vicarious infringement arises when

---

[5]*Sega Enterprises Ltd. v. Accolade, Inc.*, 977 F.2d 1510, 1517–18 (9th Cir. 1993).

[6]*MGM Studios, Inc. v. Grokster, Ltd.*, 125 S.Ct. 2764 (2005).

the entity or individual has a right to supervise infringing activities or derives a direct financial benefit from the infringement.[7]

Copyright infringement is a major issue in software generally, but it can be especially problematic for entertainment products, such as video games. Game piracy often accounts for a significant drop in a game's commercial value, and it touches on many aspects of game development, including localization, distribution, and licensing. This is because copyright protection is not universally applied—although most countries extend some kind of protection to foreign copyrights, these protections may go unenforced. Criminal penalties are nonexistent in some countries and blatantly ignored in others. As a result, game publishers must be conscious of the risks their game product may face if distributed in certain territories. Often the reward of distribution in a particular territory is undermined by the risk of prevalent piracy.

Example 1

Carol uses a torrent program to download copyrighted music. The torrent program was written by Company, which is based in Texas. The program downloads music into a shared folder, which allows other program users to download packets of data from Carol's shared folder. Carol's downloading of the song is infringement of the copyright owner's reproduction right because she's made a copy of the music on her hard drive. Carol's shared folder may be infringement of the copyright owner's distribution right.[8] Company may be found guilty of contributory infringement if their program materially contributes to Carol's infringement.[9] Company is vicariously infringing if Company charges or otherwise derives a direct financial benefit from Carol's use of the program.

Copyright infringement isn't limited to piracy or wholesale copying. A more insidious method of infringement comes from partial copying or creation of derivative works. For instance, if you borrow particular elements of another entertainment product and use those elements in your own game, the copyright owner of the original game may be compelled to enforce his copyright against you. Using a character or story that is substantially similar to a well-known entertainment product will almost certainly expose you to legal action. It is in these legal actions in particular that the legal defense of "fair use" often comes into play.

---

[7]*Ibid.* at 2776.

[8]Torrents are questionable territory depending on the amount of data transferred by any particular user at any particular time. However, it is better to err on the side of caution and approach the conduct as infringement.

[9]This isn't as cut and dry as the example suggests. There are exceptions to contributory infringement. A program that has both infringing and non-infringing uses may in some cases not be held by contributory infringers. *Sony Corp. of America v. Universal City Studios, Inc.* 464 U.S. 417 (1984).

Example 2

Studio creates a game that quickly becomes popular. Independent Producer decides to make a movie based on the game, but fails to obtain a license from Studio. Independent Producer makes the movie, and although there are several differences between the movie and the game, the movie is substantially similar to the game. Independent Producer has probably infringed on Studio's right to create derivative works.

What Is Fair Use?

The United States Copyright Act 17 U.S.C. 107 grants an affirmative defense to copyright infringers under specific circumstances. This affirmative defense is called "fair use," and may be raised by a defendant as a defense to copyright infringement. The law of fair use is intended to balance a copyright owner's commercial and artistic interest in his or her copyright against the first amendment rights of the rest of the world. A person who uses the creative work in a manner that is deemed "fair" under fair use may be able to limit or eliminate liability for the use. However, fair use is determined on a case-by-case basis and, therefore, requires some form of legal action; in other words, the only way you may prove an affirmative defense of fair use is if you're the defendant in a copyright infringement suit. Exposing yourself to litigation is typically not advisable. Relying on fair use to justify infringement without asking permission from the copyright owner is almost certainly a recipe for expensive litigation.

Nonetheless, it is important to know about fair use as a game developer. If someone claims that he is authorized to use your work under the law of fair use, it is necessary to know whether that defense is available under the circumstances. Under U.S. law, there are four factors that courts consider to determine the existence of fair use:

1. The purpose and character of the use, including whether such use is of a commercial nature or is for nonprofit educational purposes

2. The nature of the copyrighted work

3. The amount and substantiality of the portion used in relation to the copyrighted work as a whole

4. The effect of the use upon the potential market for or value of the copyrighted work[10]

---

[10]17 U.S.C. § 107

These factors operate on a sliding scale, and a particular weakness in one factor can be overcome by other factors. This makes the determination of fair use maddeningly unpredictable. For example, a not-for-profit work can fail the fair use test while a commercial parody of a work may be permissible under fair use.

Example 1

David writes a song that sounds substantially similar to another song, but he substitutes the lyrics with a parody. His use of the underlying song may be considered fair use, even if he obtains a significant profit from the use.[11]

Example 2

Lucy pays for and attends a seminar hosted by a well-known life coach, who has sold many books and conducted many lectures. When Lucy returns home, she transcribes everything she can remember from the seminar and publishes it on her personal blog, including substantial portions of the literature provided at the seminar. This may or may not be fair use, because the information provided at the seminar is probably copyrighted. Even though Lucy is deriving no profit from posting this information on her blog, a court may find that she is diminishing the market value of the seminar and may therefore rule that fair use does not apply.

Remedies for Copyright Infringement

U.S. law provides for both civil and criminal penalties against infringers. This means that both the copyright owner and the federal government may bring a cause of action against a copyright infringer. The DMCA (Digital Millennium Copyright Act) offers specific criminal charges against infringers who circumvent technology designed to protect copyrighted material.[12]

It isn't necessary to register your copyright to have a valid copyright, but you *must* register with the Library of Congress Copyright Office prior to bringing a lawsuit for copyright infringement. One of the advantages of early copyright registration is the ability to sue for statutory damages, which can be substantial. As a copyright owner, you may bring a civil suit against a copyright infringer and have your pick at a variety of legal remedies.

Equitable (non-legal, typically non-monetary) remedies include injunctive relief, declaratory relief, and temporary restraining orders. These remedies are meant to prohibit the infringer from further harming the copyright owner. If a court issues an injunction, the infringer is legally required to cease the infringing activity. This

---

[11]*See Campbell v. Acuff-Rose Music, Inc.*, 510 U.S. 569 (1994). In that case, the band 2 Live Crew's parody of the popular song "Pretty Woman" was considered fair use by the Supreme Court.

[12]17 U.S.C. § 1204

is almost always sought in copyright infringement actions, although it is occasionally withheld in lieu of profit sharing.

Legal remedies (statutory and civil damages) include statutory, compensatory, and nominal damages. Most legal remedies provide financial recourse—these remedies grease the wheels of civil litigation and provide the copyright owner incentive for copyright enforcement actions. Statutory damages are designed to punish the infringer when actual damages are difficult to prove. Compensatory damages are designed to compensate the copyright owner for any financial loss suffered as a result of the infringement. Nominal damages are minimum damages that neither compensate the plaintiff nor punish the defendant—they are damages in name only. Under copyright law, a copyright owner must choose between recovering statutory damages or actual damages.

Example 1

Violet sues Trevor for copyright infringement. Trevor has plagiarized substantial portions of Violet's book and has derived a profit from selling his own infringing book. Violet's remedies include an injunction that prevents Trevor from reproducing or distributing future copies of the infringing material. If the court finds that Trevor's infringement was willful, statutory damages may be appropriate. However, Violet may instead choose to request actual damages, which include damages Violet suffered and any profits obtained by Trevor.

With the basic principles of copyright law covered, let's move on to trademark law.

Trademarks in the Games Industry

Blizzard Entertainment, Warner Brothers, Valve, and Steam are all brand names that identify products in commerce. When those names are used in connection with a game product, you know where the product came from and the product's quality (or lack thereof) and type. If another game developer used the company name Valve, consumers would quickly become confused and may attribute the developer's product to the already established company. Trademark law is designed to prevent this kind of confusion. U.S. law recognizes that brands retain value in and of themselves. The name attached to a product connotes the quality and good will that consumers expect from the company. Trademark law protects both consumers who rely on trademarks and companies who use trademarks to identify their goods and services.

Most states have their own body of trademark law. Federal trademark law only protects service marks and trademarks used in interstate commerce. A product is in interstate commerce when it crosses state lines. Almost every product or service available exclusively online is in interstate commerce, because it's available to everyone with an Internet connection regardless of location. Commerce refers to making use of a mark in connection with selling, marketing, or otherwise promoting a product or service.

There are a few bodies of law that control federal trademarks, including the Code of Federal Regulations,[13] the Lanham Act,[14] and the Madrid Protocol. Trademarks that are limited geographically (i.e., those that operate in only one region or state) are protected under state trademark and unfair competition law.

A trademark is only valid if it is sufficiently distinct (i.e., Coca-Cola). Descriptive marks (Idaho Potatoes) typically are not given trademark protection. Those that do are only given protection if it is clear that consumers identify the mark with a specific product. This is a tricky area of the law and often leads to substantial debate within the legal profession.

When Are Trademarks Relevant in Games?

Game developers and publishers use trademarks to identify the source and quality of their games. Companies like Take 2 Interactive, Nintendo, Microsoft, Epic, and Valve integrate their brand names into everything they market and distribute. The game community, in turn, relies on those marks when making purchases. Trademarks are also relevant when we look at titles. *Grand Theft Auto* is a highly recognized franchise that has obtained substantial press and popularity. Those titles, along with identifying and unique characteristics that set the game apart in the games market, may be subject to trademark protection. This is useful to bear in mind for the same reasons that copyright is important to bear in mind—there is value to these intangible properties, and the owners must therefore defend their rights to those properties.

Trademark Infringement

As with copyright law, trademark law does not require registration; once a brand name is used in commerce to identify the source of a service or product, a valid mark exists. Registration is still advisable because it strengthens the validity of the

---

[13]37 *C.F.R. Part 2 & 3-Rules of Practice in Trademark Cases* covers requirements and rules for trademark registration.
[14]15 U.S.C. 22

mark. As with a copyright, trademark owners have a duty to enforce their rights or risk losing them.[15]

Federal trademark and unfair competition laws vary from jurisdiction to jurisdiction when determining the standards a court may establish for infringement. Generally speaking, in an infringement case concerning two or more marks, courts rely on the similarity of the marks and the risk of confusion posed to consumers. Specifically, courts rely not only on the actual statistical evidence that might be available as far as consumer confusion, but also the proliferation and exposure of particular marks, the specific industries in which the marks are used, marketing channels used, and a variety of other factors.

Infringement may also refer to trademark dilution and disparagement—if a trademark is used in a way that accurately identifies the source of a product but dilutes or tarnishes a mark, a trademark owner may have grounds for an infringement suit. Consumer confusion isn't an issue. The consumers aren't supposed to be confused about the source. Instead, the mark properly identifies the source but does so in a way that dilutes consumer perception of the product.

The most common examples of dilution are those marks that are used to describe an entire class of product, as opposed to only those products created by the trademark owner. In those cases, an extremely strong brand name may collapse under its own weight. The Band-Aid brand is an excellent example of this; most consumers use the name "band-aid" to refer to every kind of medical adhesive bandage.

Disparagement is a form of dilution that puts a product in a bad light. This is called "tarnishing" the mark, and it happens when someone uses the trademark in an unwholesome or negative context. There are freedom of speech issues that come into play here. Simply saying "Product A sucks" probably isn't going to run afoul of trademark law, because freedom of speech allows individuals to express themselves publicly. The most common example of tarnishment is using the mark or a deceptively similar mark in connection with a product of lesser quality.

These standards are further complicated when put in the context of international distribution and the World Wide Web. The Madrid Protocol is designed to simplify these issues in international trade. This treaty allows citizens of signatory

---

[15]Failing to enforce your trademark may result in trademark abandonment.

countries to register international trademark applications.[16] As of 2008, 74 countries are signatories to the treaty, including the United States. The international registry is maintained by the World Intellectual Property Organization (WIPO), which also administers arbitration proceedings when an international trademark dispute arises.

Example 1

Company DD makes high-quality games for several consoles. A much smaller, independent studio (Studio) uses a trademark that is confusingly similar to Company DD's mark. Studio makes games as well, but Studio's games are low-quality and free. Company DD may sue Studio for trademark infringement and tarnishment because Studio's games may be mistakenly attributed as Company DD's product.

Remedies for Trademark Infringement

As is the case with copyright, there are a variety of remedies available for victims of trademark infringement. This includes injunctive relief and legal remedies. Trademark is distinct in that it limits damages against "innocent infringers," something copyright law doesn't take into account for the reasons stated previously. An innocent infringer typically exists when two companies in the same industry use confusingly similar marks, but neither registered the mark and neither have reason to know of the other company's existence. The company that first used the trademark in commerce is entitled to use of the mark, and may obtain declaratory relief to that effect. The winner of the mark may also be entitled to an injunction limiting or eliminating the other company's right to use the mark. However, the innocent infringer typically is not liable for damages. Willful infringers, however, are subject to treble (triple) damages. Damages include disgorged profits and any injury suffered by the plaintiff. Reasonable attorneys' fees may also be available.

Patents in the Games Industry

A patent grants the patent owner a monopoly over a method, process, device, or other useful invention for a specific period of years. A patent doesn't give the owner the right to manufacture and distribute its invention (as is the case in copyright, where rights are conferred to the copyright owner). Instead, patents grant the owner the right to exclude the rest of the world from manufacturing and distributing the invention for a period of time. Unlike trademark and

---

[16]You can find Madrid Protocol FAQs at www.uspto.gov/web/trademarks/madrid/madridfaqs.htm.

copyright law, patents are limited as far as geographic scope. It is necessary to obtain a patent in every country where you intend to distribute your product.[17] Also, unlike trademark and copyright law, it is not necessary to actively pursue infringers or risk losing your rights. A patent owner's rights remain in effect for the duration of the patent. Due to the requirements set forth by the U.S. Patent and Trademark Office (US PTO), it is necessary for a patent attorney or agent to assist the patent application drafting process.

Patents require completion of the patent application process, which is regulated by the US PTO. A valid patent does not exist until the patent is issued from the US PTO. The patent application for utility patents must include the following:

1. Written specifications that set out the patent claims[18] and a description of the subject matter[19]

2. Any drawings that may assist in the patent issuing process

3. Filing fees[20]

4. A declaration by the applicant stating that she believes herself to be the original and first inventor of the product[21]

5. The title of the invention

6. An abstract of the disclosure

Once the patent application is submitted to the US PTO, it may take the US PTO up to two years to issue the patent. During the waiting period, there is no patent protection. People will often use "patent pending" on their invented products, but this has no legal effect. The right to exclude only attaches when the patent is issued by the US PTO.

Patents play a peculiar and powerful role in the games industry. They do not protect specific games, but they may protect certain game engines and certain unique processes and game types. Patents play a particularly valuable role in the

---

[17]The exception to this is infringing products manufactured in other countries that are then imported into the United States in conflict with an existing U.S. patent. Like trademark and copyright law, treaties do exist (The Paris Convention and the Patent Cooperation Treaty) to give citizens similar patent protections to those granted in their own country.

[18]I frequently refer to patent claims here. Patent claims set forth the specifications of the subject matter, the limitations of the scope of the claimed invention, and the "metes and bounds" of the patent monopoly being claimed.

[19]An application can have more "dependent" claims than "independent claims." Dependent claims further explain or limit previous claims in the application. Independent claims do not refer to previous claims.

[20]Effective October 2, 2008, the current basic filing fee for utility patents for 2009 is $330.00. The fee increases depending on the number of claims and whether the claims are dependent or independent.

[21]Conducting a patent search is required. This is also fairly costly.

realm of consoles, where every console developer seeks to distinguish its product in the realm of patent law.

Three types of patents exist under U.S. patent law: utility patents, design patents, and plant patents. The last literally refers to genetically engineered plant life and, therefore, isn't within the scope of this discussion. Of the three, utility patents are the most prevalent in the games industry.

Utility patents include any new and useful process, machine, manufacture, or composition of matter, or any new and useful improvement thereof. To qualify for a utility patent, the work must be novel (new), non-obvious, and useful. A utility patent's duration is 20 years from the date the patent application was filed. The term does not begin, however, until the patent is issued. Therefore, if a patent is issued two years after application, the duration of the patent is 18 years. The application process can take that long, and a complex patent application is next to impossible to complete without a patent attorney.

Design patents protect ornamental designs of articles of manufacture, such as distinctive patterns or specific packaging (which may also be protected by trade dress, which is similar to trademark in that it identifies the source of a product in commerce).

Utility patents are of particular relevance because those patents typically include game engines, consoles, and similar game devices. It's worth noting here that patent applications must be extremely specific. A general console patent application that simply states that the device is used to play video games on compact disc would not be sufficient to pass the U.S. Patent and Trademark Office standards of specificity and novelty.

Video games and software generally are unique in that they may be subject to both patent and copyright law protection. In most cases, because copyright law specifically excludes processes, methods, and other useful products, those inventions and fixed ideas that are protected by patent law are not protected by copyright law. However, because software processes operate through the use of code (literary works), that code is a necessary component of the patent. The code language is often sufficiently creative in and of itself, without reference to the underlying processes and methods involved, to warrant copyright protection. Simply stated, a particularly revolutionary or novel software application may be protected by both copyright and patent law, provided a patent application is filed with the US PTO.

The following is an actual example of a patent claim for a type of video game controller.

Example 1

"A wireless controller for a video game console, comprising: a main body including a measurement unit including a control circuit including a first amplification circuit, a control IC, a second amplification circuit, an ADC, a display circuit, and a plurality of pins for setting, a top recess, a display, two first measurement devices adapted to contact the fingers as the hand holding the main body for measuring pulse and body temperature of a user playing a video game on the video game console, and a rotation counter for counting the number of rotations of the main body; a control unit mounted in the recess; a band including two second measurement devices for measuring blood pressure and pulse of the user respectively by wrapping the band around the wrist; and a cable interconnecting the main body and the band, wherein the first measurement devices converts the measured pulse and body temperature into first signals which are sent to the first amplification circuit for amplification, and the amplified first signals are sent to the control IC; the second measurement devices convert the measured blood pressure and pulse into second signals which are sent to the second amplification circuit for amplification, the amplified second signals are sent to the ADC for converting into digital signals, and the digital signals are sent to the control IC; the rotation counter sends the count to the control; the control IC sends the received first signals, the second signals, the digital signals, and the count to the display circuit for processing into corresponding data representing blood pressure, pulse, and body temperature values; and the blood pressure, the pulse, and the body temperature values are sent to the display for display."[22]

Patent Infringement in Video Games

The repeat players in patent litigation in the games industry are console and game device manufacturers, as well as OEM (original equipment manufacturer) developers.[23] This is because the patent application process is expensive, time consuming, and almost always worthwhile when you've developed a new device or new technology. For this reason, utility patents are the major patent type to pay attention to in game development.

Utility patent infringement occurs when the infringer's product or process falls within the patent owner's claims, which is stated in the patent application. Even if the infringement doesn't literally fall within the parameters of the patent's claims, the doctrine of equivalents may still apply if the infringing product or process contains the specific elements or equivalent elements contained in the patent claim. This is only a general statement of patent infringement. However, a

---

[22]U.S. Patent Application 20080171596, Hsu; Kent T.J. (Taipei City, Taiwan).

[23]See *Gibson Guitar Corporation v. Harmonix Music Systems, Inc.* et al, where Gibson sued Harmonix for patent infringement on the claim that Harmonix's peripheral device for the game *Guitar Hero* infringed on Gibson's patent <http://news.justia.com/cases/featured/tennessee/tnmdce/3:2008cv00294/41575/>.

full-blown discussion of patent infringement claims is beyond the scope of this chapter. Because patent lawsuits are among the most complicated in intellectual property law, legal assistance is necessary before you engage in any conduct they may infringe on another's patent.

Remedies for Patent Infringement

The remedies for patent infringement claims are equitable and legal. However, patent infringement remedies are broken down as far as determining the "proper measure of damages," as stated in the Patent Act.[24] The proper measure may be a reasonable royalty rate, or lost profits. Courts are also authorized to award treble (triple) damages when they see fit. Attorneys' fees are also available.

Trade Secrets in the Games Industry

Our last discussion on the topic of intellectual property concerns trade secrets. Trade secrets are secrets that are commercially valuable only because no one else knows about them. For a valid trade secret to exist, the company claiming a trade secret must clearly determine what the trade secret is and must take steps to keep the proprietary information concealed. This includes everything from keeping people working on trade secret matters within the company isolated from other workers in the company, the requirement of non-disclosure agreements, exit interviews when employees are dismissed or quit, or otherwise ensuring that the trade secret is not revealed in any way to competitors or the public.

Trade secrets are commonly a useful tool in game development because trade secrets can protect anything, including ideas that are not yet fixed in a tangible medium. Trade secrets may include specific programming and design "know-how," game concepts and ideas, or specific marketing tools and ideas for a particular type of product.

Trade secrets are traditionally protected by mutual or unilateral Non-Disclosure Agreements (NDA). These agreements state that all proprietary information of a particular type and concerning particular subject matters are trade secrets and may not be discussed or disclosed to third parties. The contract is mostly strategic. First and most obviously, it contractually binds the employee or other party to non-disclosure. The NDA may also provide a liquidated damages clause or

---

[24]Patent Act ss. 284

some other remedy due to the speculative nature of trade secret damages. Finally, if the company does suffer serious financial harm as a result of the disclosure of the trade secret, the contract acts as evidence those trade secrets do exist and defines the terms of those secrets. Misappropriation of trade secrets is a valid cause of action in almost every jurisdiction and entitles the successful plaintiff to substantial damages.

Contracts Within the Games Industry

The subject of NDAs brings us to the contracts that exist within the video game industry. Bear in mind that almost all of these agreements in some way concern the matters discussed above. Intellectual Property is an inherent aspect of every game development transaction. This section will first set out the basic elements of a contract and the things you need to be aware of when looking at *any* contract. Next, I will discuss specific contract types that you will be exposed to during your career—namely, Publisher/Developer contracts and employment agreements.

Basics of Contracts

Contracts require several things:

- Capacity

- Mutual Assent

- Legal Purpose

- Bargained-for Consideration

- In some cases, a signed writing

Capacity is the ability to enter into an agreement. In the U.S., contracts are only enforceable against adults at or above the age of majority.[25] This doesn't mean that minors can't enter into contracts. It means that if you try to enforce a contract against a minor, the minor can void the agreement. Capacity also includes sanity or mental capacity. Inebriation, however, typically isn't a defense if someone tries to enforce a contract against you.

---

[25]Caveat: In the US, contracts are only enforceable against those 18 years old and older. Generally speaking, if a minor signs a contract and continues to enjoy the benefit of the contract upon reaching the age of majority, the contract can be enforced against the individual even if they were a minor when they signed the contract.

Mutual assent means an offer and an acceptance. Simply stated, an offer exists if the person receiving the offer could reasonably believe that acceptance would create a binding agreement. The acceptance must be an acceptance of the precise terms of the original offer. Accepting with conditions is typically viewed as a counter-offer. Counter-offers do not create a binding agreement unless the other party accepts that counter-offer. The exception to this is contracts between merchants that are controlled by the Uniform Commercial Code. In those cases, non-material conditions that do not alter the nature of the original offer combined with an acceptance creates a valid agreement, and the minor conditions are considered a part of the agreement unless the other party objects. This sounds more complicated than it actually is, as you'll see in the following examples.

Example 1

Josh calls his friend Matt and says, "I will sell you my computer for $2,500." Matt responds with, "I accept your offer so long as you include your stereo." Matt's "acceptance" is actually a counter-offer. He hasn't accepted Josh's offer under the original terms. No contract exists. If Josh replies, "Okay, you can have the stereo and the computer for $2,500," then Josh has effectively accepted the counter-offer and a contract exists.

Example 2

Merchant sells graphics cards. Retailer is an electronics shop. Merchant sends Retailer a signed price quote of $25,000 for 2,500 graphics cards. Retailer then signs and sends Merchant one of its stock order forms, which contains an order for 2,500 graphics cards for $25,000 and the following statement: "All deliveries must be made to Retailer Shipping Yard, Texas." Because this statement does not materially alter the original offer, the Retailer's order form acted as a valid acceptance. Unless Retailer contests the delivery provision, it is a part of the final agreement.

Legal purpose means that you can't make a contract for something illegal. Putting a "contract" out on someone's life isn't enforceable in any court of law.

Bargained-for consideration means that each party is getting something in exchange for something else. Consideration need not be equal or fair. It must simply be bargained for and agreed to by the parties. If only one party has obligations under the agreement, the contract is typically considered illusory or a gift. Because consideration is typically where the money and performance come into play, it is the most litigated area of contract law.

A signed writing is required in certain cases if the contact is going to be enforceable under the State of Frauds. For your purposes, you will *always* want your agreements set out in writing. Failing to do so is dangerous and rife with potential complications, especially when the subject matter concerns intellectual property transactions.

What You Need to Look for in Every Contract

Law schools do not teach attorneys how to structure transactions. Law school teaches case law, legal research, and memo drafting. Only a few courses teach students how to draft and interpret contracts. Therefore, it's no surprise that the legal profession can be dissected in two. On the one hand, you have litigators. These are the attorneys who defend and prosecute cases before the court. On the other hand, you have transactional attorneys. These are the attorneys who were at some point exposed to the world of transactions and who developed the skill set necessary to draft, negotiate, and review contracts. While many attorneys practice both, it's important to know that there is a distinction. Every attorney is taught how to litigate. Not every attorney knows how to read and draft a solid contract.

Transactional attorneys focus on two major components in every transaction: a) where is the leverage? and b) where is the money? Leverage determines who has more power to negotiate. Typically the person with the leverage is also the person with the money. Money includes money spent, money earned, and ownership and control over property with monetary value. Another important component to pay attention to is risk shifting. Who stands to lose the most if the transaction fails?

One other very important factor that should be addressed is the distinction between a material and a non-material breach. A material breach means that the contract may be terminated by the non-breaching party and may sue the breaching party for breach of contract. A minor breach does *not* terminate the agreement or entitle either party to discontinue performance. However, the non-breaching party is entitled to damages arising from the breach. Contracts should expressly state whether a failure to perform a particular duty under the contract constitutes a material breach.

It is unfortunate that most contracts are not written in plain English. This is because, as stated previously, most attorneys do not know how to draft contracts. They, therefore, rely on forms that are often decades old and are loaded with archaic and misleading language. This is doubly unfortunate considering how very slight details can alter an agreement significantly. Exchanging the word "shall" for "may" can change an obligation into a right. Words like "and," "or," and "all" are easily lost among ancillary royalty rate calculations, but those words are extremely important in determining how those rates are calculated.

Contracts are also voluminous and in many ways intimidating. This is because every single aspect of a transaction, namely where and how money is to be spent and earned, must be clearly set out in the agreement. Every provision in an agreement is important, whether because it's necessary or because it should not exist. If neither party understands why a provision is in an agreement, it should be in the agreement. This is something else you should pay attention to when signing an agreement. You should know exactly what your rights, risks, and obligations are under a contract, right down to the boilerplate.

Publisher/Developer Deals

Publisher/developer deals are in no way simple or straightforward. They span multiple pages and typically seem completely onerous against the developer. This is because the publisher in this transaction typically has most of the leverage. Publishers typically pay developers for the game's development, and then pay more to market and distribute the game. Publishers cannot guarantee the success of a game in the market, and they therefore take several precautions to ensure that the game product they receive from the developer will have the highest chance of success. This means that publishers want a certain degree of control over the creative process. A few more successful developers with several titles under their belts are in a better position to negotiate creative control. However, small independent studios that are entering the game market for the first time will likely have little to no room to negotiate. With that said, the following sections cover some of the more important provisions in a publisher/developer contract.

Milestones

Milestones are the payments advanced by the publisher to the developer during the development process and for the specific purpose of development. Milestones should always be negotiable and determined primarily by the developer. Milestone schedules will vary based on the complexity of the project, and the milestone payments should be sufficient to cover costs until the next milestone payment. This is one area where ideally a publisher and developer will work together to come up with the best schedule for the game. It is also where the developer should be extremely assertive and cautious. Publishers may demand a cure period for delayed payments—make sure that this cure period is at a bare minimum and at least *ask* that it be removed. It certainly shouldn't be the same as the cure period for a delayed milestone submission for approval. You should also ask your lawyer to make sure that delayed payment is a material breach. It takes very little effort to cut a check, but failure to pay can hinder or otherwise damage the developer's ability to produce.

Rights Ownership

Typically, a publisher picks up a developer to develop a game. In those cases, the publisher will want the game to be a work-made-for-hire. This means that the publisher owns all of the IP to the game. The exceptions to this are if, you, the developer a) brought a mostly finished or finished product to the publisher and/ or b) are using your own engines or other technology in the game that can be used and licensed for other games. In those cases, negotiation may be important. The most effective way to protect rights the developer wants to retain is to expressly exclude them from the agreement. The developer's lawyer should be able to negotiate based on what the developer is actually bringing to the table.

Contingent Compensation

Contingent compensation is the amount the developer earns from game sales. The earnings are typically in the form of royalties (i.e., a percentage of each sale). Royalties are usually based on "net receipts." This is a complicated term that is almost always determined by the publisher. Generally speaking, "net receipts" is all revenue earned through game sells minus the costs of goods sold (including manufacture, packaging, and license payments to third parties), lost or damaged goods, customary reserves for returned goods, promotional goods, and a variety of other expenses that go into publishing the game.

It is important to note that the developer's advance (i.e., milestone payments) is recouped from royalties. This means that the publisher first pays itself, at the developer's royalty rate, until the advance is paid in full. This means that if the developer has a 30% royalty rate and a $6,000,000 advance, the game will have to make $20,000,000 in net receipts before the developer is entitled to a royalty. As it's already been determined that net receipts in and of themselves are pretty tricky, the amount the game needs to make at gross may exceed $20,000,000 by a substantial margin. Game developers typically don't expect to see royalties, but in the event that the game is a huge success, the developer should be entitled to an agreed upon royalty. To that end, the language concerning net receipts should be as clear as possible. Clarification of pipeline income is also important.

Representations and Warranties

Typically, publishers won't promise much in the way of representations and warranties. However, the developer is expected to promise quite a bit. While it is important to limit your own risks, the developer may want the publisher to assume the risks for its contribution to the game product. For instance, if the publisher provides licenses for engines or other middleware, the publisher should warrant that they have acquired all of the necessary rights and licenses for the content it contributes. The developer may also want indemnification for any claims arising from that content. Indemnification is the primary form of risk shifting in contracts. It means that one party assumes liability for any claims or causes of action that may be brought against either party that arises from the agreement. The scope of indemnification is usually determined by each party's representation and warranties.

Employment Agreements

As a game developer, you will likely spend the first few years of your career working for other people. You should, therefore, have an idea of what you will be signing when you agree to work for someone else.

Most entertainment industries have unions. Sports, film, television, and even to some extent the music industry have unions and guilds that represent the interests of talent and professionals within those industries. Those unions will typically enter into collective bargaining agreements with trade or industry associations (such as the RIAA) to draft standards that are thereafter embedded into every employment contract where union labor is used.

The games industry has no such union or guild. As a result, what goes into an employment contract is dictated entirely by the employer and the prospective employee. It is therefore very important that you actually get an employment contract laying out the terms of your employment in writing. As an employee getting his or her first gaming position, you should be aware of what an employer is required to do on your behalf. You also want to make sure that your quality of life doesn't go down the tubes because your agreed-upon compensation didn't take into account things like overtime, health insurance, and revenue sharing in the event of a major success.

Do not fall under the delusion that working for a game developer means that you should be working 60-hour shifts plus weekends all the time. The terms of your employment are determined mostly by you and what you are willing to sacrifice in lieu of pursuing your chosen career. Following are the major contract provisions your employment contract will (or should) include.

Recitals/Introduction

This sets out the name of the company and the employee (you), the place of business, and so on. It sounds silly, but make sure you're actually being employed by who you think you're being employed by—in the games industry, there are a number of parents and subsidiaries, so it is always best to know who will actually be responsible for signing your paycheck.

Duties

This explains why you are being hired and the tasks that you will be required to perform. It may also include the title of your position. This section may also include a minimum number of hours you are required to work.

Term

This sets out the duration of your employment. Some states place limitations on the length of an employment contract (California being one of those states). Some employment contracts may have provisions for renewal as a result.

Non-Disclosure Agreement (NDA)

NDAs may be a separate document or an embedded provision—an NDA sets out specifically what must remain confidential, although many employment contracts with an embedded provision keep the definition of "confidential information" and "trade secrets" fairly broad. This is a bit dangerous for the employer because, unless employees are aware of what must remain confidential, it may be difficult to raise the argument that a specific piece of information should have remained confidential pursuant to the agreement.

Work-for-Hire

While employee product created in connection with the employment is automatically a work-for-hire under copyright law, some employers may seek to broaden the scope by including language that encompasses any work product created during the term of your employment. In this manner, an employer may seek to claim ownership over any invention or expression you created independently. It is therefore very important that you read this provision carefully if it is in your contract and address any issues you have before signing your contract. This is especially true if you are an independent contractor.

Compensation

This provision establishes your salary, or it will make reference to a schedule that describes your compensation. Be aware of who is responsible for paying what and what deductions will be made from your salary for tax and employee benefits purposes.

Contingent Compensation

In some instances, particularly if you are working for an independent developer and you are getting paid peanuts on the condition that you will get a bigger piece of the pie later, you may have a contingent compensation clause. This will set out the royalty you are entitled to once your company starts earning profit from the product. Profit participation should always be negotiated if the project requires a long-term commitment from the employee.

Credits

If this isn't in your contract, it should be. You are entitled to credit for your contribution to a project. This should set forth how your credit will be displayed and where.[26]

Covenants

Many agreements include covenants not to compete. While most jurisdictions legally (judicially) limit the scope of these clauses by time and geography, the covenant may be burdensome and has been held unenforceable in some jurisdictions.[27] A covenant not to compete will usually state that, upon termination of your relationship with your employer, you are not allowed to seek

---

[26]For more information on credit standards in the games industry, please visit IGDA's Credit Standards web site at www.igda.org/credit.

[27]The California Supreme Court ruled in *Edwards v. Anderson* in August of 2008 that non-compete clauses are unenforceable in employment contracts <www.courtinfo.ca.gov/opinions/documents/S147190.PDF>.

employment from a "competitor" for a specific period of time (anywhere from six months to a year, usually). This obviously creates a problem if you're only taking an entry level position and plan on moving to another potentially competing firm. A reasonable employer probably won't enforce this unless you had access to highly confidential information, and there's evidence that you disclosed trade secrets to a competitor.

Stock Option/Revenue Sharing/Pension Plan

Larger firms may offer you an opt-in to the company's stock option/revenue sharing/benefit/401(k) plan. Make sure you understand the terms of those benefit plans and what you're entitled to, as well as when you will be entitled to opt-in and subsequently collect from those benefits. It is also important to note how much of your salary will be paid directly into that plan when negotiating your salary.

Termination

Employment is typically at-will. This means that both parties can terminate the employment at any point in time on the condition that the terminating party provides notice to the other party (usually 30 days). The agreement may also include automatic termination in the event that you materially breach the agreement or breach one of the major bylaws and/or company policies and practices.

Disability

If this isn't in your agreement, it should be. If you are unable to perform your duties under the contract as a result of a serious mental or physical disability, you want to make sure that your inability to perform does not constitute a material breach of the contract and that the disability creates a no-fault termination. Yes, there are some companies out there that really can be horrific enough to sue a paraplegic because he can no longer do his job. This is also a good time to contemplate disability benefits.

Dispute Resolution (Arbitration)

Most employment contracts include dispute resolution, mediation, and/or arbitration provisions as a preliminary measure to a lawsuit. This is to the benefit of both parties because it's less expensive than going to trial. It is also less formal. You will also want to pay attention to who is responsible for attorneys' fees—depending on the language of the provision, it may be better for each party to bear the cost of their own attorneys' fees.

Conclusion

The legal issues you will face in the games industry are complex, ever-changing, and filled with potential dangers. It is therefore important to remain aware of your rights under both intellectual property and contract law. However, these are not the only legal issues that may arise. The topics and explanations set forth in this article are by no means a complete representation of the legal issues you may confront. However, having this information will hopefully provide the means to asking the right questions when necessary. If you are confronted with any of the legal issues addressed in this article, it is in your best interest to seek out adequate legal counsel and ask those questions.

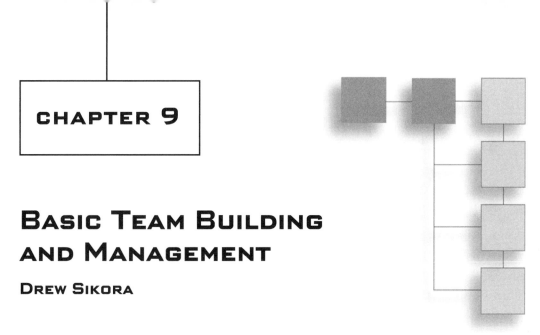

CHAPTER 9

BASIC TEAM BUILDING AND MANAGEMENT

DREW SIKORA

There are many, many ways to build and manage teams these days, and no one way will benefit everyone. Many things will dictate how you will construct your team, how you will structure your team, and how you will keep track of and manage your team. However, there are several general guidelines that you can apply to almost any situation that bear keeping in mind when you are doing any of the aforementioned things. These guidelines are aimed to help you bring together individuals who are in line with your game development goals, and then keep them happy and productive as they work together during their time with the team. Three main types of people will benefit from reading this chapter:

1. People looking to assemble a team for a project with no intention of staying together once the project is over

2. People looking to assemble a team for a new studio and retain that team

3. People looking to join an existing project or studio team

While primarily aimed at newcomers to team management who fit the first two types, hopefully experienced managers and team leaders will gain some additional insight or reinforcement as well. Additionally, if you're a developer looking to join an existing team, the guidelines from this chapter can help you decide what team would be best for you and what to be aware of while on that team.

Start with Yourself

Before you even begin to look for others to work with, you have to turn your thoughts inward and ask yourself three very important questions. The answers to these questions will guide you in your search for teammates.

Question #1: Who Are You?

An honest assessment of who you are is the most important part of the self-evaluation process. Don't make up ideas of what you *want* to be; take stock of your current situation and face this question with honesty. This includes things like your current financial situation: how much can you afford to spend on a new venture, or, if you're looking for new employment, how much money do you need to stay afloat? What is your current skill level: are you an experienced developer with a few published titles under your belt? Are you an experienced developer but have only worked on small indie or mod projects? Are you fresh out of school or coming from another profession? What's the commitment you're bringing to this venture: are you looking just to make small indie games in your spare time? Are you looking to start up a studio and work on AAA games?

I'll repeat myself one more time to drive home its importance: *be honest.* If you make yourself out to be more than you are, you're setting yourself up to fail.

Question #2: What Do You Like Doing?

When you consider this question, you're thinking not only about genre or platform, but also about the scope and difficulty of the projects you want to be working on. Scope relates to things like the size of your target audience, the breadth of content you want in your games, the number of players that can participate simultaneously, and so on. This then plays directly into difficulty, which is where you consider the assets that you have available to you and how that will affect the products. If you are a small independent studio or hobby developer, creating an MMO can be a daunting task, though not impossible. Take what you learned in the first question and apply it here. If you remain honest with yourself, you won't set goals that you cannot achieve.

Question #3: What Is Your Goal?

This final question ties everything together and gives you a direction to head in. It's the most important question when considering who you want to work with, but it requires careful and honest consideration of the first two questions beforehand. Are you looking to get into games as a hobby or pastime? Are you looking to just get some experience under your belt? Are you looking to start up a game studio and go into games full-time?

This question is important and gives you direction because you don't want to work with people who do not share the goals and desires that you do. Realize also that the sharing of goals and desires needs to be similar, and not exact. This is taken on a case–by-case basis and relies on the scope of the team's work. So don't, for example, refuse to work with someone who is looking for development experience in their spare time (like you) but wants to just continue as a hobbyist afterwards (not like you). If the scope of the team is just that project, then goals and desires past that project do not matter.

General Team Structure and Composition

Let's have a look at three different examples for structuring your team and determining its members. Obviously, these aren't the only three ways, but they do represent the various styles of development teams. Basically, you can break the world of game development into three very general categories: student, indie, and professional. Yes, the lines between these can be very blurry, but I'm just going to focus on the core aspects of each.

Student Teams

There's a reason student teams are a special breed, and that's because they have specific goals and requirements that go along with them. This is especially true for students studying in game degree programs like Fullsail or Digipen, and should be applied as well by students following a more formal degree education (whether or not that degree has anything to do with computers is irrelevant). The only major difference between the two is that students in a game degree program are often assigned projects to work on (sometimes assigned team members as well), whereas students in normal degree programs choose to work on game projects of their own volition.

There does exist a major similarity between students under game degrees and normal degrees, which is that the teams are comprised entirely of students. This is beneficial for several reasons. For one, you're all on the same schedule, and I don't mean time schedule but lifestyle schedule. You have other assignments to do, activities to participate in, parties to attend—everything that people out-side of college have largely left behind when they moved on to "the real world." This makes it easier for others on the team to understand the excuse of "I need to finish a 12-page paper due tomorrow so I can't get the build out until the weekend." Secondly, the team is usually fairly balanced in terms of experience and skill level, which means a low chance of having a prima donna developer bossing people around and refuting any claims that he is not correct on everything because he knows better. You're all learning as you go, so mistakes, while still frustrating in a general sense, are more tolerable and understandable by the team as a whole. Finally, everyone shares the passion of getting into the industry. It's not "just another project," but a shot at attaining the skills you need to become successful in the games business, which is a powerful driving force made even more so when it is shared across all members of the development team.

Don't toss the idea of an experienced non-student team member out the window entirely though. Mentorship by an industry professional can be extremely valuable to student teams who primarily need guidance more than anything. If you do acquire a mentor for your project, be sure to treat him or her properly. Mentors are *not* a direct part of your development team. They are also not meant to make any decisions for you. Consulting your mentor without first trying to solve a problem yourselves only turns him into a crutch, which you'll be crippled without later in your career. This detachment also prevents the mentor from inadvertently taking control over a project, which at best lessens the team's overall experience gain, and at worst leads to the prima donna situation described earlier.

Since student teams tend to focus on simplicity and implementation (i.e., get it done), they tend to be very small. If not a lone-wolf developer, then usually no more than two to four members make up a team. Because of this, a "many hat" structure is usually adopted, where team members partake in numerous responsibilities besides their primary focus. A programmer, for example, may have decent enough art skills to draft up concept work that the primary artist can then elaborate on. The benefit to this is that each team member can dabble in various areas of development to broaden the amount of experience they get from the project and, who knows—some might find they actually prefer another area of development than the one they originally chose to focus on. As always, however, downsides exist: make sure each team member knows his primary task and doesn't get muddled up in doing many different things all at once.

Indie Teams

The term *indie* is completely interpretive. People who develop games part-time call themselves indie. People who develop full-time but self-publish or self-fund (or both) their titles call themselves indie. People who strike out against the current and who take risks call themselves indie. Ask any developer what "indie" means, and you will always get a slightly different answer. I know—I've asked a lot. For the purposes of this subject though, when broken down to structure and goals, an indie team is generally comprised of a handful to a few dozen members who are looking to make games for profit.

The goal of profiting from your work sets a very important level of standards that your team needs to achieve. Because of this, indie teams are generally comprised of developers with at least some prior experience in game development. Sometimes student teams stick together after graduating college and go on to form small companies, while also graduating into a more formal structure. Given their background, hiring other students may not seem like a bad idea, and it certainly isn't—many students are more than qualified to work on small indie projects. Just make sure that they and their raw enthusiasm are not taken advantage of. Indies like to reach out to more veteran developers at established studios for support, but the majority are bound by clauses in the contracts against working on side projects.

The scope of games tends to be larger than student projects, hence this usually calls for a larger team as well. Given the fact that more people are around to perform tasks, positions should be more well-defined and stuck to in order to ensure that everyone remains focused on his work and decisions do not devolve into endless arguments. Blur can still be allowed, however, in some cases in order to increase efficiency. If a programmer completes a task early but is dependent on another programmer finishing before he can start his next task, perhaps he can help one of the designers mock up a new game feature. But when the time comes for his programming task, he must be able to return to his primary focus.

One of the first things people like to do when they're planning to profit from a title is promise royalties or percentages when the game is shipped. These incentives are used as bait to attract team members to the project, but more often than not they just end up causing strife within the team at a later date. There is no golden rule or formula for breaking down these incentives in a way that will be deemed fair by everyone involved. If the team starts off with eight members, that's an even 12.5% split. Now what happens if, later on in the development cycle, a ninth member is needed for the remainder of the project? Does everyone now get an 11.1% split? What if the team remains at eight for the duration of the project, but some people feel they worked much harder than others on the team? You see where this is all going.

Finally, a lot of indie teams like to work remotely, even when they live in the same geographical area. Working remotely and not in an office can keep costs down considerably, but of course it also brings along its own share of problems. How do you test a person's reliability when they're over one thousand miles away? Where do you meet with publishers? What if the build is broken but nothing can be done for six hours because your programmer halfway around the world is asleep? There are answers to these questions, but it is important that you seek them out (and many more) before you begin. Boomzap is a great company to research regarding methods of working virtually.

Professional Teams

Building atop all that's been discussed so far regarding teams, we reach a pinnacle. Here is another term that can be loosely interpreted: *professional.* Anyone in the games business to publish titles, for profit or no, can be considered a games industry "professional" to some. Others see it as a title given to someone with more than two or three years of experience under his belt. Still others see professional developers as those working on the major AAA titles, like those from BioWare or Maxis or Microsoft.

Still, teams like these are largely composed of very experienced developers due to the nature of their project's scope and the resources required to see them through to completion. When reaching out to fill positions, they are looking for other seasoned veterans of the industry. Students or members with little to no experience are slotted into "junior" or "intern" roles, but with good reason. Team sizes can balloon easily to several dozen in-house employees, and a strict structure is required to keep everyone on task and productive. If a person is there to program, he programs. Small meetings with a mix of disciplines allow for cross-collaboration, but other than that, people adhere strictly to their job descriptions, which can become as detailed as "network systems engineer" instead of just "programmer."

While this also applies back to indie teams in some cases as well, studios employing full-time developers must of course also have benefits. These include but are not limited to health care, counseling, maternity leave, vacation and sick leave. Many studios expand upon their benefits program to attract developers by offering up small signing bonuses like a video game console, or including a daycare room in the office with webcams for employees to bring in their children, weekly movie nights at a local theater, or a game room in the office. Even if you can't offer these extra benefits initially, always plan to maybe do so in the future.

Building Your Team

Now that you know what you want to do and you know how other people out there are generally doing it, it's time to find the right people to work with for your project or long-lasting team. Following are several key factors to keep in mind when reviewing applicants.

Hire Who You Need, Not Who You Know

A lot of people, when starting a new venture, like to turn to their friends and close associates first for help and support. This makes perfect sense: you're unsure of the waters you're about to step into, so for some measure of security, you want to include people you know well. But is this really the best thing to do? In some cases yes, and in some cases no.

Regardless of whether you're looking to sell your game or not, there is a certain level of standard set in terms of the quality of your product. You must also remember that quality relates to the *entire* product as well. A lot of people tend, initially at least, to associate quality with visuals. If a game looks bad, it's not a good game. But what if the game looks fabulous but also crashes every five minutes for no reason at all? That's not a game of good quality. What if the game looks fabulous and runs fine but makes people want to cut their ears off because the sound effects are out of balance? What if the game looks fabulous, runs fine, sounds amazing but after five minutes people get frustrated and don't want to play anymore? Obviously, no one will play your game, let alone dish out any money for it.

This is a consequence you can end up with if you choose friends on the simple basis that you know them, are comfortable working with them, but they aren't the best picks for the job. Don't hold up the portfolio of a close friend next to a complete strangers and, despite seeing an obvious difference in quality, choose the lesser of the two simply because "oh well, he's my best friend." This is difficult, and you may feel like you're betraying your close friend by implying that his work is not up to the task, but this slight offense pales in comparison to what could come six months or more down the road when *he* realizes he's not up to the task.

Diversity Is the Spice of Life

Games are all about creative design. In order to promote creativity, you have to have people who do not think the same way or carry the same set of skills. Of course, everyone on a team will share the same vision in regard to a project, but how they interpret that vision does not have to be the same and in fact may lead the team in an entirely new, and better, direction. A lot of people think that arguing is a bad thing when it's not. The more people you have in an argument, the more ideas you have being tossed around. What is bad is when there is no one in place to end the argument and make an assertive decision or the argument spills over into personal space, but I'll discuss that more in the next section.

Skills, too, should be varied. If you have to hire, for example, two C++ programmers and the first one you pick can also program in C#, look for a second programmer whose secondary skills lie in another area, like Python or some similar scripting language. This increases the ability of your team to take on varied projects while having on-site assistance for those who are not familiar with that aspect of development. Two artists who only know Maya will take longer to learn 3D Studio Max than one artist while being coached by the other.

Hire People for the Job They're Meant to Do

Never hire for secondary skills. If you're reviewing an artist's so-so portfolio, and then glance again at his resume and notice that he also carries a degree in law but hasn't practiced for a few years, don't start thinking how useful it would be to have an artist with lawyer's chops on the team. Obviously, it's tempting if you believe you can save money by not having to hire a lawyer for legal advice *all* the time, but don't forget that when he's not giving you legal advice, he's giving you sub-par artwork. And maybe he'll save you from signing that weighted contract, but then your game gets a bad review with many references to the "dull color" and "poor environment design."

If you stumble across someone with secondary skills you feel would be invaluable to the team, create a new position for him that takes direct advantage of those skills. If you can't justify opening a new spot on the team, consider forming a contract-based relationship in order to tap him when needed.

It's Not Who They Know, It's Who Knows Them

Take full advantage of today's networked society to research potential team members to learn who in the industry they are connected with. Many people go to great lengths to put themselves out there on Facebook, Linkedin, and many other social sites in order for people to see them and learn how they are involved in the industry. Many a fledgling studio has signed their first contract with a publisher thanks to inside connections. No one knows a team or studio name when it first forms, but they do know the people involved in that team or studio.

Don't just assume that a developer with 500 friends on Facebook and 1000+ connections on Linkedin is well-connected. They know a lot of people, but how many people actually know *them*? How many of their friends or connections, when asked, would say "Oh yes, Dan. I know Dan. Great guy!" Obviously, you're not about to go around spamming all his associates with inquiries, but looking back at public conversations and activities between him and his connections can give you an idea of how well-known he really is.

Just as you wouldn't hire an artist for their law skills, don't hire anyone for a position based solely on their connections. Still, when faced with two seemingly identically talented designers, why not choose the one who is best friends with an executive at a publisher you're hoping one day to court?

Always Remember That You Have to Work with Them

This is what decides everything. At the end of the day, it doesn't matter how talented they are, it doesn't matter what extra skills they possess, and it doesn't matter if they happen to be one of Will Wright's childhood buddies. If they don't get along with anyone you've sat them down with, and always refuse to believe that they have been proven wrong about anything (among other dubious qualities), then you don't hire them. Period. Never forget that you aren't hiring individuals, you're hiring team members who have to work closely with other people for extended periods of time. Also don't forget that over that extended period of time (months to years) even the smallest, teeniest, tiniest little character flaw you noticed in the beginning and dismissed as insignificant can grow and become a serious problem later on. True, that's not a definitive statement, but if you hear warning bells in your head at the beginning, best not to chance them growing louder as time progresses.

Let's also be clear that this applies to the obvious cases. Many across the industry slip by unnoticed, only to rear up without warning later on—perhaps they were always set to go off, or perhaps a new factor during development or in the team set the stage. Be mindful of sleepers, but that leads us on into the next section.

Managing Your Team

Here you are with a group of talented, driven, and like-minded people getting down to work on a project that can carry on for months or years, possibly with even more unseen months and years beyond that. Dedication to such a project doesn't come naturally to many people, and before long they could lose sight of their goal, look back at all the time passed, and start wondering how much farther they have to go. Soon after they start thinking it will never end, and morale starts to fall even lower. People get discouraged, fighting flares up, and some team members jump ship. Eventually, the project dies a slow, painful death, and everyone involved now hates each other because they have to blame someone, and no one wants to blame themselves.

It's a rather grim scenario that I wish never came true, but the fact is, some projects do end up like this. On the whole, you don't hear about it a lot because no one wants to talk about it ever again. Fortunately, there are several things you can do from the very beginning to help stave off such a dismal end.

Everyone Gets a Voice

For people to put stake into a project, they have to feel like they own that project. Obviously, if you're running a team of more than one person, you have a problem. Therefore, you have to make sure that whatever aspect of the game a person is working on, they feel that that part of the game is theirs. Say the design team hands down a spec for a gameplay feature to a programmer, who then returns saying that it won't be possible to implement as is without consuming too many CPU resources. Other than the design team ignoring his feedback and telling him that he's the programmer and he has to make it work, almost equally as bad is taking back the spec, redesigning it without even asking the programmer what he thinks should be changed, and then handing it back down again. This does not pass any feeling of ownership on to the programmer, and he will be less enthusiastic with carrying out the changes than had he been personally involved in their conception.

In a more general sense, don't restrict people's opinions to the position they are working in. If an artist has a thought about a programming decision, don't slap aside his argument on the basis that he is an artist. Over the years, many people gain a partial understanding of other disciplines besides their own that lets them give accurate and constructive criticism under certain circumstances. In this way, they are also helping to contribute to the project as a whole. Sticking them in their niche and telling them to stay there can be suffocating to a creative mind.

Not Everyone Makes a Decision

It's all well and good that everyone gets to share their opinions on ideas and features in the game, but it's important to remember that there are still only a select few who get to make any decisions based on those opinions. Teams are not democracies. Democracies do nothing but fail miserably because, if no one is tasked with making a final decision, decisions will not be made. Or, if they are made, they're done so under a loose agreement that will no doubt break apart again later. This is why larger teams hold to strict hierarchies of regular developers, as well as senior and lead positions. At each stage of the decision process, someone is in place to end the inevitable arguments and say, "This is what we're going to do."

As mentioned earlier, arguments between team members can be a healthy part of the development process. A disagreement is a chance at reaching a different conclusion, one that could prove more fortunate for the project. The problem with arguments is that they can run out of control very easily if they are not decisively ended by a person with the right and authority to do so. It's also a problem if animosity arises not from the argument itself, but simply from the fact that two or more people don't get along in general. It's not impossible, however, to have calm constructive arguments among team members to good ends.

Collaboration Is a Valuable Tool

People don't work well with others they don't understand, yet they don't understand people they don't know. The first thing any new team should do is "break the ice" as soon as possible and get team members working together—this is the general concept of collaboration. When people collaborate, they are sharing ideas that can provide inspiration, helping others accomplish tasks, and checking over each other's work, among other things. As a team, collaboration is essential. How do you expect to have a uniform visual style to your game if your environment artist, character artist, and texture artist never talk to one another? No, that is not the lead artist's job.

Give each department a chance to work together, and with the team as a whole. Have artists spend some time each week comparing drawings and designs, critiquing each other's work. Make them post their concepts out in the hall so passersby can leave anonymous (or not) sticky notes with their own ideas and criticisms. Many companies adopting agile development are also trying out paired programming, where two programmers share the same desk and look over each other's work. Have design meetings open to whoever from the team wants to sit in and allow them to voice opinions, but do not discuss those opinions at that time. Play music composed by your sound designer over the office's speaker system, if you have one. If everyone can tolerate a looping soundtrack all day, it's a good bet the player can while enjoying the game.

For virtual teams, collaboration is even more essential because you lose a lot of the face-to-face interaction an office environment provides. Hand gestures, facial expressions, and even vocal inflections if you're not using any VoIP technology are all important conversation factors that can be lost through virtual chat. Studies have shown that it's much easier for people to lie via e-mail, and many cases of strife between people have come from someone misinterpreting the tone of an e-mail. Also, it may be difficult just gathering people online all at one time regularly for meetings if time zones vary widely enough.

Be a Team Outside of Work

In order to truly be able to provide proper criticism of another person's work, you have to know and respect (or at least like) that person. If not, your criticism will be either conservative and ineffectual or harsh and unconstructive. Both cases are bad because conservative criticism will most likely not sway a person to change his or her work, and harsh criticism will serve no purpose other than to bring down a person's morale.

Avoiding this isn't always easy, but it certainly helps when most, if not everyone, on the team are on good relations with one another. Fostering this should not be left up to the individual team members, either, but is a responsibility the company as a whole should take on, whether this means office parties, summertime barbeques, movie nights, or other such events. These events should also be regular, as one-off events don't have a lasting impact on people, both in terms of their effect and their perceived importance, and team members should also include their families. Friendly rivalries in the office are also something that can be encouraged as well as closely monitored.

While this is harder for larger teams to arrange, it's also vastly more beneficial. Imagine trying to get to know everyone at a large company during your first few weeks. It's not possible to go from door to door and chat with people who are mostly working. You end up close to the people you work with every day, and slowly bump into new people as time goes on, but you forget many of them when you don't see them again for a time. Regular office gatherings provide the proper social setting for everyone to meet everyone else and build friendly relationships.

Recognize and Handle Conflicts Immediately

Things can still go bad in teams despite all the precautions you may have set in place. Therefore, your last precaution is to be ready when all of your other precautions fail.

Hopefully, if you've managed to keep people happy and working well together, nothing bad will ever come of it. If something does, then there's a good chance that it will be brought to your attention right away so that it can be dealt with. If your team doesn't get along well and/or people don't communicate well, it could take days, weeks, or months for problems to make themselves readily apparent. Under these circumstances, you could end up losing team members or the entire project.

The moment it becomes apparent that you have a problem involving two or more people, you need to solve it. There are two ways that you solve problems: you lead all parties to reconciliation, or you fire people. It really is that simple because without reconciliation you're going to end up losing someone anyway, so it might as well be the person you *don't* want sticking around. This means that if the parties involved cannot settle their differences, and these differences are beginning to spill over and affect the rest of the team, you need to let go of the people who will continue to cause disturbances in the future. Just as when you hire people you can't look only at their personality, so it goes for firing people. Yes, you may be losing the best programmer on your team, but what happens if you decided to send off the victim instead of the perpetrator because he held less programming skill? What's stopping the next programmer who comes on the team from also being rubbed the wrong way by the senior coder? Now you're in the same situation all over again.

Any dispute between team members can grow to affect others on the team. Some people will take sides while others will want nothing to do with any of it. One person will refuse to work with another and their task will screech to a halt, which will create a cascading effect as dependencies slowly grind the whole project to a standstill. Morale will plummet, and some team members will simply quit before any resolution is reached. Total decimation of a team is the sole result of the failure to recognize and handle brewing conflicts between team members as soon as they arise.

Conclusion

It's hard to believe that with all this text, we've only scraped the very surface of team structure and management, but scrape we did. The interaction of people in a team environment has launched countless studies, whole books are written on the subject, and an untold number of outcomes have resulted from seemingly similar situations. The individual members who make up the team dictate what needs to be done in order to keep people working together and focused on their task. Sacrifices are made on a daily basis, and new lessons are learned every day. Hopefully, this article gives you enough forewarning to stave off the more extreme examples of human behavior, but never think you've seen it all. None of us has.

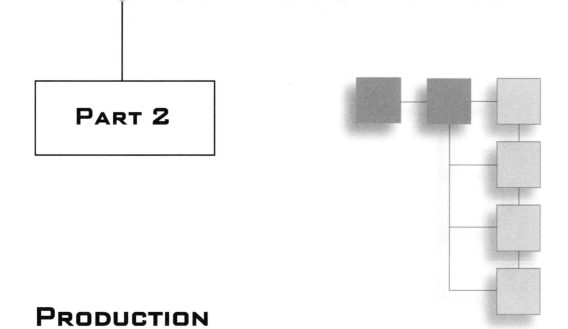

PART 2

PRODUCTION

CHAPTER 10

LONE WOLF KILLERS

MASON MCCUSKEY, CUTTLEFISH INDUSTRIES (WWW.CUTTLEFISHINDUSTRIES.COM)

In this great land of game development, I've seen more than my share of death. If I had one dollar for every game development team I've seen fail, I could fund the development of *Duke Nukem Forever*!

It's always a sad thing when a group goes down for the count, leaving only a half-baked demo that crashes on startup as the only reminder of their great game idea. It's too easy to say that every dead development team died because of lack of dedication. There are many circumstances where all the dedication in the world won't help the situation. By carefully looking at my own experience with now-dead development teams (both amateur and professional—in my pro career I've worked on a couple of cancelled titles), I've come up with several ideas about why teams fail and what can be done to prevent them from dying.

I'm presenting these ideas in "development order," meaning design comes first, because that's what you do first when building a game, and implementation comes second.

Design Document? What Design Document?

For a team to succeed it needs a common vision—that is, everyone on the team must know exactly what he or she is aiming for. The best way to get that common vision is by writing down your idea. In the original version of this article, published on GameDev.net, I wrote, "The best way to get that common vision is through a big, fat, detailed design document.'' But that's misleading—while you certainly need something about your design written down, a "big fat design document" isn't generally appropriate for indie teams.

The most important thing is to nail down the areas of ambiguity. You should be able to play your game in your mind and answer every question that starts with, "What if the player does *this*?" You don't need 800 pages detailing every option, but you do need to think about the big issues before you start developing.

Developing without a design document is like driving without a destination—ultimately, you'll burn a lot of fuel and end up somewhere you don't want to be. Learn to resist the "start developing it now!" impulse that always comes with a new idea, and instead concentrate on getting that idea fleshed out and on paper. *Never* start developing a game the same day you think up the idea for it. Wait, and write about it instead.

Continuing with the driving analogy, if your design document is your map, remember to follow your map. Don't develop technical features that your design doc doesn't call for. As an example, if your design document doesn't specifically mention that you need seamless travel through your huge city, then don't spend time coding it. Many programmers go insane about creating functionality and "building an engine." If that's what you want to do, that's awesome—making an engine can be just as rewarding as making a game—but if you want to *release* a game, you should realize up front that the game, not the engine, is the priority. Aim for developing only what you know you need.

Too Many Requirements, Not Enough Resources

History has proven that the people who think they're invincible are the ones who usually get clobbered. Game development is no different, so it's important to make sure that you keep your head out of the clouds. I'm not saying you should be forever content with making 2D Space Invader clones. I'm saying you should think about the scope of your game and your own abilities. It's okay to challenge yourself and reach for a couple of features you're not sure you can do; but in general, you shouldn't be completely overwhelmed by your game design. Think realistically about the resources (number of people, tools, and amount of time) you have at your disposal, and don't bite off more than you can chew.

Also, tasks that are technically easy can still take a lot of time. The fact that it's easy to make one level doesn't mean it will be easy to make 10 levels. Numbers have a way of tricking developers into thinking something's easier than it is. Saying "this game will have five levels, with five different enemies on each level" makes it sound easier to do than saying "this game will have 25 different enemies." Be careful about such things, and be positive that you know for sure what you're dealing with.

The "I Can Do Anything in a Week" Attitude

Along that same line, many indie game developers severely underestimate how long something will take, assuming an "I can do anything in a week" attitude. The vast majority of programmers significantly underestimate how long it will take them to code up a feature.

It may not seem very important at first, but if you can accurately estimate how long things will take, and then design milestones around those estimates, good things will come to you. Your game will get done, your teammates will respect you, and your team members will have a good reason to feel proud of themselves.

Good estimates, however, are very difficult to create. A good rule of thumb is to take your absolute worst-case estimate, double it, and then use that as your best-case estimate. You laugh now, but it's true.

Here are some additional tips for making better estimates. There are enough books written on this subject to fill a library—do a web search for "software project management"—but here are some basic tenets:

- **Break down complex tasks**. Say you've got a task like "create a renderer." That's huge. Break it down. What features do you need? Particle system? Okay, maybe a week, but break that one down, too. Mesh particles, sprite particles, or both? How do they spawn? Do they collide? Continue breaking down complex tasks until you get an outline full of smaller, easy-to-estimate tasks, and then add up all the times. A good rule to follow is that no single task should take longer than three days. If a task looks like it'll take longer, it can probably be broken down further. Software that creates Gantt charts—like Microsoft Project—can be helpful here.

- **Track your estimates**. During development, revisit how long you thought it would take you to code that enemy versus how long it actually took. This will ground your future estimations, ideally giving you a "scaling factor" that you can apply. And of course, conduct postmortems on things fairly often to bring inefficiencies to light. For example, if creating those three levels took you way longer than you thought, is it because your editor sucks or is crash-prone? If so, it may be worth fixing that problem to streamline the development of the remaining levels. That's an oversimplified example, but you get the idea.

- **Find similarities in tasks**. Relating a task you have to estimate to a task you've already done (or estimated) can give you better estimates. For example, if you have to estimate a task like write an octree to speed up rendering, think to yourself, "Hmm, that's a lot like that one time when I had to convert our renderer to using octrees. What did that take?" That's an obvious parallel, but you get the idea—often a task that seems very unique is similar to one you're more familiar with, and comparing how it's similar, or how it's different, can bring to light subtasks or approaches you hadn't initially considered.

The Ego War

There's another, more subtle danger related to the "I can do anything in a week" attitude—the war of egos. Quite frequently, members of indie game development teams will start competing against one another, showing off how quickly they can get something done. Programmers might race against artists or other programmers to see who can get the most done over a weekend. With restraint, this can be helpful and inspiring; but if it gets even slightly out of hand, it can burn out your team, lower the quality of your game, and possibly jeopardize its completion. In an ego war, otherwise-sane programmers will rush insanely through code without properly testing or integrating it, and artists will rush ahead with their creative work without first making sure it's within code requirements. People stop talking, and problems start appearing.

It's always better to spend time doing something right the first time. Keep team competition in check, curb your developer's egos (this is easier said than done), and remind everyone that they're all fighting on the same side of the battle.

The Dictatorship

A common symptom of a dictatorship is a team whose leader considers his fellow teammates "employees," even though he or she isn't paying them. Decisions are made on the "employees'" behalf, reducing them to unpaid cogs in a very badly run machine. The truth is, team members are paid in two main ways: money or enjoyment. If you can't afford to pay money, you had better make sure that there's more than enough enjoyment to go around. Promising future royalty cuts is *not* the same thing as money. Regardless of how great you feel about your team and your idea, the fact is that the odds for failure are so high that royalty cuts are useless. Unless you're signing paychecks, your team does not work for you.

So, it's imperative that your team is having fun. Your team members should be your friends. Your team should tackle tough decisions as a group, debate the design document as a group, and share in the grand game creation experience as a group. Developing games is fun. For some people, it's so much fun that they're willing to work 80-hour weeks for half their potential salary. If your team isn't having fun, there's something seriously wrong. Just because you've gathered everyone together doesn't mean that you can tell them what to do. The best teams are the ones where everyone is given equal input into things, and where everyone's considered an equal. The first rule managers learn is that they are enablers—their job is not to lord over everyone; their job is to clear obstacles and make sure that the team can move forward. They work for the team.

But in some cases, some people are more equal than others. If you've put hard cash into something, you deserve to say where you want your money to go. If I put up $1000, and my team members each chip in $50, then nope, it's not a democracy—I get more say than everyone else. If I buy the snacks for the weekly meeting, I have final say over whether we're drinking Dr. Pepper or Coke. But these are easy-to-spot exceptions; in general, the team should make the decisions, and make sure everyone has a reason to remain interested.

Exclusive Membership

Bad teams are more concerned about membership than creating games. If your team spends most of its time debating whether or not Johnny gets to join, you may want to get out of game development and go build a tree house instead.

The only good reason why you shouldn't let new people join your team is size—it's more difficult to lead a 50-person team than a five-person one. In general, however, you should be very open about who joins. If you must rely on criteria, I would suggest that you focus on dedication and follow-through potential instead of raw talent. It's better to have an average programmer who's dedicated and excited about the project than a guru who "might find time for it in a few weeks."

Keep your doors and minds open, and don't waste valuable development time debating whether someone new gets to join.

Of course, make sure that the people who are on the team—the people who are taking up a precious slot—are contributing. If someone's just along for the ride, that's a problem the team needs to address.

Eating Dessert First, and the Infinite Alpha Syndrome

Beware of the Infinite Alpha syndrome. This is where the project for some reason or another never manages to progress from alpha to beta (or, more rarely, from beta to gold). Far too often, it goes like this. An alpha version is made, showing off something cool. Six months later, another alpha version is made that shows off something else cool, but completely different. When asked about the change, the developers say something like, "Yeah, the old code was good, but it was a bear to work with. This new code is much better, much faster, and much cleaner." In effect, the game gets repeatedly rewritten, each time getting "faster" and "cleaner" than the last iteration, but never getting any closer to finished.

A common cause of the Infinite Alpha syndrome is that too many developers "eat dessert first." That is, too many developers think that game development is all about implementing cool things; they don't realize that a significant chunk of time on each project needs to go to mundane (and less-tasty) things: in-game menus, saving/loading games, resource management, compatibility, scalability, and so on. The game developers ignore these more healthy dishes and insist on eating dessert first.

There are quite a few facets of game development that are flat-out boring, technical, complex, and arduous, and these facets do just as much (or more) for the game as the "cool" technology. Don't let your development team fill up on the tasty desserts of game development without also paying attention to the more bland (but essential) staples.

Burnout

Burnout is one of the greatest threats to the success of an indie project. All of a sudden, a project that used to be fun to implement is now boring, hopeless, and arduous. Tired team members start to lose passion for the project, and they begin refocusing their efforts on other things. Developers say things like, "This project's become too complex. What we need is a really simple diversion game we can develop in a few weeks so that we can 'take a break' from this project and get back to it later." The sad truth is that 99.9% of the time, developers never return to a project they'd previously vowed to "get back to later."

It's important to realize that burnout can never be completely eliminated. Burnout occurs at different times for different teams, but eventually, it will happen on your project. However, there are several things you can do to subdue its effects. Most importantly, don't bite off more than you can chew. The best way to limit burnout is to make sure that by the time it starts to affect your team, you're finished (or nearly finished) with the project. Everyone likes to see the light at the end of the tunnel; if the game will soon be complete, team members won't get burned out as easily.

Hot/Cold

The symptoms of this are easy to spot—your team members will work on the game for two weeks straight without sleep, and then won't touch it for two months. Then, after two months, they'll work nonstop for another few days. They're impatient, yet oblivious to the fact that they spent so long not doing the game.

Hot/cold isn't the same thing as when your developers work all weekend on the game, and then ignore it during the week because they have other priorities (job, school, and so forth). Developer focus doesn't need to be constant day after day to be useful. But at the same time, if a developer ignores the game for two months, then takes a week off of work to do nothing but code. . .that's hot/cold, and that's something to watch out for.

Hot/cold developing leads to all sorts of problems. For starters, your team is much more likely to fall victim to burnout. Their attention will drift more easily, the things they produce will appear disjointed, and they may have problems seeing the big picture. Also, it's hard to re-establish a context after you haven't touched something in a long time, which makes it too easy to slip backward and redo things you'd forgotten you'd already done, going around in circles.

The best way to fight the hot/cold syndrome is by setting a good example for your team to follow. Stick to deadlines, and set realistic goals. Consider starting a blog—even if it's private, it'll force you to keep context and will provide an excellent way to refresh your memory should you have to set your project aside for a while. This will be very helpful to any new members you pick up midway through development.

Tunnel Vision

Developers are notorious for what's known as *tunnel vision*. Tunnel vision is closely related to eating dessert first—someone has tunnel vision when he lacks the ability to see the big picture. For example, if, two weeks before your beta release date, your programmer is obsessed with getting 10% more frames out of the rendering pipeline while ignoring the fact that there are no enemies, weapons, or powerups in the game, that's tunnel vision. He or she is concentrating on one very small and often nonpriority aspect of the project and ignoring the stuff that really matters.

Prevent tunnel vision by keeping a big prioritized list of everything that has to be done. Continually ask yourself, "Is there anything more important than what I'm working on right now?" If so, drop what you're doing and concentrate on the other thing instead.

Lack of Commitment

If you're trying to assemble a team, sooner or later you're going to run into people who are not dedicated but are instead all talk. These people care more about impressing others than they do about getting things done; they're the ones who show a small sample of amazing work, but then fail to produce anything more. They often lie about the status of their work, using high-tech variants on the dog-ate-my-homework excuse, like "my drive crashed, and I lost everything," or "I accidentally deleted the folder."

Learning to recognize and avoid these people is easier said than done. It's very difficult to spot a lie in an e-mail message or in a chat room, and everyone makes mistakes. I've deleted stuff I've needed, and I've had hard drives crash on me. Knowing how to discern who's not dedicated to the project is tricky, but it gets easier over time—the people who are dedicated will have produced something, and the people who could care less will still be making excuses. After a few months of solid development, you'll be able to separate the people who walk the walk from the people who simply talk.

The best way to combat lack of commitment is for your team to brush the noncommitted people off to the side of the project—have them do the lower priority tasks with fewer dependencies. Your team should demonstrate through example that the people who do the most work are the ones who are trusted when it comes to the big, fun stuff. Don't assign the task of developing your main character animations to the slacker artist; give him the background animations instead. The nice thing about this system is that the big projects are often also the exciting ones, so team members who work more get to do the fun stuff.

The Mutual Admiration Society

Lone wolf developers don't have the resources to do play-testing and market research like the pros. However, even the most "independent" game developer can take steps to ensure that the finished product is one that gamers, other than the people who developed it, actually want to play.

It's perfectly okay for developers to test the game, and of course the game should be dictated by what they want to do. But, simultaneously, it's important to get outside opinions. The outside opinion can act as an arbitrator should the team get split about which approach would be more fun. Remember this: as you develop something, you spend many hours playing it, and you naturally get good at it. This fundamentally skews your perception of the game's difficulty and learning curve.

To get an accurate measurement of how fun your game is, think about your target audience, and recruit game players to play what you've created. Just watching them—seeing what they smile at, where they get lost, what awesome thing they never even tried—can be incredibly useful.

Conclusion

This is but a sketch of several issues that can arise for the lone wolf developer or development team. There are many great books on the process of software development and project management. If you want to learn more about project management, check out some or all of the following:

- *Code Complete: A Practical Handbook of Software Construction* by Steve McConnell (Microsoft Press, 2004). I can't recommend this book highly enough. If you read it and follow its advice, you *will* become a better pro-grammer, estimator, and software development team member. A must read.

- *The Mythical Man-Month and Other Essays on Software Engineering* by Frederick P. Brooks (University of North Carolina at Chapel Hill, 1975). Considered by some to be one of the most important books on software project management.

- *Dynamics of Software Development* by Jim McCarthy and Michele McCarthy (Microsoft Press, 2006). A collection of short tips and scenarios designed to highlight problems in software teams. It's simultaneously entertaining and informative, and one of my favorites. Don't flip the bozo bit!

- *AntiPatterns: Refactoring Software, Architectures, and Projects in Crisis* by William J. Brown, Raphael C. Malveau, Hays W. McCormick, and Thomas J. Mowbray (Wiley, 1998). In the same vein as the previous book, with the same mixture of entertainment and information, but from a slightly different angle.

If nothing else, remember the main things that influence the quality of your project—your vision, your dedication, and the solidity and consistency of your team's work. A shortcoming in any one of these will seriously jeopardize your project. Hard work can't make up for a lack of vision, but even the best idea can't make up for a lack of commitment and hard work.

Keep your expectations realistic, your team happy, and your nose to the grindstone, and good things your way will surely come.

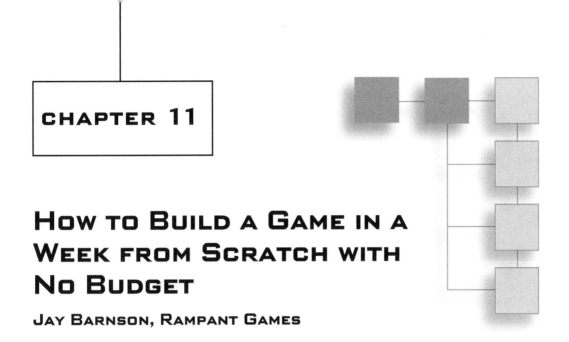

CHAPTER 11

How to Build a Game in a Week from Scratch with No Budget

Jay Barnson, Rampant Games

I did it on a dare.

A few years ago, I found myself sucked into a discussion about the expense of various game development tools and engines. As a former professional mainstream game programmer and active indie game developer, I was very impressed with the amount and quality of resources available to small, budget-conscious independent game developers.

I found myself squaring off against some potential game developers who complained that their progress was stymied by the lack of access to expensive development tools and game engines. I got onto a soapbox and expressed my opinion that, if you were to give me a week, a fresh install of Windows, and a good Internet connection, I could build a game with no further budget whatsoever. No, it wouldn't be something capable of competing with the latest *Halo* or *Final Fantasy,* but it would be reasonably amusing and playable. Lack of budget was no excuse!

Tom Bampton, who ran a monthly "Game in a Day" competition at the time, said, "You're on!" He knew I was capable of it and dared me to put my money (or lack thereof) where my mouth was and prove that it could be done. He added one additional contingency—I had to do it without the benefit of one of the (free) game engines out there. I could only use a basic library/API.

At first, I dismissed the idea. For one thing, I didn't have an entire week to take off of my day job and my current game development project to do something like this. But then I thought, "What is a week?" A work week is typically defined as 40 hours (unless you work in the video game business, where it tends to be closer to 60). How about taking 40 hours to create a game, over the course of two or three weeks? I thought I could pull it off.

When I'd made my statement, I was thinking of something simple, like a Space Invaders clone. But I didn't want to settle for something like that. I wanted to do something I could really sink my teeth into. How about something really challenging, almost impossible? What about one of the most complicated game categories in existence? How about a small role-playing game? Would it be possible?

I accepted the challenge.

I decided to take it a little farther than this. Since I realized I was taking on a nearly impossible task and going through the development process compressed to microscopic time, I decided to document the entire process. I thought it might be interesting to game developers—or at least an entertaining record of how I fell on my face if I failed. The end result was a long, rambling, stream-of-consciousness record of my hourly activities.

I've tried to edit it down to something a little less yawn-inducing here. So this article is my record of how I created a game in a single week from scratch, with no budget.

If you want to skip to the end and see what the final product looked like in all its buggy, imperfectly realized glory, you can download the Windows version of the game at www.rampantgames.com/hackenslash.html.

The Plan

Create a game over the course of 40 hours—one work week.

The Goal

Create an RPG in the style of the old, early 1980s "top-down" RPGs like *The Temple of Apshai*, *Ultima III*, and *Telengard*. The player will move through rooms in a stereotypical dungeon, doing battle with various monsters using magic and combat. Along the way he'll improve his capabilities through gaining "levels" of experience, and magical equipment.

It won't all be about combat, however. The player will also have the ability to sneak past or negotiate with monsters. There will be locked and trap doors and chests, and unique dungeon features that may have strange effects. The game will not be long on plot, characterization, or dialog—it's mainly a hack-and-slash affair. You go up the level treadmill until you are powerful enough to face the final boss, retrieve a great quest item, and bring it safely home (your "starting room").

The Rules

- **Rule #1: A limit of one work week (defined as 40 hours)**
  Game development time should be restricted to 40 total hours. These will be actual game development or research hours. Breaks of longer than 10 minutes won't count towards the total time. This will be an "ideal" workweek of 40 highly productive hours.

  The 40 hours only include development to a feature-complete "alpha test" stage. Debugging and packaging the game for distribution won't count toward the development time, but no new features should be implemented. Documentation of the process doesn't count.

- **Rule #2: All free tools**
  Except for the software that comes with a Windows install, only free/open source software tools will be used. The point of this whole exercise is to show how you don't need expensive (or even not-so-expensive) tools to develop a game. Hardware such as a scanner, microphone, and digital camera are exempted from this rule—if you don't own these, you can probably borrow them from someone.

- **Rule #3: No engines, only basic libraries/APIs**
  The game must be created from scratch without the benefit of a fully featured game engine. No cheating and creating a game using some kind of "click-and-play" game-maker software to throw together a game.

The Tools

Code:

- Python 2.3 (www.python.org)

- PythonWin

- PyGame (www.pygame.org)

- Py2EXE to compile this into an executable for distribution (www.py2exe .org)

Art:

- GIMP 2.0 (gimp-win.sourceforge.net)

- MS Paint (which comes with Windows) for pasting up screen shots grabbed by hitting the PrintScreen key (GIMP doesn't like these for some reason)

- Texture resources with free licenses available on the web (like Toob's Tiled Textures at www.tiledtextures.com/shoppe/)

Sound:

- Audacity (audacity.sourceforge.net) plus my microphone or free sound samples

The (Intended) Schedule

Schedules are made to be broken, but it's important to have them as a baseline to compare your progress with and make corrections as necessary.

- **Hours 1–10: Basic architecture**
  Design the engine and the main components. Get the world displaying on the screen. I should be able to move a test player around the world to look at things. In fact, I should allow the test player to be turned into a full-on editing tool if I can swing it.

- **Hours 11–20: Player interaction**
  Implement all core interactivity for the player—moving around, attacking things, opening doors, dying, picking up and using inventory, and so on. Bare-bones representative objects in the environment will be created to test the interactivity.

- **Hours 21–30: Making the world active**
  Add the AI, game events, traps, and special effects. By the end of this period, the game should be a pretty complete tech demo of all of the game's major features.

- **Hours 31–40: Adding content and rules**
  Take the project from tech demo to game. Add all additional content. Complete and balance the gameplay mechanics. Apply polish where time permits, adding special effects, animation, and so forth.

- **Post-Hour 40: Testing and game release**
  Fix bugs (no adding features!). Package up the game and release it. Finish documentation.

The Development Diary of *Hackenslash:* A Game in a Week

Hour 1: Wild Freeform Design and Base Classes

I spend this hour creating some basic classes for the game and using these to help guide my design. The world is represented as a series of rooms connected by portals. Everything in the world is room-relative, similar to how old Adventures and MUDs are designed. Most objects in the game are represented by a `GameObject`, which has a position and contents (which include other objects—a map might contain rooms, a room contains a box, a box contains a sword, and I guess the sword could contain more rooms, but we won't go there).

- I create a `creature` and `player` object.

- I generate a set of attributes off the top of my head for creatures and put this in a class. Apparently I'm a game geek who has played way too many RPGs. I don't know exactly how the game mechanics will work yet. This really is seat-of-the-pants game development!

- I make a `room` object, derived from `GameObject`. Rooms have width, height, and walls, but not much else right now.

I figure out how things will work and make corrections as I go. I don't even have PyGame linked in at this point—I don't even have anything other than a console for output. But I feel like I've made great progress!

Hour 2: PyGame 101

The goal this hour is to initialize PyGame and start putting things on the screen. Actually, I spend most of my time going through the PyGame documentation and figuring out how to do things, since I have almost no experience with PyGame or SDL.

I end the hour bringing up a blank screen filled with black. So far, it's not very impressive. Actually, there's quite a bit going on behind that black window—sort of like the Black Triangle story (www.rampantgames.com/blog/2004/10/black-triangle.html). There's a functional game loop, page-flipping, the calling of several classes, and a lot of stubbed behavior. But that doesn't make the black screen any more impressive.

Hour 3: If the Walls Had Ears, I'd Be Cussing at Them

This hour's goal is to get a room's walls to display on that black screen. To make this happen, I need a room, and I need graphics. I spend a lot of time in GIMP touching up some textures downloaded from Mayang's Free Textures so that they tile. I create a texture manager class, and I fill out a sample room structure. I also spend a bit more time looking through PyGame's docs to see if there's anything else I can use that might make the job easier.

At the end of the hour, I still don't have walls on the screen.

Hour 4: The Inn Now Has Room

After fighting some syntax errors, I finally get the walls to appear on screen. But they aren't displaying *correctly*—they are in the wrong positions, with gaps between segments. It's horrible. But with a little bit of tweaking and bug-fixing, I have something resembling a 10-square by 10-square room on the screen (see Figure 11.1).

Without a highly detailed project plan, it's really easy to get lost when you get to one of those points where you wonder, "What next?" It's very easy to get stuck chrome-plating what you've already done without moving on to the next task. I decide that if drawing one room is good, drawing two rooms is better, and I move forward toward this goal.

■ I create a "minidungeon" file to handle the generation and storage of these rooms.

■ I start adding logic for portals—holes in the wall that lead to other rooms (and provide all the offset information necessary to draw the adjoining rooms).

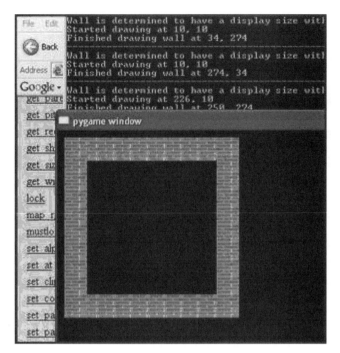

Figure 11.1

Hour 5: *Hackenslash* Gains More Rooms

- I change the title of the window to "Hackenslash!"—just because it's cool.

- I create a Map object to contain rooms, and a MapMaster class to hold multiple maps.

- I add a second room connected to the first via a portal.

- Neighboring rooms connected to the current room via portals are now displayed.

- I fix some clipping bugs where the walls aren't displaying correctly when partially outside the viewport.

Hour 6: Wherein We Practice Our Mad Drawing Skillz

- I add a door class and set up the maps to accommodate doors (since these need to be shared by two rooms). *(Editorial Note: Too bad I never got to actually use these!)*

- I create three more wall tiles and combine them together into one "sheet."

- Wall graphic changes based on type.

- I make a simple top-down player graphic.

Hours 7–8: Rotations and Exclamations!

- I figure out how to have PyGame rotate bitmaps.

- I have the test player spin slowly in a circle. Lots of tweaks are necessary to correct for size changes as he rotates.

- I learn how to use fonts in PyGame, and I build some classes to display and animate text.

- I add a manager class to automatically handle all this animated text. Having them be "fire and forget" means they'll be much easier to maintain, and I'll be more likely to use them in the future (see Figure 11.2).

Hours 9–11: Feature-ific!

Once again, I face a troublesome "What next?" decision.

Rooms need more interesting features, so a "feature" element goes onto the list. I don't know what sort of behaviors features should have, so I decide to go from

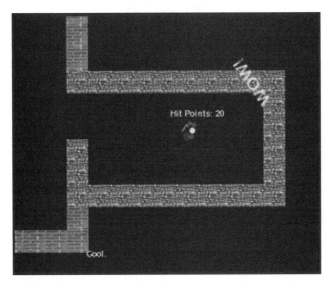

Figure 11.2

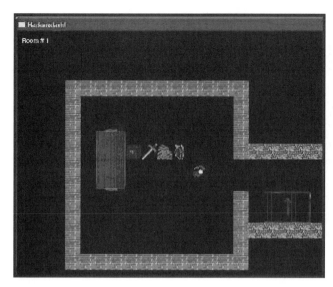

Figure 11.3

specific to general. I decide on three static features that could be found in a dungeon room: a rug (visual only), a pillar (blocks movement and line of sight, like a wall), and a staircase (blocks movement from some directions along some tiles, and teleports you to a new location at the end.) See Figure 11.3.

I determine that features can be larger than a single square and should be able to be rotated any ninety-degree step. *(Editorial Note: In retrospect, a very dumb decision—I spent way too much time on this feature and derived very little benefit from it.)*

I end up spending about three hours working on "features," between graphics and fighting some poorly designed code.

Hours 12–13: We Want Loot!

I create art and code for items. It's amazing how much time can get sucked away doing artwork. It's particularly annoying when it still ends up looking like dumb programmer art no matter how hard you work on it.

I add a lot of details for items, including their value, size, equipment slot, graphics image data, and so forth. They aren't interactive yet, but at least they are being drawn in their correct locations in the room.

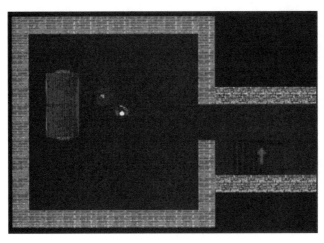

Figure 11.4

Hour 14: Carpets

I'm clearly behind schedule, and what do I do? I decide that the black background is too ugly, and I put in floors.

After working on the floor graphics, I discover that I'd forgotten to put a transparent background on the player and item graphics. So I spend more time fixing them.

But the floors look cool—cooler than black, at least (see Figure 11.4).

Hours 15–16: Click! Click!

- I implement mouse control and event handling.

- Add player responses and movement to mouse events. The movement is blocky, not yet smooth-scrolling.

- The player isn't yet leaving the rooms or checking for collisions.

- I fix several bugs.

- I create a prettier-looking staircase in GIMP.

By now, I've already crossed the threshold of Hour 17, so I start to get a little bit nervous. I should now be 2/5ths of the way done with this game (the second "working day" of development). While what I've got up and running is pretty impressive thus far, I recognize just how much I've got left to do. I now have four more working hours to finish up basic player interaction according to the schedule. It's going to be tight—but I still don't regret putting those floors in!

Hour 17: Smooth Move, Until You Hit the Wall

- More time is spent cleaning up graphics and fixing bugs.

- Add collision detection and smooth-scrolling to player movement.

- Player can now move multiple steps (turns) on a single mouse click.

Hour 18: Crossing the Threshold

- The player now goes through portals into other rooms.

- This exposes a cosmetic bug with overlapping walls and floors between adjoining rooms that is really jarring.

- More bug fixing on rotated portals not allowing/prohibiting movement.

Hour 19: Stairway to Heaven, Menu Hell

My brother volunteered to do some music for the game. He did the music for *Void War* (www.rampantgames.com/voidwar.html), and he is really good. This reminds me that I need to do sound (and now music) for the game. This looks pretty simple in PyGame, so it shouldn't take too long. *(Editorial Note: I never did get around to this, sadly.* Hackenslash *ended development as a silent game.)*

My next goal is to handle interactions with creatures and items in *Hackenslash.* I'm really fond of how *The Sims* and *Neverwinter Nights* did context-sensitive pop-up menus that appeared when you wanted to interact with a game object. I'm thinking of doing something very similar here.

- I get stairways to properly teleport the player to a new room.

- I do some research on the Internet and through PyGame docs to see if anyone already has some kind of menu system in PyGame already done with an open license that I can use. I don't find anything.

- I start work on the menu system.

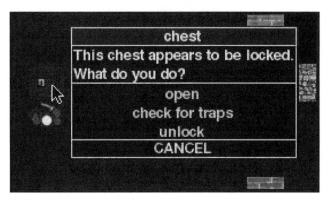

Figure 11.5

Hours 20–21: What's on the Menu?

- I continue work on menus. Menus can be associated easily with the object that spawned them, making it easy to call back to the originating object with a callback to handle the player's selection.

- I start work on item menus. They simply pop up and allow a selection at this point—clicking on an option does nothing but close down the menu (see Figure 11.5).

Hour 22: Falling Asleep at the Wheel

- I continue work on items, trying to make them functional and have them respond to menu commands. This includes putting more contextual information about the menu in the player's "action" queue. Right now, there's still not much that the item actually does, except create an animated bark reflecting command information.

- I improve how movement is calculated for performing an action, which allows more flexibility.

It's getting very late—I'm finding myself zoning out while working on this. If I wasn't paying attention to the total time—sure, I'd work through it. Since I'm on a limited number of work hours for the development of this game, having a less-productive hour is really bad news. It's interesting how your priorities shift when you consider time a limited resource. So I go to bed.

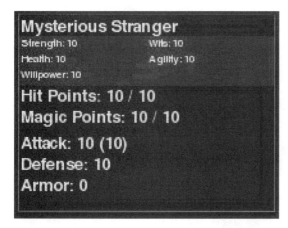

Figure 11.6

Hour 23: Stat Attack!

- I modify (and actually start *using*) some of the `attributes` class that I created in Hour 1.

- I create a window in the upper-right corner to actually display those stats.

- I optimize said window so that it is just a bitmap that quickly blits on screen, rather than writing out font instructions every frame. I update the bitmap only when I detect a change in the stats (see Figure 11.6).

Hour 24: Player Menus

- I wrap up optimization on the stats window.

- I create a pop-up menu that appears when the player clicks on his avatar.

- I create submenus for potion usage, casting spells, and so on.

- I fix some bugs in the menu response handling.

Hour 25 : I Take a Saw to Floors and Walls

This morning I had an idea in the shower (why is it that the shower is such a great place to have ideas?) for eliminating the overlap problem for walls shared by rooms (see the Hour 18 entry). What if I only draw half of the exterior walls (walls 0–3) in a room—the half facing into the room? That way there'll be no overlap with walls of neighboring rooms, and I don't have to add some complicated logic to detect and resolve overlaps.

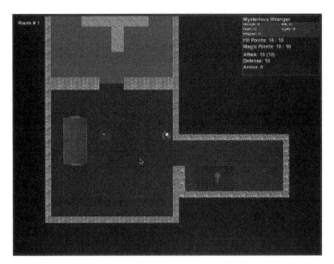

Figure 11.7

I begin work (yet more engine/foundation work) on this "quick fix." Unfortunately, it really complicates my room drawing routing (for floors as well) and turns out to not be as quick of a fix as I had hoped. It takes about an hour to create and debug this system to make rooms more seamless, but the results are much nicer.

While debugging the code, I discover a few more movement bugs related to crossing portal thresholds with negative offsets, and fix those (see Figure 11.7).

Intermission: Crisis Management!

At this point, I realize I'm more than 3/5ths of the way through my schedule, and I have less then 15 hours left to finish the game. I go through my list of things to do, and assuming one hour per feature, it'll take around 25 hours to finish it all. That's 10 hours over my limit. I'm halfway through the time I'd allocated to getting the environment active, and I've not really started on it yet. *The project is officially in jeopardy.*

Going overtime is really not an option that I'm allowing myself. Hiring additional help or buying some more code/resources isn't an option either. Since I'm only counting real "development" time for my 40 hours, I'm already pretty maxed out on productivity—I can't think of any way to be more efficient. Aside from spending a lot of time on the Internet looking for magical free solutions to my problems, I really have no choice here but to cut features and see what I can do to simplify my design.

- **Doors: CUT!** I *Really* want doors in this game. This is the most painful feature to cut, especially since I've already spent some time working on them already. But there is too much work to be done on them, especially considering the AI has to deal with them. I probably need two to three hours to get them working, and I don't have the time.

- **Inventory: SIMPLIFIED!** Forget having a back inventory of usable items you don't currently have equipped. Anything you aren't equipped with gets converted into money immediately.

- **Traps: SIMPLIFIED!** I wanted to have all kinds of nasty traps with interesting, debilitating effects. Not gonna happen. Traps will have a simple visual when they go off, and just do damage and temporarily increase the chance of running into a random (wandering) monster.

- **Bows (missile weapons): CUT!** It's going to be just melee and spells in this game.

- **Saving/loading the game: SIMPLIFIED!** Only your character will be saved and loaded, not the state of the world. *(Editorial Note: I didn't even do this!)*

- **Particle effects: BACK-BURNERED!** These are getting dropped to the bottom of the priority list. I really doubt I'll get to them. I wanted some cool particles for animations for spell effects—but that is unlikely to make it.

- **Spells: SIMPLIFIED!** I had a concept for spells where you could find spells in the game via scrolls, and that there'd be over a dozen spells you could use. Well, as much as it pains me, I don't see that happening. I'm going to have only a handful of spells available now: Heal, Damage, Debilitate, Buff, and Recall. To deal with increased level, I'm going to allow the player to beef up the spells by increasing the number of magic points that go into the spells.

- **Monster and player animations: CUT!** I don't have the artistic talent to do a great job anyway.

While deciding what I won't do (or what I'm dropping down in priority to highly unlikely status), it's equally important to decide what I absolutely must do and what needs to be made top priority.

There are a lot of elements to the planned game that I consider very important, like searching for traps, finding secret doors (well, secret portals now), and unlocking chests. But the core of the game is combat. If that's not there, nothing else matters. So I decide I must focus on that—getting combat working is top priority. I set a goal that by Hour 30, monsters will be working, at least enough that the player can kill them.

With my adjusted priorities in place, I move on to continue development.

Hour 26: The Roll of the Dice

I work out the core "dice" mechanic, something I've had in mind for about the last week—how the random chances come into play. Since we're not limited to using real dice, we can make a random number of any range we want. Like 1–33, or 6–17. So what I do for a standard roll is a weighted, random roll against the total of the attacker's score plus the defender's score. If the number is above the defender's score, the attacker wins.

For example, let's say I have a total attack rating of 15. I'm attacking a monster with a total defense rating of 10. My odds are 15:25 (25 is 15 + 10), or 3:5. So the game will generate a number between 1 and 25, and if it's above a 10, I win.

Damage uses a slightly different type of roll. I add the defender's armor rating together with the attack's damage rating. I generate a random number between one and this total, and then subtract the armor rating. If the total is less than one, the defender takes no damage; otherwise, he takes the amount indicated. So if a monster with a damage rating of 10 attacks the player with an armor rating of 5, the game will roll a number between 1 and 15, and then subtract 5 for the damage.

This explanation took more time to document here than it did to write. The dice-rolling code looks like this:

```
from random import randint
def StandardRoll(attackerScore,defenderScore):
    # If the attack rating is 0, the attack always fails
    if (attackerScore<1):
        return 0
```

```
    # Otherwise, automatic success on defense rating of 0
    if (defenderScore<1):
        return 1

    roll = randint(1,attackerScore+defenderScore)
    if (roll > defenderScore):
        return 1
    return 0

def DamageRoll(attackAmount, defenseAmount):
    # 0 attack rating? No damage will be done
    if (attackAmount<1):
        return 0

    # Man, don't screw with us with negative numbers
    if (defenseAmount < 1):
        defenseAmount= 0

    total = randint(1,attackAmount + defenseAmount)
    total -= defenseAmount
    if (total < 1):
        return 0
    return total
```

Filling out the hour, I decrease the window size for drawing the dungeon to get a slight frame rate increase—the section to the right will now be entirely user interface stuff. I also make sure the player's movement is corrected for frame rate.

Hour 27: Building a Monster

I have a lot to worry about to get monsters working. I have to change the game update system to make it turn-based. The player needs a variety of ways to interact with creatures (bribery, combat, spell-casting). The monster has to interact back. There are AI and path-finding considerations. And graphics! Do I display the monster with the same top-down perspective?

I can't worry about all these at once—I need to start small. Just putting a monster in the room and displaying in the correct position on the screen is a good start.

- I create a `monster` class, derived from `creature`.

- I create an ActiveAI list for the main game loop to deal with activated monsters.

- I work on art for a monster, which takes me the rest of the hour. (And it still doesn't look very good—I should have just used a smiley face.)

Hour 28: The Monster Appears, and the Player Has to Change His Armor

- I get the display routines working for monsters.

- I make the monster block the player's movement.

- The perspective on the monster is totally different from the player, but I don't care. The player graphic looks more terrible by comparison, so I redo the player graphics.

Hour 29: Time to Come Out Swinging

- I create a menu and menu responder for the monster (see Figure 11.8).

- Player attacks are working.

- Main loop responds to the monster dying.

- Experience points are awarded for killing the monster.

Hour 30: With This Sword, I Thee Slash

- I create the first truly equippable item (a +1 sword).

- Monsters drop their items when they die.

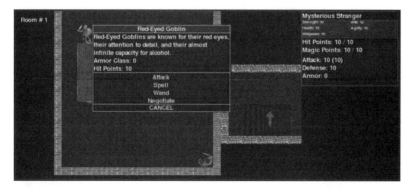

Figure 11.8

- Game loop update gets broken into turn-based and non-turn-based updates.

- Massive changes to player movement/actions based on the turn-based architecture.

Hour 31: Entering the Final Stretch

- Monsters get emotional—I give them three attitudes toward the player, which can be adjusted by player actions.

- Money is added to the game in the form of silver.

- I get the `negotiate` action working, where you can bribe the monsters to leave you alone if you haven't attacked them yet.

- Monsters attack a player if the player is right next to them (and they've not yet been bribed).

- I fix a bug where the player decides to treat a monster like a chest, and runs up to them to begin the negotiation. This gives the monster a free attack before the negotiation happens. That kinda ruins the point, but it's funny.

Hour 32: Why Can't We All Just Get Along?

- Finish negotiation logic.

- Add monster hunt/chase routines.

- Monster chooses between spell-casting attacks (stubbed out) or melee combat.

In order to save time, I cheat on monsters chasing players through a portal. I just assign a random chance of the monster going through the portal each round. This gives the player a better chance to escape anyway.

Hour 33: Wandering Artwork

- Monsters now wander around if they aren't actively attacking the player.

- Artwork for some items and potions.

- I add potions as items—they don't work yet, but they appear.

Hours 34–35: Drink Me!

- Potions get added to the player's potion inventory.

- Potions have the appropriate effect on the player's stats. Healing potions restore hit points, and essence potions restore manna points.

- I add pure treasure (which gets converted immediately into silver) as an item.

- I start working on equipment items.

Equipment items are a little tricky. Since I don't have an inventory of unused equipment, you can't carry a spare sword around with you. If you pick up an item and you already have another item in the slot, the game asks you if you want to replace the old item or cash in the new item for treasure. For items where only a single slot is permitted (like a weapon or armor), that's not too hard. Wands and rings are more complicated, since those can be in one of several slots.

After almost an hour of working on this, I realize that I've got the player running through two menus (one to pick up an item and another to choose what to replace); for items this is really ugly. It's far better to have the game be "smart" about it and reflect these options in a single menu. I end up overhauling some of what was already done, throwing away a little bit of code, to make this change to a simpler system.

Hour 36: *Hackenslash!*

- I create a "Hackenslash" title panel with a sword graphic and link this bitmap into the right UI panel display.

- Add the logic for the "monster display" panel to display the information on whatever monster last had the mouse pass over it.

Hour 37: We Don't Need No Stinkin' Word Wrap!

I create a scrolling text box class to display game mechanics information (see Figure 11.9). This is useful both for player feedback and for debugging purposes. Without any user controls (like scroll bars), development goes extremely quickly. It actually takes more time to send it lines of text from various events in the game (picking up items, attack results, etc.).

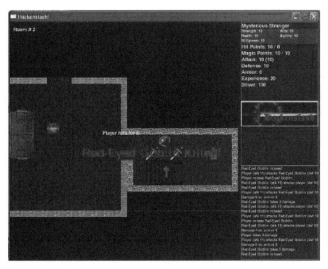

Figure 11.9

Some of my preliminary work back in the first 20 hours is *finally* paying off. There's a good framework in place for calculating the bonuses for skills based on equipment. All items have a *dictionary* (a great Python construct) of bonuses and penalties to *something* (the name of the roll). So when I get ready to make a roll, say, an attack roll, I just run through the equipment list and apply all adjustments with an `attack` key. I'll do something similar for spell effects.

Next, I work on the menu for opening chests—and decide to simplify it significantly. Why not just assume the player is *always* going to check it for traps and will *always* attempt to unlock it if it's locked? The extra steps in there are tedious. No sense in having trivial choices floating around.

Hour 38: A Little Bit of Magic

I'm frantic now. Three hours left. I have to work on *only* what *must* be in the final game.

- I generate five types of spells—three that are cast on the player, and two on monsters.

- I add extra "levels" for the spells to give them slightly more variety. The levels vastly increase the power (and cost) of the spell and are only available as the player's "magic" skill increases.

- I make the player menu non-static, so I can add menu options that become available only under certain circumstances.

- I add the ability to "level up" through a set of menus that becomes available from the player menu when the player's experience points exceed a certain level-based threshold.

Hour 39: Crisis Management, Part II

Here's what I'm missing:

- Searchable secret doors and items

- Quest items (and a place to return the quest item to win the game)

- Sound effects

- Music

- A merchant from whom to purchase equipment

- A place to rest

- Random equipment with different bonuses and names

- Random monsters

- Graphics for the new equipment, monsters, and merchant

- Random chest traps and locks

- Creatures casting spells

- Wands

- A larger dungeon with a quest item (and maybe boss monster) at the end

- The ability to sneak around (?) to avoid being attacked by the monsters

There is no way I can get all of these in with a little over 100 minutes to go. I can handle maybe three or four if I'm fast. What is the minimal set of items needed to make a playable game? I decide on the following:

- The player must be able to rest to regain health and magic points.

- Monsters and treasure should respawn while the player is resting.

- Random equipment types and abilities should be generated with the treasure, and should gradually scale up by player level.

- Random monsters should be created with abilities and numbers that scale up to the player level.

The initial room (the one up the stairs) becomes the "rest" room (pay no attention to the awful pun—aw, heck, it's part of the charm). There will be no monsters in this room, ever. I add a new dynamic entry into the player menu when he's in a rest area (the "rest option"). Then I create a routine to re-initialize the dungeon while the player is resting. Right now it's a stub.

I add the remaining equipment graphics in GIMP. I have no time to make them look any good. I simply draw them in 32 × 32, blur them in areas to hide my awful artwork, and then sparingly add some highlighting so they don't just look like a blurry mess. Now they look like a touched-up blurry mess.

For the random equipment generator, I have the game pick one or two random abilities and slap them onto the item, with a possible range based on the player's level. *(Editorial Note: Unfortunately, the player's level is never actually displayed on the screen anywhere. D'oh!)* Certain items have mandatory effects—a sword has to improve either your attack or your damage rating, armor must improve your armor rating, and a shield improves your defense rating. I add these constraints, and we're now already well into hour 40.

Hour 40: The End Is Near

I have no time to create actual unique monster types, so I frantically work on just changing the names and stats of the one monster I have—the goblin. I throw some silly-sounding adjectives in front of the goblin names, and I have them "level up" similarly to the player based on the player's level. I finish up the re-initialization routine to repopulate the dungeon while the player rests. I finish up some routines to deactivate monsters that are far away from the player and to make them become active when the player enters the room.

I add a couple more rooms to the dungeon, and then I'm out of time.

Post-Development Work: Wrapping It Up with a Bow

After talking with a friend, I'm convinced that I shouldn't work on fixing any bugs except the ones that crash the game. Since the purpose of this project is to

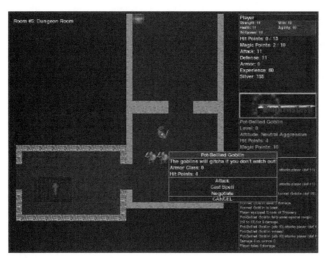

Figure 11.10

show off what can be done in 40 hours, I leave it in that state (see Figure 11.10). There are lots of non-critical bugs: stats aren't being displayed properly in the right-hand panel, I don't think goblin hit points are increasing with level, I'm not convinced monsters are properly de-activating, monsters are ignoring collision detection, treasures are appearing inside interior walls, monsters are ignoring magic attacks from long range. . . .

I leave them, and focus on the crash bugs. This means playing the game quite a bit. It's actually pretty fun. Not play-this-game-for-hours fun, but certainly an amusing diversion. Once the crash bugs appear to be mostly quashed, I work on the distribution.

Py2exe is supposed to make things ridiculously easy, allowing you to package a Python program as a native Windows executable, including everything you need so that users don't need to have Python installed to run the program. It's not quite as easy as all that. First, it tells me there are missing modules, and the executable crashes in the font code. I check on the Internet, and find that the "missing modules" are red herrings, and what I'm missing is a font file that needs to be copied over manually.

After I do this, I get another crash in the executable. This is much harder to track down. It turns out that I need an icon for the window—something that didn't seem required in the non-compiled version. Once I have that in place, everything works. I run a few more tests—and I seem golden. WHEW! I create a zip file of the distribution (I'm not going to bother with an installer/setup program), and I'm *done*.

My week-long project actually took two-and-a-half weeks of real-world, part-time effort. It's definitely not everything I hoped it would be, but I'm pretty proud of what I accomplished.

Aftermath: The Postmortem

Interestingly enough, the lessons I learned from working on a game with such impossible constraints are very applicable to the development of any game, on any budget and schedule. A lot of the lessons *Hackenslash* taught me weren't completely new to me, but these sorts of things often bear repeating. Without further ado, following are the top ten lessons *Hackenslash* taught me.

Lesson 10: Doing Something Like This Really Was Worthwhile

I didn't think I'd have time to do something like this when I first found myself challenged. But now that it's done, I found it not only taught me a few things, but it increased my enthusiasm for continuing work on the project I put on hold for this. You wouldn't think that working on *yet another game* would feel like a vacation, but it did. And after all, I didn't lose that much time—only 40 hours. This was a fun experience, and one I'd be happy to repeat in the future.

Lesson 9: Cutting Features Isn't Always Free

Some of the last-minute changes to *Hackenslash* really blew the game balance out of whack. The inability of monsters to cast spells, and the lack of need for the player to conserve resources as he pushes deeper into the dungeon trivialized some of the challenges of the game. If those features were going to stay gone, the game needed another design pass to rebalance it and improve the modified gameplay. In other words, cutting features introduced an additional cost to the development of the game. This made me wonder how many retail games were released in a terrible state because the development team didn't have time to revisit the game design after features were cut in order to meet the schedule.

Lesson 8: Do the Important Stuff First

I found I tended to be more productive, efficient, and make more progress on the game when I was in crisis mode, realizing how tight my deadline was and making a conscious decision to (usually) only work on the pieces that made the biggest difference in the game.

I think I may run through a similar exercise with all of my future projects: I'm going to try to break my development time into, say, eight-hour segments and play a little game with myself: If I pretend that I only have those eight hours to finish the game, what could I do that would make the biggest difference in those eight hours? I don't know if it would pay off as well at the end of the project as the beginning, but it's worth trying.

Lesson 7: Scope Will Expand to Exceed Your Budget and Schedule

Every programmer I've ever met tends to underestimate the time required for him or her to complete a feature. Add to that the dreaded "feature creep," and you can guarantee your project is going to be way over schedule. I'm not one of those guys who believed that feature creep is always a bad thing. I think some of the most killer features—the ones that turned games into hits—often came about as a form of feature creep. But new features are seldom free. You will have to make room for them in your budget, and that often means cutting other, less worthy features. This project taught me a little bit about being ruthless in cutting features. In truth, if I had the option, I should have added an extra 10 hours to make the game truly "work," but only after cutting all the fat (like doors, magic wands, and so on).

Lesson 6: Get the Game Playable as Fast as Possible

The sooner you are able to get things on screen and start playing around with it, the sooner you can revise and improve your design, weed out the things that don't work, and come up with great ideas for making the actual game better. It also helps you catch bugs (especially those ugly design bugs) earlier, which makes them much easier (cheaper) to fix. It also aids you in sorting through priorities.

Lesson 5: It's Sometimes Much Faster to Throw Away Old Code and Start Over

I only ended up completely throwing away some code and starting over once in this project. While I can't know with certainty if I really saved time by doing this, I suspect I would have been fighting the design flaws of the original method all the way to the end of the project. On the flip side, throwing away the old rotating feature code and starting over with a better design might have saved me some trouble.

Lesson 4: Python Rules!

I can't believe how quickly many features came together using Python as opposed to, say, C++ or even Java. Things like typeless variables, dictionaries, and extremely easy-to-declare lists (allowing a mixing and matching of object types) made it very easy to implement content lists, attribute handling, spell effects, and so forth. I was already a fan of the language, but now the prospect of using Python, tied into a high-level 3D engine, has become extremely appealing to me.

Lesson 3: Don't Underestimate the Art Requirements

Looking up source art, drawing, tweaking, testing, and re-tweaking artwork, even little 32 x 32 bitmaps, consumed a great deal of my time. And the results weren't nearly as satisfying as what I'd have gotten if I had devoted those hours to programming.

Would an experienced artist have taken less time? Undoubtedly, though the difference probably wouldn't have been too extreme. Would their results have been better? Absolutely. Be careful not to trivialize the effort it takes to generate art for your game, whether you are doing it yourself or getting someone else to do it for you. It can suck up a great deal of time if you aren't careful.

Lesson 2: I Need to Be More Efficient in My Use of Time

A night where I'd devoted four hours to working on the game often ended with only two hours (or less) of actual development time taking place. Some of the time went to documenting what I was doing, but I also found myself losing focus, taking extended breaks, not immediately returning to work after a minor interruption, surfing the Internet, playing (quick) games, or whatever. Now, taking breaks during long stretches of development is a good and healthy thing. But by recording my actual productivity, I was pretty surprised at how inefficient I was with the usage of my development time.

I'm not getting paid by the hour. Better use of my time means I can get more done *and* have more free time to do other things. So I'm going to be making a concentrated effort to improve my use of time when I am "on the clock."

Lesson 1: It Can Be Done

While *Hackenslash* in its current, 40-hour incarnation is hardly a poster child for high production values, I think it demonstrates how much can be done, on a fairly complex game, with no budget and very little time by a single developer. Given more time—and even a fairly insignificant budget or the help of a few friends—who knows how much better it could become?

The bottom line is this: If you want to develop games, nothing is stopping you. You can find the time. You don't need a big budget or fancy tools. You don't need a team of specialists. You don't need years of training. All you need is the will to make it happen.

And that's the most important lesson of all.

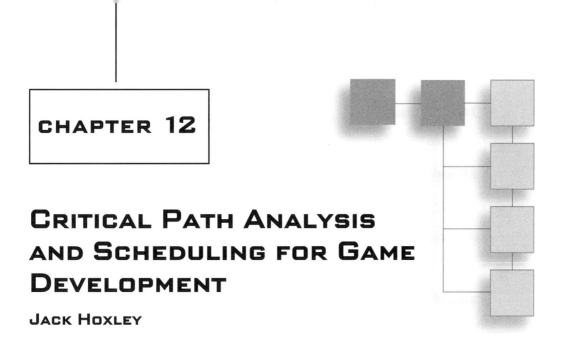

CHAPTER 12

CRITICAL PATH ANALYSIS AND SCHEDULING FOR GAME DEVELOPMENT

JACK HOXLEY

So, how do you go about developing your projects? Maybe you will have just worked out what you need to do, and then got on with it, picking and choosing tasks in some sort of correct order, and working from the foundations upward. While there isn't anything particularly wrong with this method, it's hardly an efficient and quick way of completing the project. In this article, I'm going to cover a method that will help you complete your project in the most time-efficient manner.

The first time you get the feeling that the first method (the "old" one) doesn't work is when you forget to do something and have to go back and do it, pausing all other development in the process. This is particularly bad when working as a team. If this happens, you may be working your socks off trying to correct what you missed while the rest of your team is twiddling their thumbs because they can't do anything till you've finished. If you'd planned it properly, you could have gotten someone who wasn't busy earlier on in development to do it, while you (and others) were still working on other things.

By the end of this short guide, you'll be able to work out, in almost no time at all, the quickest and most efficient route to completion.

Critical Path Analysis: Step 1

The first step to using critical path analysis (CPA) is to set out the activities that must be completed in order for the project to be completed. If you take a simple game framework, it might look something like this:

[A] Graphics Engine

[B] Sound Engine

[C] Music Engine

[D] Input Engine

[E] Gameplay/General Programming

[F] Physics

[G] 2D Artwork

[H] 3D Artwork

[I] Sound Effects

[J] Music Recording

[K] Level Design

Anyone who's completed a game will probably realize that there's much more to it than the preceding list; this is only an example—and it can easily be extended. You could go as far as doing a separate analysis for the development of the graphics engine. It's only limited to the detail that you include.

Critical Path Analysis: Step 2

Now that you know what activities you must complete in order to finish the project, you need to decide what dependencies there are. This will involve creating a hierarchy for the activities—what activities must be completed before you can start this activity? Notice that the original list (in Step 1) has a letter for each activity. This is just for convenience. Later on when you start drawing out diagrams, it'll get a little crowded and complicated to put the complete activity name in, so I'm referring to them by letter:

[A] depends on:

[B] depends on: I

[C] depends on: J

[D] depends on: A

[E] depends on: B, C, D

[F] depends on: E

[G] depends on:

[H] depends on: G

[I] depends on:

[J] depends on:

[K] depends on: F

The preceding list is what I think the dependency list should look like. You may well disagree, but you can change it all around when we're done. Notice that [K] only depends on [F]. You may be thinking that level design doesn't only require physics to be completed; it requires almost everything else to be completed as well. But if you look closely, [F] requires that [E] is completed, and [E] can't be completed until almost everything else has been. Therefore [F] effectively implies that everything before it has been completed (in this case [E]), so Level Design [K] does actually require that (almost) everything else is completed.

Critical Path Analysis: Step 3

You're now starting to get a clearer picture of what will need to be done to complete your project efficiently. However, this is still very murky compared with the final result. This step is the beginning of things getting complicated. In this step, you must draw a graph.

But this isn't quite like the normal graphs you're used to, with bar charts, scatter diagrams, and so on. This graph doesn't represent a series of data. If you've done much discrete mathematics/path finding algorithms, chances are that you'll know most of this, so feel free to skip forward. The rest of you will need a quick crash course in graph theory. A graph as I'm using it can also be referred to as a *network*—a series of points (nodes or vertices) connected by lines (arcs or edges). Nodes represent events or positions (of buildings, for example), and the edges represent a path between them (a road, for example). Edges are normally straight lines (and don't actually represent the real-world path). For critical path analysis, I'll be using a *digraph*—a graph with directed edges. These edges will have an arrowhead on them indicating that you can

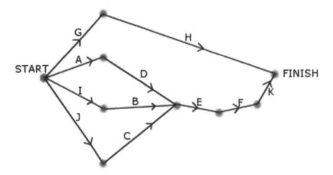

Figure 12.1

only travel in that direction along the edge. Finally, a couple of conventions: (1) Where possible edges should not cross each other and (2) for critical path analysis graphs, time is represented across the graph from left to right; it's not fixed to any scale. All it really means is that the start is on the left and the finish is on the right.

Bet that was confusing! It's best if you look at an example graph. Figure 12.1 is basically the dependency list (Step 2) converted into a graph.

Not too complicated really, but trust me—they can get unbelievably complex in some cases. Each of the edges in the graph shown in Figure 12.1 represents an activity (or task). The red dots (nodes) represent the completion of that task, and they also represent a junction where you can possibly enter/exit from multiple routes. The length of the edges isn't important, nor is the positioning of the vertices; just juggle it around until it fits together nicely.

Critical Path Analysis: Step 4

You're starting to get somewhere now, but you need to put some information on your graph. Currently, all it represents is the dependency list, and you require more. The first step is to add the activity lengths. This is very ambiguous—how can you tell how long it takes to develop the graphics engine? You can take a good guess, but you can't always be sure, especially if you are part of a part-time team (where you don't always do an eight-hour working day, for example). The algorithm does take this into account though. Events that are important (on the critical path) will dictate the length of the project, so if one activity on it is delayed, the whole project is delayed.

The following list is my estimation for the length of time (in days) that it will take to complete each activity. The predictions made here will be the basis for the final path. Putting strange numbers in here will mean that you get a strange (and probably inefficient) path.

[A] Graphics Engine = 14 days

[B] Sound Engine = 5 days

[C] Music Engine = 5 days

[D] Input Engine = 10 days

[E] Gameplay/General Programming = 31 days

[F] Physics = 7 days

[G] 2D Artwork = 14 days

[H] 3D Artwork = 21 days

[I] Sound Effects = 14 days

[J] Music Recording = 9 days

[K] Level Design = 21 days

Chances are you will have a different prediction for all of these, but bear with me; it's the process that counts here. Also note that the times given are for a single person doing the task, assuming that he or she works on the task for all of the hours they can (be it an eight-hour working day).

Now that you have some times, you need to add them to your network. By convention, they go in brackets after the activity label. The graph now looks like Figure 12.2.

Critical Path Analysis: Step 5

Now you have analyzed the project, worked out what activities are involved, decided what the dependency list is, and calculated some times for those activities—and it's all included in your graph. You can now start the algorithm.

There is one final thing that you must do (to make it easier for you)—add in events. So far you've just added activities. Events are actually already in the graph

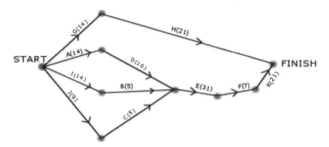

Figure 12.2

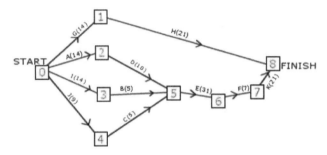

Figure 12.3

(the red dots), but you need a way of identifying them. As you're already using letters for activities, you'll use numbers for the events. The revised graph is shown in Figure 12.3.

Now, on with the algorithm. The first step is to work out what the earliest times are for each of the events (the numbered boxes). The value that you calculate will be the earliest possible time that you can arrive there with all incoming events completed. To work them out, you scan forward through the network adding the previous events' earliest time and the activity length together. If there are multiple activities coming into an event, you must select the *largest* one—this is simply because you cannot get to the event until *all* activities are complete, and you know all activities are complete when the one with the longest duration is complete.

While the previous concept isn't too complicated, I'll work through the example graph to see how it all works. You're going to use a simple table to accumulate all the results:

EVENTS	0	1	2	3	4	5	6	7	8
Ei									

Starting at Event 0, there are no incoming activities, and because it's the start, you know the earliest time it can be reached in is 0 (days).

EVENTS	0	1	2	3	4	5	6	7	8
Ei	0								

Moving to Event 1 now, this only relies on activity G being completed, which has a duration of 14 days. Therefore, the earliest time that you can get to Event 1 is 14 days.

EVENTS	0	1	2	3	4	5	6	7	8
Ei	0	14							

Event 2 only has activity A to depend on; therefore, the earliest arrival time will be 14 days.

EVENTS	0	1	2	3	4	5	6	7	8
Ei	0	14	14						

Event 3 only depends on activity I being complete; the earliest time is, therefore, 14 days.

EVENTS	0	1	2	3	4	5	6	7	8
Ei	0	14	14	14					

Event 4 only depends on activity J, so the earliest time of arrival is 9.

EVENTS	0	1	2	3	4	5	6	7	8
Ei	0	14	14	14	9				

Event 5 has three incoming activities; therefore, the three earliest possible times are as follows:

$(2)\text{->}(5) = 14 + 10 = 24$

$(3)\text{->}(5) = 14 + 9 = 23$

$(4)\text{->}(5) = 9 + 5 = 14$

You must choose the largest value (see the rules at the top), so the earliest time you can get to Event 5 is 24 days.

EVENTS	0	1	2	3	4	5	6	7	8
Ei	0	14	14	14	9	24			

Event 6 only depends on activity E, so the earliest time of arrival is the earliest time of arrival at Event 5 plus the duration of activity E, or $24 + 31 = 55$.

EVENTS	0	1	2	3	4	5	6	7	8
Ei	0	14	14	14	9	24	55		

Event 7 only depends on Event 6 and activity F, so the earliest time is $55 + 7 = 62$.

EVENTS	0	1	2	3	4	5	6	7	8
Ei	0	14	14	14	9	24	55	62	

Finally, Event 8 depends on two activities:

$$(1)->(8) = 14 + 21 = 35$$

$$(7)->(8) = 62 + 21 = 83$$

You must choose the largest value, which in this case is 83.

EVENTS	0	1	2	3	4	5	6	7	8
Ei	0	14	14	14	9	24	55	62	83

Hardly a complex task, but if you have a complicated network, it can get a little tedious after a while! From the data that you've just calculated, you can tell that the earliest time the whole project can be completed in is 83 days. If nothing goes wrong, then this is how long it will take.

You aren't finished yet, though; you need to calculate another set of numbers (and then some more). The next set of numbers is the latest time that you can arrive at the event and still complete the project on time. You'll see why this is important later on in the process.

To calculate the latest time of arrival, you use a very similar method to the earliest time method. The only main difference is that you start from the end and go backward, and in the case of multiple choices, you choose the lowest value (instead of the largest value). Here goes then.

Event 8, the same as with the start node. The latest you can get here and still complete the project on time is the total project length, or 83 days.

EVENTS	0	1	2	3	4	5	6	7	8
Ei	0	14	14	14	9	24	55	62	83
Li									83

Event 7 only has 1 activity coming out of it (K), so you take K away from 83 and you'll have the latest time of arrival: $83 - 21 = 62$.

EVENTS	0	1	2	3	4	5	6	7	8
Ei	0	14	14	14	9	24	55	62	83
Li								62	83

Event 6 only has activity F coming out of it, so the latest time of arrival is $(7) - F(7) = 62 - 7 = 55$.

EVENTS	0	1	2	3	4	5	6	7	8
Ei	0	14	14	14	9	24	55	62	83
Li							55	62	83

If you're starting to notice a pattern here, you're on the right track. I'll explain this pattern later.

Event 5 only has E(31) coming out of it, so the latest time of arrival is $(6) - E(31) = 55 - 31 = 24$.

EVENTS	0	1	2	3	4	5	6	7	8
Ei	0	14	14	14	9	24	55	62	83
Li						24	55	62	83

Now Event 4, which only has activity C(5) coming out of it. The latest time of arrival is, therefore, (5) − C(5) = 24 − 5 = 19.

EVENTS	0	1	2	3	4	5	6	7	8
Ei	0	14	14	14	9	24	55	62	83
Li					19	24	55	62	83

The pattern seems to have stopped, you may be thinking. But you don't know what the pattern means yet. . . .

Event 3 only has B(5) coming out of it, so the latest time of arrival is (5) − B(5) = 24 − 5 = 19.

EVENTS	0	1	2	3	4	5	6	7	8
Ei	0	14	14	14	9	24	55	62	83
Li				19	19	24	55	62	83

Event 2 only has activity D(10) coming out of it, so the latest time of arrival is (5) − D(10) = 24 − 10 = 14.

EVENTS	0	1	2	3	4	5	6	7	8
Ei	0	14	14	14	9	24	55	62	83
Li			14	19	19	24	55	62	83

Event 1 only has activity H(21) coming out of it, so the latest time of arrival is (8) − H(21) = 83 − 21 = 62.

EVENTS	0	1	2	3	4	5	6	7	8
Ei	0	14	14	14	9	24	55	62	83
Li		62	14	19	19	24	55	62	83

Finally, Event 0 has four activities coming out of it:

$$(0)\text{->}(1) \text{ via } G(14) = (1) - G(14) = 62 - 14 = 48$$

$$(0)\text{->}(2) \text{ via } A(14) = (2) - A(14) = 14 - 14 = 0$$

$$(0)\text{->}(3) \text{ via } I(14) = (3) - I(14) = 19 - 14 = 5$$

$$(0)\text{->}(4) \text{ via } J(9) = (4) - J(9) = 19 - 9 = 10$$

You have to pick the smallest value, which in this case is 0. So your final table looks like the following:

EVENTS	0	1	2	3	4	5	6	7	8
Ei	0	14	14	14	9	24	55	62	83
Li	0	62	14	19	19	24	55	62	83

Critical Path Analysis: Step 6

You have now collected a fair amount of data about your project, but I haven't really explained what it all means:

▪ **Earliest Time of Arrival:** If you were very quick and worked hard, then this indicates the earliest time that you could get to that event.

▪ **Latest Time of Arrival:** This is more important as far as the analysis goes. The value you have for the event indicates the latest time of arrival while still completing the project on time. Take Event 1 for example: you could get there by day 14, yet you could put it off until day 62. If you start it before day 14, any other dependencies won't be ready (therefore, it's impossible). If you start after day 62, the project will be delayed; yet you can start on any day between 14 and 62 and not hold the project up at all.

Those people who are working quickly today will have realized what the pattern means—the pattern where the earliest time and latest time are the same. All it really indicates is that you must be at that event by that day, or the project will be delayed. If you only get to Event 5 on day 26, the whole project will be delayed by two days, meaning that you cannot complete it until day 85.

You have a further calculations for this called the *float* and the *slack*. Float is for activities, and slack is for events.

$$\text{Float} = \text{Dest\_Max} - \text{Src\_Min} - \text{Activity\_Length}$$

$$\text{Slack} = \text{Latest\_Time} - \text{Earliest\_Time}$$

If the slack and/or the float is equal to 0, it is a critical event/activity; a critical activity must be completed on time and in order to avoid delays to the project.

A slack at any event means that if a person has completed the activity(s) prior to the event (and is ready to go on to the next event), he can rest/pause for that much time. A slack of 0 would mean that he can't pause at all and must carry on, but a slack of 10 means that he could spend 10 days spinning around in his chair. Later on, when I discuss scheduling, I'll examine the possibility that instead of letting him spin around in his chair, you get him working on another activity.

The float is similar, but it indicates how much extra time you can take—if it's a 10-day task and has a float of 3, then you can take up to 13 days to complete the task without delaying the project. It, therefore, makes sense that critical activities have a float of 0, because that activity must be done in the specified time period (or the project is delayed).

The revised table (see Table 12.1) now shows the slack for each event. You can immediately see that Events 0, 2, 5, 6, 7, and 8 are all critical events and are said to

Table 12.1

EVENTS	0	1	2	3	4	5	6	7	8
E_i	0	14	14	14	9	24	55	62	83
L_i	0	62	14	19	19	24	55	62	83
Slack	0	48	0	5	10	0	0	0	0

be *on the critical path.* You can use this to find out what the critical activities are—those activities between 0–2, 2–5, 5–6, 6–7, 7–8. It's not always that simple, so I'll do it the proper way—work out the float for each activity:

A = 14 − 0 − 14 = 0

B = 24 − 14 − 5 = 5

C = 24 − 9 − 5 = 10

D = 24 − 14 − 10 = 0

E = 55 − 24 − 31 = 0

F = 62 − 55 − 7 = 0

G = 62 − 0 − 14 = 48

H = 83 − 14 − 21 = 48

I = 19 − 0 − 14 = 5

J = 19 − 0 − 9 = 10

K = 83 − 62 − 21 = 0

I've made all the critical activities bold, and you can see what sort of float the other activities have. Combining this information, you can calculate the critical path from start to finish, as shown in Figure 12.4.

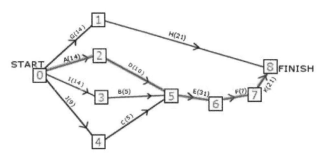

Figure 12.4

This critical path indicates that you must complete these tasks back to back with no delay:

[A] Graphics Engine

[D] Input Engine

[E] General Programming

[F] Physics

[K] Level Design

Makes sense really, and it is quite likely that you would have come up with something similar without using the algorithm. But this is only a simple example. However, that doesn't mean you can skip the other activities. They're still just as important in the overall plan. The key point is that the critical activities and events must be reached by the designated time, or the project will be delayed.

Critical Path Analysis: Step 7

You've now finished with the actual CPA algorithm, and now you're moving on to synthesizing the data you've gathered. The most popular and easiest method of doing this is through scheduling, which is usually done by Gantt charts.

Designing Gantt charts and scheduling using them is done purely by eye—there is no magic algorithm to find the most optimal pattern. It does have its weaknesses, though, and one particular example is specialist skills. The algorithm doesn't take into account any differences between the workers. For example, Bob can't do graphics engines, but he can do general programming. You may well find that the optimal route only works properly in some cases, where there is always someone who can do the task at the given time; if there isn't, then you have to wait until someone is available, and this could delay the project.

The first part of a Gantt chart is to plot all the activities in the correct positions. You'll use two rows for each activity: one being the earliest start/completion, and the second being the latest start/completion. The end result will look something like this:

- The earliest start of an activity is the earliest arrival time at the event before

- The earliest finish of an activity is the earliest start time + duration of the activity

166   Chapter 12 ▪ Critical Path Analysis and Scheduling for Game Development

- The latest start time of an activity is the latest arrival at the destination event – duration of the event

- The latest finish time of an activity is the latest start + duration of the activity

Therefore, the completed table for the earliest start and earliest finishes is as shown in Table 12.2.

From the graph in Figure 12.5, you can see the earliest and latest times that you can start activities. Each little block can be moved backward and forward, as long as it's always after the earliest start time and before the latest start time. It is this fact that allows you to do the next part—scheduling.

Scheduling is where you shuffle all the little blocks around to form the most efficient way of completing the project. This is where it gets complicated. You must do it by eye, as mentioned—there is no algorithm to do it for you. There is often more than one possible arrangement, and you also have to take into consideration any skills-based factors (can Bob actually do this task?). The first step is to redraw the Gantt chart so that you have people down the side (instead of activities). You can go about it two ways from here: either to use up all the

Table 12.2

Activity	Earliest Start	Earliest Finish	Latest Start	Latest Finish
A	0	14	0	14
B	14	19	19	24
C	9	14	19	24
D	14	24	14	24
E	24	55	24	55
F	55	62	55	62
G	0	14	48	62
H	14	35	62	83
I	0	14	5	19
J	0	9	10	19
K	62	83	62	83

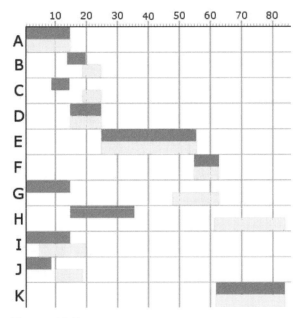

Figure 12.5

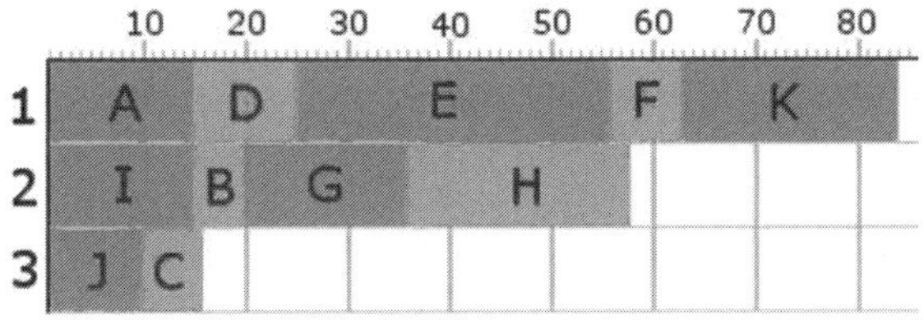

Figure 12.6

available people, or try to arrange it so that you use as few people as possible (yet the few people you use are always busy). For this example, I'm going for the latter approach.

To get things started, it's easiest to assign the first person to do all the critical activities. This person will then always have something to do, and it reduces the amount of juggling you have to do. One possible way of organizing things is shown in Figure 12.6.

It's a bit annoying organizing the I-B and J-C pairs; both have to be completed before E (on the critical path) can be started, yet you can't arrange them so that only one person does them. You could (in a real-world situation) have persons 1 and 2 as full-time team members, and make person 3 a temporary person—once he's completed tasks J and C, he goes away.

Conclusion

I hope this article has been of some use to you. As you've probably already noticed, this method has limited use for a one-person development team, and even with a multi-person team, it still has its weaknesses. But ignoring those, you can still get some very useful data from spending half an hour with this algorithm.

CHAPTER 13

INCREMENTAL DEVELOPMENT

DREW "GAIIDEN" SIKORA

Everyone wants to make games, but few people actually do. Why is that? This can be attributed to several factors, such as skill, knowledge, dedication, and goals. You can take those four variables, assign them any values you want, and mix them up every which way, but doing so will still not reveal whether a person will succeed or fail. See, all those attributes describe the person's willingness and ability to achieve what he or she has set out to do—but it says nothing about how he or she goes about actually doing it. And *that's* where a lot of people trip up.

This article will introduce you to a method of development that will supplement the four previous properties in order to enable you to achieve your goals. This isn't some new-age method I thought up—it's a tried-and-true formula. Perhaps you've already thought of it yourself, since it's nothing complex. If you haven't, or just have no idea what the title of this article means, then read on.

Why Planning Is Good

I know you're just itching to read ahead to the section that says "Incremental Development" so you can find out just what the heck I'm blabbering about. Well be patient with me for a while longer as I take a little time to explain why planning your projects is important. And I don't just mean big projects. Don't stop reading this because you're doing a dinky tic-tac-toe game.

If you think of constructing games as constructing a building, you'll get a good idea of what will be expected planning-wise. The first thing that goes into making a building is laying down requirements. These requirements are then used as guidelines in creating the blueprint. The blueprint is then used to determine, before construction begins, if there is anything that looks wrong. What do you think is easier and cheaper, changing the placement of a wall on a blueprint or moving the actual wall itself? Finally, the blueprint is used during construction to create the actual building.

To complete the analogy, let's look at constructing a game. Instead of requirements, you have rules. These rules are then used as guidelines to create the design document, which in turn is used to help create the technical specs. These two documents are your blueprints. You can guess where it goes from there, on to construction, debugging, testing, and so forth.

Yeah sure, you may think extensive planning for a game of Snake is unnecessary, that you may spend more time planning than it would take to actually code the game. This may be so for some people. However, that shouldn't matter. The fact is that you will be forced to plan out larger projects, so why not practice on the smaller ones that are easier to comprehend? It's important to get into the habit so you can't rationalize your way out of planning later on, when it's even more important to do it.

I would also wager that those who choose to dive straight into coding would actually end up spending more time sifting through buggy and disjointed code than it would have taken them to plan it first and code it second. It's hard for people to believe that planning is a timesaving method because they think of the hours spent with pencil and paper or in Word, drafting or typing up the rules and specs as a total waste. The common belief is to fix bugs when they pop up, instead of trying to squash them before they ever manifest themselves.

Even with simple projects, you'll start out with a clear idea of how everything will work. This "big picture," however, will soon become muddled in your head once you get knee deep into code. Having hard copies of design material to reference while coding is well worth the time and effort. So now that you know planning is good, let's learn how to take your planning to the next level: construction.

Incremental Development

The concept of incremental development centers on the construction phase of the project. By now you have already completed the design document, the technical specification, and the system architecture (which is sometimes blended with the tech spec). It's important that you have these things because they will aid you during development, as that is their purpose.

Loosely translated, *incremental* means "bit by bit." Therefore, you can assume that I'm talking about steps in development. "Oh great!" you think. "Milestones!" Not quite. Milestones are a bit too big for the purposes of this article, both in terms of length and importance. Check points would be a better description, although I prefer a term already well known to programmers: *builds*.

Let's take a scenario where you are a programmer attempting to create a simple game of Breakout. You briefly sketch out the interface and list the modules you'll need, such as a ball object, a brick object, a paddle object, and so forth. You then start constructing these modules one by one, laying out their properties and filling in the routines with executable code. Then you create the main source file and integrate everything. Finally, when everything is in place and with a flourish of the hand, you start the compile. Sure, you're bound to get errors—let's be realistic here. But, you figure, you can just go down the list and wipe them out one by one. The compile finishes. No, it aborts. You have so many errors that the compiler refuses to continue. No problem, you say, it'll just take a while. This is the whole point of debugging, right? You find a missing semicolon and recompile. Only 15 errors now. Ha! You fix another error and recompile. Now you have 24 errors. What?!?

Yes, it's true. A lot of people think they can get away with build first, debug later, not realizing that fixing one error doesn't mean more won't pop up. Even if you were to compile the first time with only three errors, you would most likely fix those three (say, missing header files) and then, all of the sudden, you'll end up with 98 *real* errors. This can be quite devastating for any programmer.

Now, let's take a look at this problem from another perspective. Say you're the designer, and you decide to include a new feature in your Breakout game in order to make it unique among the countless Breakout clones in existence. You receive the first completed game build from your programmer and hand it over to your best friend to play. Your buddy loads it up and starts knocking out bricks, but after a few minutes he stops playing and says that your feature is getting in the way. You look at it yourself—did the programmer incorrectly implement the feature from the design document? No, it's as specified, but when you actually play it, you realize it's just not fun.

Now, Breakout isn't a very complex game compared to the bigger, more expansive titles in existence today. You can reiterate that design flaw isn't a huge issue, but take that example and stick it in the middle of a AAA development cycle, and you can immediately grasp the significance. If not, think back to the analogy I gave earlier of moving a wall. In this case, it could be an entire *floor*. The point of incremental development is to prevent these scenarios from happening.

Breaking It Down

The whole idea behind incremental development is to keep the time between compiles as short as possible. You want to take baby steps for two reasons:

- **Theoretically, the less code you add to the existing structure, the less chance of bugs and errors popping up with the next compile**. This is, of course, not always true—there will still be times when the errors stack up no matter what. Even so, this can become a rare event if the amount of new code added between compiles is reduced.

- **When the errors do pop up, they're a lot easier to get rid of when you know exactly what was added since the last stable build of the project**. The more you add, the easier it is to lose track of things as they tend to spread out. This is why, when adding new code, it should be an encapsulated module or localized to a set of files for easy debugging.

Reading the previous two points, you can begin to define the term "baby steps" into something workable. Incremental development emphasizes constant compiles, but the problem is deciding when to compile. Obviously, you don't want to spend half of your total development time compiling the project, even if it can drastically reduce errors. There *is* a point where incremental development can actually become time inefficient, and that's when you spend more time compiling than coding or debugging.

Another thing to consider when deciding build points is that, when you compile the project, you want the new build to *run* and actually *do something* on top of the old build. Don't do a compile just to debug a routine that isn't even called yet in the game's execution. Wait until you've added a whole game function. For example, if you had a space game, you might compile to simply display the player's ship. Then you would code in all the weapons programming, and then compile to test and debug the shooting of the lasers. You *wouldn't* compile the project until you were able to actually shoot the lasers. For example, compiling to display the guns themselves would be a waste—they should have been shown with the ship the first time, or you should have waited until the lasers could fire. Just showing weapons adds nothing of testable value to the previous build. While showing just the guns might code errors, you also want the designers to be able to receive feedback from each new build as well.

With this is mind, it's a lot easier to decide when to compile. Keep these guidelines in mind:

- If you are adding an entirely new game object, depending on its size and complexity, you may want to break the object down into smaller pieces. For example, a space ship would be broken down into its display, movement, weapons, shields, and so on, if possible. Compile, test, and debug each of these pieces, not separately, but on top of each other.

- The amount of new code to add depends on its localization. If the new code is spread out over many files, you should not add too much. If the code is localized to a single file, more is acceptable. The whole point is to make it easier to determine where you screwed up when the errors come marching in.

- It's important to plan out your entire build order, rather than take it as it comes. This is because it makes no sense to compile and test weapons when you can't even see the game object that's shooting them. Make sure each additional build adds onto the previous builds.

- You should *always* have a playable version of the project on hand as a previous build. This is good because it's a stable version you can fall back onto when things get hairy; you always have something to show to impatient clients, and as a visual aid to other team members, it's priceless. Don't do a build that adds nothing to the playability.

Let's take one more simple example, again to showcase that even small games can benefit from this process. Pretend you're making a basic Asteroids clone, with a parallax star field, a rotating ship that can fire lasers, and asteroids careening randomly around to shoot at. Let's have a look at what the first build would entail.

Build #1
- Implement game API
- Create full-screen application
- Display simple star field
- Allow for exit in ESC key press

The purpose of this build is to prove that your game can start up and run in the environment that it is destined to be played in. If you are supporting multiple platforms, testing this basic build on all those platforms will ensure a solid foundation for future development. Now if for some reason down the road the game works on Mac and Windows but no longer on Linux, there's a greater chance of the cause being just the latest implementation, and not some basic architectural function, like graphics rendering that you've been building on top of the entire time.

Build #2

- Implement asteroids

- Implement collision

It's a good thing to lay down framework that will be used later on in the process of developing your game. Your spaceship will have to detect when it collides with an asteroid, but why implement the spaceship first when you can have asteroids bouncing randomly around the screen and colliding with each other? Since the asteroids should collide with each other as well as the spaceship, this double dependency means they should be implemented first.

Build #3

- Implement parallax star field

- Implement player movement

Here's another interesting example of where you can cut your build length short yet still remain a step ahead. In order to ensure that the parallax effect is working properly, you're going to have to see it moving. If you're going to make it move, you might as well make the player able to move about the limits of the world. So why not implement the player's ship? Because seeing the player's ship has no effect on whether or not the parallax effect is working properly. However, by allowing the player to move about the world, you're testing out the parallax effect and already partially implementing the ship functionality.

Build #4

- Implement player ship

- Implement player weapons

This doesn't sound like much, but that's because a lot of the basic functionality is already in place to make things easier. Implementing the ship is simply displaying a sprite object; the movement is already there. The collision of the ship with asteroids is already in place. When an asteroid is shot, it can already spawn new, smaller asteroids, just like the world itself spawns asteroids. Basically, the only real big new thing is the weapons system shooting particles out into space.

Build #5

- Implement HUD

- Implement game menu

Now place your head-up display, showing information like score, a radar screen for tracking asteroids, and lives remaining. Also put in a menu so you can choose to pause the game and confirm the player's choice to exit the game.

Putting It Together

Now that you've learned how to break a project down into builds spaced realistically apart, let's look at actually putting them all together.

Several problems can arise from incrementally developing your project. As I briefly touched upon in the last section, dependencies can be a hindrance. In the case of implementing the parallax star field effect, you had to make sure the star field would animate properly when the player moved; however, you had not yet implemented the player object. You could have skipped the build, built the player object up to the point where it would function in this case, and then have come back to do the parallax effect. This is an acceptable option, but in some cases, like this one, it's just easier to emulate the object you're dependent upon. Plus, this emulation allows you greater control over the input given to the object being tested.

Another thing involving dependency is the calling of nonexistent routines by an object. The object may need the data provided by these routines to function properly. Once more, you could jump ahead and develop the object containing these routines, but again, a better way exists. Just like the emulation method, supplying dummy routines for the object is a great way to control the data the object receives from the routines. Think stubs—instead of coding the actual routines, you can just have them return values. Since you can then manually tweak the values, you can stress test the heck out of the object. You may not have had this level of direct control if you had gone ahead and built the actual object.

As your project gets larger and larger, the possibility of getting a lot of errors in your code and gameplay, even with small additions, increases. If you've planned your builds carefully, you should be able to determine exactly where the new functionality interacts directly with the old functionality. These contact points should be listed as hot spots for debugging. Keeping a record of these contact points for each build is invaluable to the debugging process. This is because you can then use these contact points as a map to trace your way back through the build order to locate problems at various junctures when necessary. It also creates a structure for the project—you can chart the points visually and determine, for example, if changing this routine will affect the function of another.

You can easily work around dependency problems like those previously described by planning in advance. If you set up a "scaffold" around the code being built, you can create a controlled environment for testing. This scaffold would support the existing code by providing input that the code uses to perform its functions. The preceding two problems are solved using this scaffold example. Scaffolds can remain in place as long as necessary, usually until they are replaced with the actual code that performs the functions they are emulating; these should be simple constructs to ease in the debugging, since they are really nonessential components. Having a scaffold in place is important in team environments because each person will be working on a different portion of the code. A team member may be constructing an object that requires input from another object being worked on by another team member. Instead of hassling that team member to finish or provide the latest build of the object, he can just use the scaffold to emulate the input.

Conclusion

Incremental development helps to reduce errors and speed up construction. It allows you to identify architectural problems sooner rather than later, thanks to the constant building and checking. It can provide a map of checkpoints allowing you to trace the relationship of objects. It can improve testing by providing to objects highly tunable input.

Sure, it's common sense to build the project every now and then to check for errors, but not everyone may actually take the time to determine *when* the best time would be to build and check. Furthermore, not everyone stops to determine how these incremental builds can help them in other ways. Hopefully, this article has given you a broader sense for what incremental development can really do to make construction of a project, big or small, much easier.

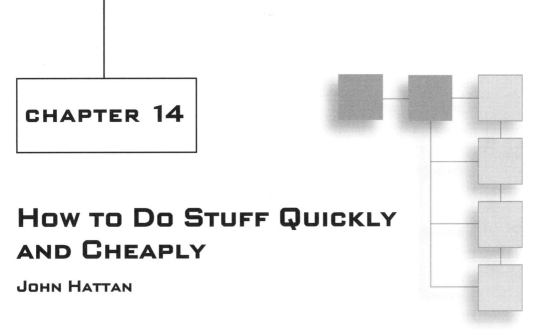

CHAPTER 14

How to Do Stuff Quickly and Cheaply

John Hattan

While the budget of a computer game can be an indicator of its potential success in the market, it isn't always. One thing the budget always is, though, is the measure of how long your project will take before the product starts making a profit. A game with a budget of $1 million will need to sell a lot of copies before it starts showing a profit. A game with a budget of $5000 needs to sell a lot fewer copies. Although it's usually a foregone conclusion that a low-budget game will sell fewer copies than a high-budget one, that isn't always the case. And a lower budget necessarily entails lower risk.

Lower budgets also correspond directly with shorter development schedules, mainly because of smaller scope. A casual puzzle-game, even one with high production values, will usually take less time to develop than a fantasy role-playing game. And a shorter development schedule means that you will be able to make more games. While a colorful and quick-playing puzzle game might not be the epic-length project that you've been envisioning since childhood, a small project's development can be rewarding and, if you're lucky, pay off in fairly short order.

There are many decisions you can make and products you can buy that don't justify cost very well. If you spend $1000 to get something developed just to find that an off-the-shelf tool could do the job as well for $50, then the decision places you farther away from your game making a profit upon its release.

So here are a few penny-pinching tips regarding sound, graphics, and your development team. This list is by no means comprehensive, but hopefully it will get you on the road to "on time and under budget." Some of them might seem trivial and would only save you a couple of dollars, but hopefully a few of them added together will get your game done quickly and under budget—maybe even way under budget.

Sound

The sound and music in your game is, almost by definition, an afterthought. Very few game design documents stress the quality of sound compared to, say, the quality of the graphics and animation. Graphics and animation always come first. Unless you're working on a project with professional voiceover work that you're matching with animation, your graphics, animation, user interface, and control scheme are going to come first.

But you can't ignore sound completely. While good sound won't make a bad game good, it can make a good game excellent. So don't put off the sound and music in your game until the last minute.

You have a few choices for game sounds. And there wouldn't be the need for choice if each option didn't have its own inherent advantages and disadvantages.

Canned Sound Effect Libraries (aka "Audio Clip Art")

Large libraries of sound effects are the cheapest and easiest ways to get sounds into your game. They are available in easy-to-purchase "five zillion WAV files for your projects" packages on software store shelves. You'll also find them on web sites where you can listen to samples of sound effects to buy individually or with a volume discount if you buy an entire game's worth of sounds in one go.

Be aware, though, that there are web sites out there that offer gigabytes of free sound clips for download, but these sounds aren't properly licensed and are not available for your royalty-free use. For example, one sound download site that used to be very popular had an entire section devoted to Monty Python clips—the "license agreement" on the site did not spell out your rights to use the sounds, but it absolved the site's maintainers of any wrongdoing if you ended up getting sued for using unlicensed clips in your game. Do not pretend to be a lawyer and assume that you can use a sound because you think it's "fair use" or your game is freeware or you cannot identify the source of the sound. If you use sounds in a game, make sure the license terms for all your sound effects are explicitly spelled out and you are 102% certain that you have the rights to use them.

Also make sure that the sound effects you buy can be used for games without any further agreements. A few sound effects libraries and web sites have a default license that only allows the sounds to be used in one-off presentations or videos with limited distribution, and you will need to shell out more money for a mass-market product like a game. There are other sound effects libraries that allow the sounds to be used for games but require more fees if your game sells more than a few thousand copies. If you license any sounds that require more money above a certain sales threshold, make sure that the extra licensing fee is spelled out first. Imagine having to change all your sound effects after you sell 1,000 copies because you just found out that the next tier of licensing is prohibitively expensive. Not only would you be upset, but your users wouldn't be too happy to find that they're suddenly buying a different-sounding game than the demo they downloaded.

Another disadvantage of audio clip art is that you might not be able to find precisely the sound you need. If you hire a professional Foley artist to create the sound of an overripe pickle being pulled through a slow-moving fan, you'll probably get what you want. And if it doesn't sound quite right, you can make a few extra passes with the professionals until you have just the right sound or your sound budget runs out. If you're relying on "Big Bob's Super Sound Effects Collection CD-ROM," you'll probably find a nice collection of splats and splorks, but you might not find exactly what you want. If this is the case, you will have to do the following:

- Lower your sights and accept something that sounds close

- Change the animation to something more closely matching the sound (an overripe eggplant perhaps)

- Change the sound to something more closely matching the animation

- Hire someone to make a one-off sound for you

- Grab a microphone and try to make the perfect sound yourself

By far, the quickest option of the group is to lower your sights, although this might cause trouble for your inner perfectionist.

One thing to note when it comes to sound effects is that the range that will properly "fit" your game is much wider if the theme of your game is more abstract. If you have a game where a cream pie is dropped on a tile floor, you'll only find a few sound effects that will sound right and won't sound like you settled for something close. If you have a game where a blurgoplaxz undergoes mitosis, sending out a flock of glipnorks, there are a whole host of beeps or clicks that will work, as people don't have any kind of preconceived ideas as to how that would sound.

Finally, be sure that your sound effects are high quality. Some sound effects, especially sounds that are necessarily recorded outdoors, have so much background noise that they're useless for a game. Put on some headphones and make sure your sound effects are clean before you commit to putting them in your game.

Canned Music Libraries

While you would think that music and sound effects would be so similar that music wouldn't warrant mention, there are a couple more considerations when it comes to music.

There is a pretty big divide between music and sound effects. The services that sell sound effects usually don't offer full musical scores beyond little 10-second orchestral punches for presentations. And the places that sell music just sell music. You won't find many places that offer one-stop shopping where you get on a web site with your credit card and emerge an hour later with every bit of sound and music your game needs. So plan to do some shopping, and don't get enamored with a single source.

Canned music libraries offer the same advantages as canned sound libraries. They're usually high quality, they're cheap, and they're very quick if you're in a time crunch at the end of a project.

The disadvantages are similar, but licenses for music are usually even more restrictive than sound effects. Music is often licensed for a single project, so you'll need to buy the song again if you want to use it in another game or even for an animated demo on your web page. Sales limits are common, requiring extra fees if your game sells above a certain amount. You'll even find music that is limited by platform, requiring an extra license if you decide later that a mobile phone version is just what you need.

Another minor disadvantage of using canned musical scores is the possibility that people will recognize a particular piece. While there are some sound effects that are now firmly cemented in our neurons (like the infamous "Wilhelm Scream"), people usually don't catalog sound effects in their heads. Sound effects play quickly, and by the time someone realizes that your alien ship's explosion sound is the same as the one they heard in a game last week, the game has already moved on to a different sound. Music is different. Your audience is more likely to notice if your musical score is identical to one in a game they played before, and whether this is acceptable is up to you.

People are, by and large, forgiving as long as the music is a good fit for the onscreen action. A great example of this is the lovable "Mahna Mahna" song that became a cornerstone for the Muppets and Sesame Street. It's still popular today despite the song's first public appearance in a Swedish soft-core porno movie. Nobody cares that it was a porno theme because it fits the Muppet skit so well.

Despite the disadvantages, canned music can improve your game quickly and cheaply. A good musical theme can make a user more tense during an arcade game or more relaxed during a "coffee break" puzzle game. There are disadvantages to canned music, but if you are smart about how you license and use existing music, it can get you a great return on your investment. There are loads of talented musicians who make their music libraries available for a low price, and a quality musical score can really improve a game. Just make sure that the license for a musical score is within the budget of your project.

Hiring a Professional Musician

Contracted music created by a professional artist and designed to exactly match your game is the game developer's dream. When you imagine music for an A-grade title, you often think of your game running on a musician's monitor while he, desk covered with synthesizers, builds a lilting score that exactly underscores the action in your game.

Something like this is possible, but if you're reading this chapter, you likely cannot afford it. Any musician you hire is going to be charging you by the hour of composing time or by the minute of music created. And while you'd think that the music created would be 102% yours given that you created it as a work-for-hire, you'll often find the license even more restrictive than buying some "musical clip art" off the web. Professional musicians like to keep their good reputations in the industry, and they don't want to see that reputation besmirched when you need to convert their beloved composition into a 20-second mono low-quality MP3 clip for a cheap web game that you wrote on the side.

So if you plan to hire a professional musician, especially one who has a name in the industry, plan to get out your wallet. And plan to get your wallet out again if you want to reuse any part of the composition, and again if you want to use a short clip in an ad, and again if someone films your clip and plays it on television.

And, not meaning to be indelicate, professional musicians have a not-undeserved reputation for being less than professional about deadlines. If your project is running late, and your musician promises that his composition will be complete in seven days, you should plan for it to take longer. When dealing with hired music, make sure that your deadlines are spelled out explicitly and that you get some benchmarks in place. If you need music in two weeks, ask that you receive progress reports every two or three days, preferably accompanied by some clips of the composition in progress. This will not only ease your troubled mind about the deadline, but it will give you a good idea as to whether or not your musician's result is going to fit your grand vision for the game.

And, while this is not always something on which a professional musician will agree, try to get a bailout provision in your work-for-hire agreement. Unlike canned music, where you can listen to the completed piece before you get out your credit card, you are going to pay for professionally contracted music whether you like the results or not. And while you will probably be allowed a couple of passes to tweak the score more to your liking, if you feel the music is completely wrong, you are still going to pay for it. If you can (and this is a big *if*), try to work out a bailout provision where you can pay a percentage of the fee and let your musician keep his score to sell elsewhere.

Hiring an Unprofessional Musician

While professional music can get you the best possible fit for your game, it is neither cheap nor quick. But all is not lost. You can still get custom music for a low price if you look for professionals who aren't yet established in the game music world. There are actually plenty of musicians out there noodling away with keyboards and guitars who will write your music for a low price and resume credit.

A good place to find them is on the music/sound discussion boards of game development web sites (like GameDev.net). Post a call for musicians, making it clear that you are looking for music for a genuine project and that you're willing to pay genuine money, not just a nebulous chunk of royalties that they may never see. You will get a few hits. Also make your license terms clear from the onset as to whether or not the music will be exclusive to your game or if they're allowed to resell it to someone else later.

And if someone is interested in using your game to get some professional credit for their resume, make sure that the license gives *them* rights to post samples of their music to music web sites. After all, there is a difference between saying "I wrote the love theme for Blurgoplaxz Mitosis" and "I wrote the love theme for Blurgoplaxz Mitosis and here is how cool it sounds." Not only will you get some karma points for helping a starving artist get some professional credit, but they will be advertising your game on their "Hire me for game music" web site for free.

If you're buying "unprofessional music," make sure that your musician is of legal age to enter a licensing agreement. If you find a 15-year-old guitar prodigy who was born to score your game, you will (at least in the U.S.) have to make the license agreement with his legal guardian, lest you find out years later that your music hire is now a 20-something star with a platinum album and a desire to regain ownership of all of his earlier recordings.

When dealing with unprofessional music, it is even more important that you receive regular updates and "sketches" of the music as it's being composed. And this is not so much for checking progress as it is for your assurance that they are actually doing the composing. There are plenty of people out there who would be more than happy to sell you five minutes of somebody else's music for $50, and if you discover after shipping that the "original composition" you bought is actually an obscure B-side from Pink Floyd, you have a real problem.

Graphics

Unless you are writing a revival of Infocom text adventures, graphics are important. Graphics are very important. Graphics are your game's "curb appeal," and a great game with cheap graphics will not get the amount of attention that a game with great graphics but mediocre gameplay will get.

Having bad graphics will also make your game a target for cloning, especially if it is a casual title. If someone can knock off your title's gameplay but give it better graphics, then their title will get all the attention. While you will have bragging rights for having done it first, bragging rights do not pay the bills.

Drawing It Yourself

This is certainly the most convenient and cheapest route, as drawing programs are either installed with your computer's OS or, failing that, are readily available for free on the Internet. And with a few strokes of a brush, you can have your Blurgoplaxz ready for play.

But there are plenty of disadvantages to this approach. For one, you might not have any art skills whatsoever. Even if you do consider yourself to be a reasonable artist, you're very likely not as good as you think you are. Still, if you are putting together some simple items like arrows or buttons, your own handiwork might suffice.

Hiring an Artist—Professional or Unprofessional

Hiring an artist is not unlike hiring a musician, although the licenses for art are usually much less restrictive than music. While a musical score can be reused in other projects, a professionally drawn sprite of a purple alien in an avocado green prom dress is really only useful for the plot of your game.

Artists, like musicians, exist in both the professional and unprofessional varieties. Like musicians, it is important to get progress sketches so you can ensure that your artist is not selling you someone else's work.

While you will be leaning heavily on an artist's skill for the look of your game, you will need to do a modicum of programmer art as a placeholder while your artist-for-hire makes the sprites and backgrounds for the finished product. And here is a little-known commandment if you are working on a project that has an artist who will be drawing the game's look—make your programmer art as *awful* as possible. Launch MS Paint, grab the scribble tool, and draw up your art in hot pink on an avocado green background.

Why intentionally make your art look horrible?

So it will be replaced!

If you spend a little time making nice antialiased fonts, or you make up some cute glowing aliens using your favorite paint program's "add green glow" plug-in, your game will look better at development time, but you also run the risk that your art will not be replaced by the professional artist. You, your development partners, and your artist will start taking the "look" of your game for granted. The art will not be improved out of sheer inertia or, even worse, everyone will decide that your art is good enough. And then you can end up with a program with mostly professional art but some leftover programmer art. And if your game has a lot of art assets, it's easy to miss some.

But if your art looks like something drawn by a three-year-old with a love of magenta, it will beg to be replaced. Your artist-for-hire will start improving the look of the game just on general principle. Your game will be less likely to ship with graphical inconsistencies because all of the graphics will have been drawn by the artist.

Graphical Clip Art

Clip art, by and large, has a bad reputation. And most of clip art's bad reputation is richly deserved. That little cartoon wizard with his hat pulled over his eyes might be a cute and clever metaphor for your application's "document settings wizard" functionality, but it makes it glaringly clear that your graphics budget was exactly zero and consisted of a floppy disk's worth of bitmaps that installed with Visual Basic.

That doesn't mean that clip art is entirely useless. Clip art can be great for some things.

First off, clip art is great for graphics that are trivial. There are a very limited number of ways that you can depict a smiley face, an arrow, a playing card, or a stop sign. In fact, some things like road signs are based on international standards, so getting them from a clip-art collection is more likely to look "correct" than something you drew from scratch. If you need such a demonstrative symbol in your game, it is better just to use an accepted version than to make a custom version that is more clever but less obvious. A great example of this is a set of chess pieces. While there are dozens of very clever chess games out there (physical and computer) that use some innovative piece styles and animations, people who think chess is more than a shiny board that is kept dusted on the coffee table prefer the classic pieces. In fact, the chess pieces used in competitions are very restricted in size, weight, and appearance just so the pieces are clearly distinct and are identifiable from across the room. And in this case, clip art is a good way to ensure that your game is not sacrificing usability for cleverness.

Another good use for clip art is in placeholder art, which, as mentioned earlier, is art that is intended to be replaced with professional art nearer to ship-time.

While programmer art is just fine for filling in gaps, it might not cut it if you need to demonstrate your game to a potential buyer. In this case, some clip art might give your client a better idea of your "vision" for the game. Just make sure to point out the art that will be later replaced, lest your client think that the cartoon wizard is going to end up in the finished product.

Clip art is convenient and is absurdly cheap. Those "Clip Art Bonanza 100,000" collections most likely do contain 100,000 pieces of art. And the licenses are generally very liberal and wide open for use in games of all types. Just be sure to check out what you are buying. A couple of the clip-art collections out there claim to offer "one million images" but are actually just a CD with a smaller number of pictures coupled with a limited-time membership to an online clip-art service.

Also make sure that the format is something you can use. Most vector clip art is easily converted to bitmap, but the reverse isn't as easily done. Some packages appear to have a lot of 3D, but the actual content is either a collection of rendered bitmaps or is in a proprietary format that can't be easily imported into a modeler. Some bitmaps look great against a white background but will require a lot of work to get them to look properly antialiased in the setting of your game.

Development Teams

When working with software teams, you have two choices. You can have a team of one (e.g., yourself), or you can have a team of more than one. There are advantages to each, and you should not just assume that your game is too simple to require a team or is too complex to be done with one person.

A Team of One

The advantages to having a team of one are the following:

- You get all the money.

- You get all the glory.

- There will not be any conflicts over the design or code.

- Your resulting program will match your specs (or at least your capabilities) exactly.

And there are also disadvantages:

- You have nobody on whom to blame the bad reviews.

- It may (but not necessarily will) take longer.

- You can get lonely.

- Your scope is necessarily limited to your own capabilities and available time.

Of all of these factors, the last one is most important. While there have existed some pretty impressive one-person projects, there are limits. The possible scope of your project is roughly proportional to your experience. If you're just starting out, your first one-person project is going to be necessarily simple. If you have a few years and completed projects under your belt, you will be able to create more impressive results.

If you don't need programmers or designers, but you need some simple art or music for your game, do not go searching for partners to share in a percentage of your revenue. If your game doesn't make it out the door or has no success upon release, then your artist or musician will at best receive a copy of the game. You will feel guilty about it, and they will feel resentful. If your game turns out to be an enormous success, then your partners will receive much more than their work would justify even though you took most of the risks, thus rendering you a sucker.

Much like a musician hiring session players, try to negotiate a reasonable flat fee for their efforts. If you cannot pay a single flat fee, try to negotiate a payment plan. If your sound and music people get a flat payment that arrives in a timely manner, then they will be happy, your conscience will be clear, and all of the risk will be right where it belongs—in your lap.

A Team of More Than One

If your project justifies it, you will need to have a team of more than one person. If your design is complex and your scope is non-trivial, then a larger team is necessary. Just be aware that having a team requires a larger investment in time for management and communication. As the project commences, you will find yourself making design decisions by committee that you wish you could be making yourself. You will write e-mails and instant messages instead of code. Your days of blissfully hacking together a game that is uniquely yours will be done.

It is a big price to pay, but it may be worth it if the result is more impressive than something you could do yourself.

Just be aware that if the reason you are recruiting a team rather than implementing your design on your own is because your own design and implementation skills are deficient, then you are on a rocket sled to failure. If it is an independent development team, then managing the team will require that you have *more* programming skill than if you were doing the programming yourself.

This point bears repeating. Managing a team of programmers for an independent production requires *more* programming skill than doing it yourself. You are going to need to know how everyone else's code works. You are going to need to integrate modules written by people who may or may not have made the calling interfaces compatible. You will need to debug code that is not yours. If you have decided that you are going to manage a game project because you think the programming will be done better by others, then you are making a mistake. The reason you should be recruiting other programmers is because there is only one of you and you do not have time to do everything. Offloading the programming on others does not make the programming easier for you. In fact, it makes it more difficult. If you and your team fire on all cylinders, then you will end up integrating more code from the group than you could do yourself, but you will need to be the most talented programmer in the group in order to do this.

And, while this shouldn't bear mentioning, it happens every day in programmer-oriented message boards all over the world. If you are starting up a team to write a large-scale game, your programming experience is weak, you have no experience managing a multiple-person software project, and your professional game-design experience consists of having played lots of games and knowing how you would have done things better, then prepare for Epic Fail.

Partnership Terms

You must make the terms of your partnership known from the onset. In fact, the terms of the partnership (in both time and money) is the second most important factor of a partnership behind your partners' role in the project. If your partnership's terms are along the lines of "work with the time you have available, and you will get paid equitably once this project makes some money," that is the same as saying "while you will initially be enthusiastic, your time investment in this project will quickly drop to zero, and you very likely will not make a dime." If you are hiring a partner for a particular part of the project (musical scores, programming the animation subsystem, and so on), then make his role clear from the onset as well as the amount of time that you expect him to invest per week until his part of the job is completed. And if you must negotiate a percentage deal, make it explicit and have some benchmarks that he (and the project itself) must complete, or else the partnership should be considered dissolved.

If your programming team consists of two people, then read up on *extreme programming*, aka programming in pairs. While pair-programming is most effective when you have two people crammed together in a cubicle completing each others' sentences by the time the job is done, it can be done remotely. Read up on it.

Conclusion

Doing things quickly and cheaply is not necessarily something that is only used by risk-averse penny-pinching misers (like your author). It can be a choice that, if well planned, can get your project into profits faster and with less stress than a large budget and team can. Planning ahead for a small budget and schedule can make game development easier and more rewarding than can fewer constraints, more people, and more money.

CHAPTER 15

WHAT A PORTAL WANTS

JOE LIEBERMAN, HEAD OF BUSINESS DEVELOPMENT, ARCADETOWN.COM

Remember that movie *What A Girl Wants*? Well, this article is just like that movie, only shorter and actually worth the price you paid to see it. The most common question I get when I tell people it is my job to accept or reject games for online distribution is, "What do you look for in a game?" It may surprise you to learn that many developers don't ask this question until *after* their first game is finished (and in many cases their third or fourth game). Oh, yeah, did anyone else notice I get paid to play games? Take that, Mom!

So, after reading this article, you will no longer be able to claim ignorance of at least one portal's opinion. Keep in mind this is just what we look for at ArcadeTown—every portal is different and looks for different things. ArcadeTown takes a more cutting-edge approach. We are bold enough to embrace more traditional games, from first- and third-person shooters to RPGs and beyond. We also sell plenty of traditional casual style products, like action puzzles, but my point is we're more diverse than many other "casual-only" destinations—and this affects what we look for in a game.

Acceptance Guidelines

First, there are things that are absolutely going to hamper your acceptance:

- **Requiring a connection to a third-party site.** Whether it is to register for a multiplayer or to submit a high score, a requirement to connect to your web site (and therefore leading people away from ours) is a major strike against accepting your game. If we like the game, we may ask those features be removed in our version; but then it becomes a pain for you to rework your game, and more trouble for us to keep track of the fact the versions are different. My advice: Keep it in the game guys!

■ **Gore, excessive violence, language, sex.** Sex may sell on a porn site, but we run a family-friendly portal. Guns are okay, shooting things may be okay, but limbs being torn off in a fountain of blood is not okay. Basically, focus on keeping your game T for Teen or E for Everyone in rating.

■ **Download size.** Download size is less of an issue than it used to be. There was a time when any game over 5MB had serious sales problems. Currently, we try to keep things under 40MB for the demo, but we do occasionally distribute larger games. Still, the higher you get over that 40MB mark, the harder it will be to get a deal with portals. And don't forget, even with people at home having access to broadband, the smaller the game, the more likely it is to be downloaded, and therefore played and purchased.

■ **In-game branding.** Sometimes developers get the great idea that they are going to place their own branding inside the game. To a limited degree this is okay, but all of that has to be hashed out. If you submit a final build and a portal sees that you are still branding your game heavily, we're going to ask you to go back and remove it. It's a needless hassle for everyone and could create some animosity, which may impact your future dealings. Branding is really anything beyond your company logo. Some developers commonly place a splash screen with their company logo, but placing your web site's URL inside the game isn't going to fly. Other portals are far more strict about this, so be up front with the portal and ask how much branding you're allowed with specific examples of what you'd like to do. Communicate—it's worth it.

Reviewer's Opinions

With those rules in mind, there are a lot of other factors that are far more subjective. The personal tastes of the reviewer, in this case me, play a large role in what gets into a portal. Here are some major factors that I find influence my opinion:

■ **Cute versus gory.** Make it cute and cuddly. It isn't actually the cuteness that I look for, it's a lack of aggressive imagery. A lot of our (and most other portals) fans are female. Not to stereotype, but aliens with dripping fangs don't do so well with my mom, wife, or daughter. A cute game always seems to win out in sales and downloads over an invasion of greasy aliens.

- **Will it sell? Is it a good game?** Funny that I thought the game should be cute before I thought it should be good. This is a complicated issue, though. We accept any game that we feel is good. However, we let our users decide what sells, and oftentimes being good just isn't enough. What makes the game sell are the little features, referred to as *polish*, which make a good game great. These would be great graphics and sounds, smooth play, unlockable bonuses, little animations that do nothing but make you smile, good music, and so forth. The list goes on for ages, but if you take a look at the top games on every portal, you'll begin to see a sharp contrast between them and most other me-too games that don't have the right amount of polish, appropriate basic concept, or appropriate originality. You should also be on the lookout for similarities between all 10—they're typically pretty obvious. Again, being good will usually get you a contract, but just because we believe the game is good doesn't mean the game will sell by the boatload.

- **Which genre?** ArcadeTown is less picky when it comes to genre. You have an FPS? We'll look at it. Still, we know for a fact certain genres outsell others on our site, whereas other portals may concentrate on other categories that aren't as strong on our site. Action puzzles (the *Mystery Case Files* series, for example), shooting games, adventure games, RPGs, and strategy games are all pretty hot categories for us, but all of them need to be casual in nature. A hardcore turn-based strategy game may not do so well here. Games like *Aveyond*, *Cute Knight*, *Westward*, or *Age of Castles* are what we're looking for. The farther you get from a casual design, the less likely we are to accept it. Also we aren't too big on generic me-too clones of other games, unless you can surpass their level of polish or provide a twist that is truly unique that will appeal to users.

- **Professional developers.** We like working with people who are reasonable and easy to work with. Developers need not acquiesce to our every whim and desire, but returning calls, e-mails, and builds on time, as well as considering any suggestions we make, is key. The stark reality is, most of the games out there are average (that is, the definition of average); so in a sea of mediocrity, we'll work with the people who *appear* professional to us in their response and willingness to work with us over the classic closet developer who believes social graces have no place in business. My advice to any of you out there who hate social/business e-mailing, just pretend it's an RPG, and you're playing a business executive who has a penchant for profit-based world domination. Oh, should I have used my "not to stereotype" line again? Oh well!

- **The name.** I hate to name names, but I have seen some awful game names. A horrible name can seriously turn a submission into an instant reject; though these are few enough, I didn't feel it fell into the first list. A bad name can hurt sales though, and we may ask you to change it. If we do ask, it isn't because we're egomaniacs; it's because we think your name is actually going to decrease sales! Don't take it as an insult; take it as advice from someone who knows their audience. It may just be that our audience will react negatively, while your own direct audience couldn't care less. What's in a name? A whole lot! Just ask a guy named Joseph Lieberman (and no, I am not related).

- **Online web versions.** Having a solid online playable web version of your game definitely helps a lot on our site. Users will keep coming back to play your game over and over, helping to drive eyeball exposure, downloads, and sales. Web versions also help nicely on some other portals. Many developers also report that web versions help to re-invigorate sales of their older good-selling titles. Unfortunately, some large portals don't provide web versions to their users, even when available, so some developers don't see the value. Trust me, web versions are good!

Conclusion

That's really all there is to it. I would also offer the following advice: We don't e-mail replies to everyone who submits games. If we love the game, we obviously reply and begin negotiations. If we do not like the game, there usually isn't any reply at all. It's got nothing to do with disrespecting you or your game; it has more to do with saving us time and the inevitable argument-reply we get on why we should accept it. Even if you are mistakenly insulted, it is important to follow up with us even when we don't reply. If you make a new build with significant improvements, submit it again and let us know! We'll look at it once more. If you make a new game entirely, submit it! Even if we didn't get back to you on your first game, there's a good chance your second game will be improved enough that we'll get in touch. With that said, if you *do* get an e-mail back from a portal, that is not a "let's talk about a contract"; it instead focuses on things we liked or wished were improved—take that as a great sign! It means we're interested but not convinced. This e-mail is the opportunity you have to make the game into something that works for us and likely for other portals as well. I would say about half the e-mails we send of that nature never bear fruit, which translates into an opportunity for you to capitalize.

The final note I deliver is ArcadeTown is not evil. We're here to make money, and in the process, help you the developer make money, too—simple as that. A lot of people seem to have a vision that portals do everything in their power to bleed the developer and that working with a portal is the death knell for direct sales from your site. The opposite is true: When a game goes on a major portal and does well, it is almost always coupled with an increase in direct sales on the developer's site as well. Working with portals should be a win-win situation, and if it is not, let the portal know and try to sort it out. You'll find that most portals are professional and responsive to your needs; but we can't fix a problem we don't know exists!

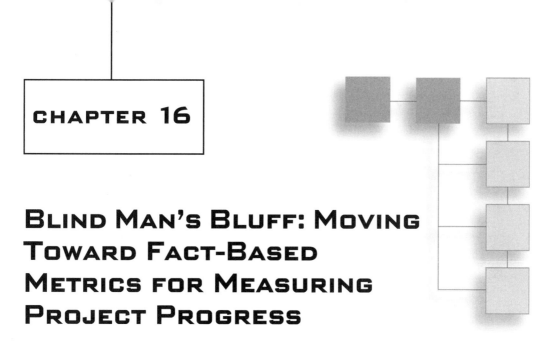

CHAPTER 16

Blind Man's Bluff: Moving Toward Fact-Based Metrics for Measuring Project Progress

Dean Margerison

Companies involved in software development traditionally spend a significant amount of time, effort, and heartache trying to ascertain how a particular project is progressing. Even with the benefit of having the development team located in the same building, the success rate is poor; more often than not the experience has much more in common with a hi-tech game of blind man's bluff than a measured and repeatable means of visualizing progress. Looking ahead to ever-increasing complexity and the greater use of external development teams, the picture can look very bleak indeed.

Thankfully, the last few years have seen the development of a number of tools and techniques that can offer a quantum-shift improvement in this area. This article provides a brief insight into the current problems that many projects face, as well as what can be done to transform the situation for the better.

Our Current Challenges

The most common means of tracking progress can be characterized by the following:

- One member of management will be assigned the task of collecting progress data and disseminating this to a wider audience (generally senior management). This person can be the hands-on manager of the team or a dedicated project manager who handles a number of projects at the same time.

- The manager will talk to the development team members individually to gauge what progress has been made. This might be with the aid of a task list generated from the project plan.

- During the conversation, the manager will try to find out the developers feeling for how well it's going. Based on experience and knowing the individual developer, they themselves try to build up a picture of how well the final delivery is progressing.

- The manager then writes a progress report that includes edited highlights of the conversations with the team, amended to include the manager's educated guess as to how things are actually going.

- Usually some form of project plan or Gantt chart is updated to complement the progress report, and these are then e-mailed out or saved to a shared folder.

The difficulty of achieving the previous points when the development is being done by a third party can at times make the whole process feel more like playing blind man's bluff and Chinese whispers at the same time.

Using the preceding methods of visualizing how projects are doing has had an extremely patchy success record, one which can be better understood if you look at some of the major drawbacks inherent in this process:

- Progress can appear to be going fine in so far as all the allocated tasks are being completed, but the project plan does not reflect the body of work that really needs to be completed.

- Being primarily a subjective process, it relies heavily on a complex blend of skills to collect, collate, and translate the information gained into an accurate picture.

- The process is time-consuming and can constitute significant overhead on the individual team members.

- Team members do not see any direct benefit of going through the process and tend to view it as getting in the way of their actual work if you are lucky, or as a "management-sponsored spying mission" if you are not.

- There is no real measure for the quality of what is being produced.

- You cannot really see who is doing the work.

- You cannot measure progress over time to gauge trends or patterns —that is, three more developers have been added, but are we actually doing more?

- This type of process is almost impossible to replicate from one project to the next, as its success is based on the skills and experience of a very small number of people.

Fact-Based Visualization

Taking advantage of the readily available facts that are currently being ignored can transform our understanding of development progress to a level that most senior developers aspire. Making this level of understanding readily available to the whole team and its managers provides you with the timely facts on which to base decisions, and also to see what impact these decision have on progress.

In order to achieve the quantum shift in the capability to visualize progress, there are six key guiding principles:

1. Metrics must be based on facts.

2. The facts should have a historical element to track progress over time.

3. An automated process should be in place to extract/transform and deliver the metrics.

4. When statistics are gathered from several sources, they should be delivered to the end user via one mechanism. The currently preferred delivery mechanism is via the web in HTML.

5. You must be able to re-use metrics in planning new projects and comparing progress between projects.

6. The tools used to achieve the previous points should be easy to install and maintain.

Looking at some of the available tools and techniques, you can investigate how the guiding principles can be practically achieved.

Source Control Management (SCM) Metrics

Linking into a project Source Control Management (SCM) tool is a vital element in unlocking what is actually being achieved by a project. As developers go about their daily tasks, they are continually updating the contents with their SCM tool.[1] As this information builds up over time, it is generally totally ignored. The view is that SCM tools are really only there to protect and manage the source code. By taking this view, you throw away the biggest source of concrete facts that can be used for tracking purposes, namely:

- Lines of code and its growth over time

- Number of files and their growth over time

- Which developers are active?
    - What percent of the code base they have contributed
    - In what areas they are working

There are a number of tools on the market right now. There are three worth mentioning in the context of this paper: CVSMonitor, StatCVS and Bloof, which are all open source projects[2] and so are freely available. They provide insight into what can be achieved and tend to work in a very similar manner in that they parse the change logs produced by the SCM system in order to produce graphs and text-based description as to what has happened over time. Incorporating this into an automated process can deliver pseudo real-time statistics to all interested parties. Figure 16.1 shows a project's code growth over time using Bloof. Figure 16.2 shows the kdebase project's file count growth over time using Bloof.

Seeing the code base grow over time can be an invaluable means of understanding the day-to-day progress being achieved. Some of the patterns you might see include the following:

- A vertical rise in the number of lines of code/files could be an indication that an awaited piece of development has been introduced into a project. It could also point to code being copied from a previous project for re-use. (This is particularly interesting for third-party developed projects in that it shows they are not necessarily developing all of the delivered code base for your sole use.)

---

[1]If your development teams are not currently using an SCM tool, you should start worrying now.

[2]Visit the Open Source initiative web site for more info at www.opensource.org.

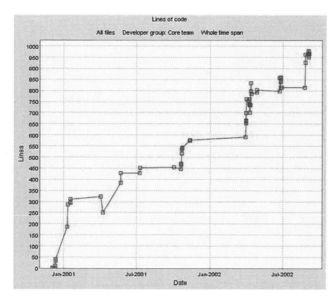

Figure 16.1
Lines of code and its growth over time

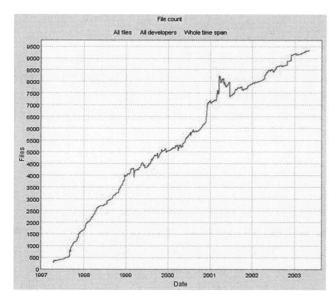

Figure 16.2
Number of files and their growth over time

- A drop in the number of lines of code/files could indicate a refactoring process going on to optimize the code or that functionality is being removed.

- A sustained period where the number of lines of code is not changing significantly could indicate a period of bug fixing.

User	Changes	Lines of code	Lines each change
Top 10 Developers			
jra	7118 (20.3%)	350610 (19.1%)	49
tridge	7058 (20.1%)	269750 (14.7%)	38
jerry	2520 (7.2%)	251843 (13.7%)	99
jelmer	1442 (4.1%)	156437 (8.5%)	108
lkcl	3442 (9.8%)	125348 (6.8%)	36
tpot	3484 (9.9%)	124114 (6.7%)	35
abartlet	2714 (7.7%)	94362 (5.1%)	34
samba-bugs	2257 (6.4%)	84113 (4.5%)	37
herb	465 (1.3%)	66469 (3.6%)	142
jmcd	326 (0.9%)	58247 (3.1%)	178
Sum	30826 (88.1%)	1581293 (86.3%)	51

Figure 16.3
Which developers are active and who's doing the work?

The project's *velocity* (code growth) is a very key metric. Having access to several of these graphs for similar projects coupled with graphs from your own projects can make estimating the final delivery date much more accurate.[3] Figure 3 shows who is contributing what to the project (StatCVS).

The power of the chart in Figure 16.3 is quite obvious, and before I use one example to prove the point, I would like to say that *this metric needs to be handled with extreme care.* While there is a strong correlation between the number of lines coded and the overall contribution to a project, there will be instances where the creation of a relatively small piece of code can take a disproportionate amount of time to produce and deliver an equally disproportionate benefit to your project.

If developers feel that this metric is being abused, they can easily change their code to skew the results and make them meaningless: Quantity is not necessarily an indication of quality!

Let's say that you commissioned a piece of work from a third party-developer and, as part of that work, requested that they use the Concurrent Version System (CVS) SCM tool. CVS is open source, so it would not cost money to buy, and it means that you can use tools like StatCVS, CVSMonitor, or Bloof. From this you could then see who is doing the work for you. If, for example, you noticed that the users jra and tridge from the chart in Figure 16.3 suddenly stopped contributing code to the project, alarm bells would start ringing straight away, and you would probably want to meet with your third-party developer for an explanation.

---

[3]This relies on establishing the final code size, which can be estimated or derived by benchmarking your project to others that you have statistics for. You can also use www.sourceforge.net, which has 70,000 projects for you to benchmark against.

Without these types of tools, you really would be playing blind man's bluff. Being blissfully unaware that the two people who had contributed 40% of your code had suddenly stopped is not a situation you would want to be in. I wonder how often this has happened in the past?

Code Complexity

Using other metrics tools can also add to the body of knowledge you build up over time to increase your level of understanding of the progress being made. Tools like JavaNCSS work directly from the actual code base and, as such, are independent of any SCM tool, but they are specific to a particular language or set of languages. These tools can generally be integrated into an automated build process to generate complexity metrics, such as McCabes Cyclomatic Complexity Number (CNN).

The CNN is one of the most popular methods of representing complexity/ functionality using a single ordinal number. Project teams can use this information to decide if areas of code are potentially too complicated and so can aid code review. You can also collect this information over time to represent the total complexity/functionality of your code base and plot this along with your other code-related metrics. Figure 16.4 shows the complexity of some of the JUnit samples code base using JavaNCSS.

Unit/Regression Test Results

There are numerous testing frameworks available for you to utilize. Taking JUnit as an example, you can integrate this into an automated system to generate daily statistics on the quality of the code being produced and the overall health of the project. Collecting these statistics over time and plotting them graphically can also provide a much-needed confidence that projects have a good level of quality and greatly reduces integration issues that could dramatically effect project delivery (see Figure 16.5).

Code Coverage

Having automated unit tests in place is an important element of establishing a quality-based metric. But to really appreciate how good your tests are, you really need the ability to see just how much of the code base is actually being exercised. For example, you might have 200 unit tests running every night and feel good

Functions

Nr.	NCSS	CCN	Javadoc	Function
1	1	1	1	junit.samples.money.IMoney.add(IMoney)
2	1	1	1	junit.samples.money.IMoney.addMoney(Money)
3	1	1	1	junit.samples.money.IMoney.addMoneyBag(MoneyBag)
4	1	1	1	junit.samples.money.IMoney.isZero()
5	1	1	1	junit.samples.money.IMoney.multiply(int)
6	1	1	1	junit.samples.money.IMoney.negate()
7	1	1	1	junit.samples.money.IMoney.subtract(IMoney)
8	3	1	1	junit.samples.money.Money.Money(int,String)
9	2	1	1	junit.samples.money.Money.add(IMoney)
10	4	3	1	junit.samples.money.Money.addMoney(Money)
11	2	1	1	junit.samples.money.Money.addMoneyBag(MoneyBag)
12	2	1	1	junit.samples.money.Money.amount()
13	2	1	1	junit.samples.money.Money.currency()
14	8	6	1	junit.samples.money.Money.equals(Object)
15	2	1	1	junit.samples.money.Money.hashCode()
16	2	1	1	junit.samples.money.Money.isZero()
17	2	1	1	junit.samples.money.Money.multiply(int)
18	2	1	1	junit.samples.money.Money.negate()
19	2	1	1	junit.samples.money.Money.subtract(IMoney)
20	4	1	1	junit.samples.money.Money.toString()
21	1	1	1	junit.samples.money.MoneyBag.MoneyBag()
22	4	3	1	junit.samples.money.MoneyBag.MoneyBag(Money[])
23	3	1	1	junit.samples.money.MoneyBag.MoneyBag(Money,Money)
24	3	1	1	junit.samples.money.MoneyBag.MoneyBag(Money,MoneyBag)
25	3	1	1	junit.samples.money.MoneyBag.MoneyBag(MoneyBag,MoneyBag)
26	2	1	1	junit.samples.money.MoneyBag.add(IMoney)
27	2	1	1	junit.samples.money.MoneyBag.addMoney(Money)
28	2	1	1	junit.samples.money.MoneyBag.addMoneyBag(MoneyBag)
29	3	2	1	junit.samples.money.MoneyBag.appendBag(MoneyBag)
30	10	5	1	junit.samples.money.MoneyBag.appendMoney(Money)
31	3	1	1	junit.samples.money.MoneyBag.contains(Money)
32	14	11	1	junit.samples.money.MoneyBag.equals(Object)
33	6	4	1	junit.samples.money.MoneyBag.findMoney(String)
34	6	2	1	junit.samples.money.MoneyBag.hashCode()
35	2	1	1	junit.samples.money.MoneyBag.isZero()
36	7	3	1	junit.samples.money.MoneyBag.multiply(int)

Figure 16.4
JavaNCSS: The NCSS column represents non-commented source statements, and the Javadoc column represents the number of comment lines in the code.

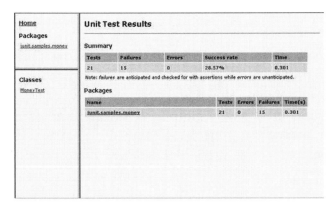

Figure 16.5
Results of running JUnit tests

that they all pass on a regular basis, but your tests might only touch 5% of your code base. This is where code coverage tools really come into their own (see Figure 16.6).

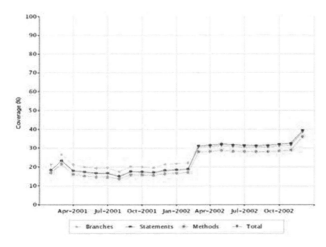

Figure 16.6
Percentage of code tested over time using Clover

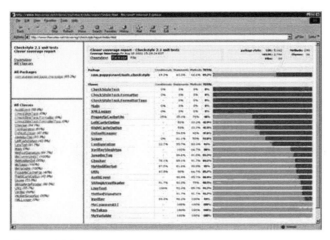

Figure 16.7
Detail code coverage report by class using Clover

With these tools, you cannot only see how much of a particular class or module is being tested, but also what the figure is overall. This particular class of tools can be illustrated by Figures 16.6 and 16.7. They come from Clover, which is a commercial product that can be incorporated into an automated build process in order to report on the coverage of Java-based tests.

Using Clover and tools like it allows you to greatly improve the quality of your projects in such a way as to make a very positive contribution to a successful delivery. These tools can also be used as a key enabling strategy for implementing ISO 9000 or improving your company's Capability Maturity Model (CMM) status.

Automating the Process

The glue that brings together all of the tools and technologies that appear in this article is a robust build tool. The likes of Ant[4] provides for award-winning cross-platform capabilities with unrivalled third-party integration. This means you can bring the generation of all of your key metrics into one build system. Doing this reduces the complexity of the generation/transformation and deployment of the metrics and means that the minimum manual intervention is required.

Benefits

Hopefully you can see how some of the elements covered in this article are applicable to your environment. In summary, I would say that the major benefits of adopting fact-based visualization can be categorized as follows:

- Establishes a repeatable process.

- Removes a major part of the guesswork from the equation.

- Requires minimal effort to produce the statistics.

- Allows for comparison to other internally and externally developed projects in a consistent manner.

- Taking advantage of open source technologies provides you with an ultra low cost of adoption.

- Aids in project estimation.

- Makes the impact of decisions on project delivery much more transparent.

- Enables the project team to gain valuable insight into how they are progressing, allowing them to take corrective measures early in the lifecycle.

A Word of Warning

Having access to such a body of information is a very powerful tool for your company, but there are a couple of points to bear in mind:

- Make the information freely available to the project team.

---

[4]Ant is a widely used cross-platform build tool http://ant.apache.org.

■ Don't make it appear that you are using the data to beat the team up. This is one sure-fire way of destroying all of the benefits that can be gained and alienating the people you rely on to deliver projects.

Ultimately, the team members should gain the most by being able to more accurately judge how they are doing so that they can be the first to take corrective action.

Useful Links

SCM
Concurrent Version System—the premier open source tool (www.cvshome.org/)

SCM Metrics
CVSMonitor (http://ali.as/devel/cvsmonitor/)

StatCVS (http://statcvs.sourceforge.net/)

Bloof (http://bloof.sourceforge.net)

Code Parsing Metrics
JavaNCSS (www.kclee.com/clemens/java/javancss/)

Code Coverage
Clover (www.thecortex.net/clover/)

Build systems
Ant (http://ant.apache.org/)

Unit Testing Frameworks
JUnit—Java unit testing (www.junit.org/index.htm)

NUnit—.Net unit testing (www.nunit.org/)

General links to testing frameworks (www.xprogramming.com/software.htm)

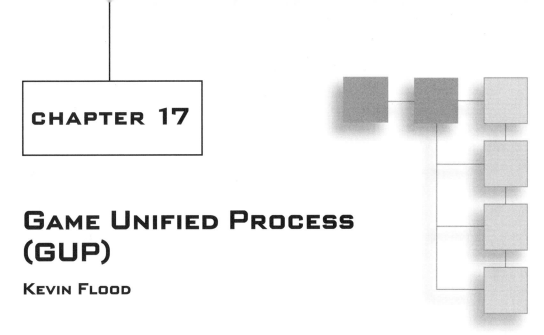

CHAPTER 17

GAME UNIFIED PROCESS (GUP)

KEVIN FLOOD

Game development post mortems all sound the same. The game was late. It had too many bugs. Functionality was not what was originally intended. Getting the game out the door took too many development hours, and the development team was under too much pressure. Even when the game was launched, management was not pleased.

What is missing from all these evaluations is the resolve to overhaul the game development process. Why? Perhaps there's something about the macho aspect of game development, the love of bragging about difficulties overcome and pain endured. I'll reserve comment, not being a sociologist or a psychologist. As an executive and manager, I know that these problems have a cost, measurable in misused resources, problems in the game, features that have little value, or slipped target dates. All of these have business implications. Isn't it time we tried to address these issues?

Before I take a crack at this, I have a confession: my background is software engineering, not content development. If you are a producer, artist, or audio engineer, you may be tempted to stop here. This would be a mistake because the content developers are the ones who have a big influence over how the entire game development process operates.

A Sample Project

To illustrate how I think the game development process usually works, I'll cite a project I once managed. It was large, involving the development of games (casino

211

games) and a complementary platform to support high-volume Internet gameplay.

Client-side technologies included Flash, animation, audio components, and logic to support gameplay. On the server side, we used BEA's J2EE-compliant WebLogic platform, Enterprise JavaBeans (EJBs), servlets, Java coding, and an Informix database web development combined HTML, Javascript, and JSPs.

The team included artists, producers, Flash developers, programmers, architects, database developers, product managers, project leads, and so on, working in three main groups. Responsibility for the games' look and feel as well as the supporting client-side logic belonged to the content group. Server-side logic was the responsibility of the system platform group. A third group handled web development; they floated between the content and system platform organizations.

There was an overriding development process, but its role was more project management, tracking where we were on the project, who was working on what piece, and what had to be delivered when to achieve our objectives. Each group had the latitude to define the actual process of getting the work done, on time, with the features that they signed up for and at the quality level that was expected of a production or golden master product.

The content group and the system platform group used different development approaches, affording me the opportunity to see how each organization defined and executed a development process. It allowed me to assess the pros and cons of each and to determine which methodology resulted in a better outcome. (I'm leaving out the web development group. It was small and was subject to the development strategies of either the content group or the systems group.)

The groups did not sit down and explicitly say what the overriding development process would be. Instead, each group used the methods with which they were most familiar. Despite some differences, essentially they followed a similar process. I call it the *game waterfall process* (GWP).

Waterfall Development Basics

The waterfall development process is the one commonly used in game development. It has distinct phases that need to be completed in a certain order. Once a phase has been completed, there is no turning back, and it is on to the next phase.

Waterfall processes occur at various levels of complexity. Following are the larger categories found in game development, described in a common sequence of execution.

Conception

The business analysts, product managers, and senior development personnel get together and discuss what the game should be. Among other issues, they may discuss the following:

- Audience

- Platform

- Development time frame

- Some of the features of the game

- Some of the high-level technical and artistic challenges

The group may (or may not) produce a document describing all of the expectations for the game and some of the detail about how a group might approach development. In some cases, a series of discussions results in a go or no-go decision.

Game Specification

If the team gets the go ahead to proceed, a document is crafted by the product manager and/or producer that describes what the user experience will be in the game. This involves play characteristics, platform decisions, and potential artistic mockups of the game. It is a description of the game from the end user's perspective. This document is circulated to high-level art directors, game designers, and architects.

Art Bible/Story Bible

I have compressed the art and story bible into one phase. They are different, but they are executed at about the same time in the process. They are linked because the producers and artists need to work together to create these documents.

The art bible contains what the name implies. It defines the overriding art style that will be used, the tools to develop this art, and mock-ups to validate that approach. The story bible describes how the game will flow. It discusses the overriding objective of the game and how that objective will be expressed in various scenarios.

Technical Specifications

In this document, the engineers detail the architecture of the game. It could be expressed in unified modeling language (UML) or with system diagrams. If development is to be object-oriented, high-level objects and their interactions are defined. Core fundamental tools are defined, and a platform for the game is recommended. The interactions between art assets and programming code are defined. Security and access methods might be part of the game technical specifications.

Construction

The decision is made to go ahead, architecture and concept documents are completed, the platforms have been established, the full team is hired, and the development environment is up and running. *Then* people begin to construct the game. The producers, managers, and project leads form the organizational glue within their respective disciplines and across organizational lines. The artists and developers begin to develop the game using all of the documents that have been previously developed.

QA System Test

Upon completion, pieces of the game go to the quality assurance (QA) organization, which takes all of the previously mentioned documents and tests the game against these documents. Any problems found are logged and reported back to the development teams. The development team responds by fixing the problems, redesigning certain key modules, or adding additional functionality.

Play Testing

Once the QA organization has an opportunity to give feedback to the development teams and the game is up in some working order, play testing begins. In this exercise, producers organize group sessions to demonstrate the play characteristics of the game. These sessions are usually attended by product and marketing managers as well as members of the development staff. The goal is to validate or critique the play characteristics of the game at that point in time. These sessions may occur a number of times during the testing cycle. Each play test session involves feedback that must be addressed by developers. The feedback can require cosmetic or fundamental changes to the game.

Alpha Testing

When producers, product managers, and developers agree that the game is ready for a wider audience, the producer will release the product to a select group of evaluators that provides feedback on the game. This feedback can result in required changes to the game. Some of these changes could be substantial. The assumption is that the changes will not be drastic in nature.

Beta Testing

In this phase, the game is released to a much wider audience that has little knowledge of the game. People play the game and provide feedback on problems that occur, features they like or dislike, and the overall game experience. For console games, it is difficult to get a comprehensive beta test because the game is usually kept inside the company that is making it. On the web, the first release of a game is frequently considered the beta test. Sometimes this is called release 1.0 and is quickly followed by a subsequent, more robust release.

Golden Master or Final Release

With all the feedback received and changes made, the game is released to the general public.

Defects in the GWP

So what is wrong with the waterfall process? It has been used for years. It results in feedback along the way, and everyone can be made aware of when each phase is complete. This way the development group and all people involved in the process are aware of the progress against the target date.

If you look closely at this linear process, you see that each phase exposes the game to different classes of observers. The test team does not see the product until after the developers determine it is time for them to see it. In some cases, the product managers will not see the game until the developers schedule a play test. If play tests are not scheduled early in the cycle, product managers may not see the game until late in the cycle. Alpha evaluators may not see the game until very late in the cycle.

The reality is that, as each of these groups sees the game, they may request drastic changes. This has a cascading effect, introducing problems into the game and sending the game back into phases that were expected to be complete, possibly forcing the development team into emergency mode very late in the development cycle. The actual process may become very chaotic because the sequence of the waterfall development process has been broken. Development activity that should have occurred early in the cycle is actually occurring late in the cycle. Also, many unplanned minicycles may be occurring at the same time. These issues are common themes in game development post mortems.

This is precisely what occurred in our project, and watching it from a management perspective was very unnerving. I was responsible for the delivery of this project. The company's future depended on finishing this game platform and these games on time. I set about to understand what alternative development process would be better.

These are Not New Problems

Software engineers will recognize our experiences because they've been plagued with them for quite some time. The response has been new techniques, such as agile modeling, rational unified process (RUP), extreme programming (XP), and other hybrid processes to address the waterfall process's pitfalls. There are differences between the new approaches, but they all have a common theme. They all recognize that the software development process is iterative, not linear. Issues are identified, and problems arise all through the development cycle that need to be addressed.

These techniques also seek to get more disciplines involved early in the development cycle, including QA personnel, product managers, business managers, developers, and others. The goal is to get as much interaction, dialogue, and goal setting done as early in the cycle as possible. It also establishes formal communications between all vested parties. These communication mechanisms help as the product moves through the iterative process. All of the parties stay involved in all phases of development.

Rational Unified Process

For RUP, documentation (that is, artifacts) and *use cases* in particular play a key role in keeping the development process on track and well communicated to all participants. Use cases are collaboratively developed user expectations for the product, visually and verbally representing how an end user will interact with it. (In some cases, the user is another application or machine.)

The *user case forum* and its resulting artifacts help to force interdisciplinary communication as well as the documentation of that communication. RUP continues from the initial use cases to more detailed artifacts that reveal the technical specification for the product. RUP acknowledges that at each phase of development, facts may be revealed that cause a return to an earlier phase. In fact, RUP encourages this iterative recycling as opposed to discouraging it. The use of RUP lets a project stay on track, despite the existence of many minicycles, by forcing all groups to collaborate. Everyone is aware of the state of development and can make adjustments. Documentation plays a key role because it gets continually recycled to reflect the actual state of the project. This combined with the emphasis on multidisciplinary collaboration creates a communication feedback loop that lets decision makers make the right calls to keep the project on track.

The discipline required to follow and document the iterative phases ironically contributes to less iteration in the development process. Recognizing the collaborative nature of development and the religious demand for documentation together decrease the need for changes.

The RUP process is not endlessly iterative; it doesn't allow gross changes to design and specifications to the bitter end. It does assume that this process in itself will result in fewer and fewer changes to design and specification as the project proceeds toward the release date.

XP and Agile Modeling

The XP and agile approaches are philosophically similar to RUP, but with some key differences. XP is not documentation-centric in the traditional sense. It is geared toward short cycle development and projects that are engineered in relatively small development groups. XP is very interactive-centric and proposes that through the process of peer programming and intense small group interaction, the program and product itself become the documentation. A key differentiator for XP is its emphasis on testing early in the development cycle. It proposes that test cases, test harnesses, and test examples should be created before the application code is developed. This discipline forces the development team to think about the end result of the development before development begins. I believe this discipline, by forcing agreement on what the product is supposed to do before development begins, achieves the same results as use cases.

XP is perhaps more iterative-aware than RUP because it does not explicitly establish phases, such as use cases, design documentation, or test cases. XP is a scrum type development cycle that facilitates rapid development by discarding formal documentation phases; it substitutes, from the start of development, unit tests for documentation. The project moves along the cycle and continues to add unit tests as the product becomes more sophisticated. With each build, these unit tests are executed to make sure that the product is working according to the understanding of what the product should be doing. XP development is meant to be fast. Six months appears to be the average term of the development cycle. It also assumes a very close working relationship for all of the parties involved in the success of the product. If any group is not well represented throughout the cycle, the development could suffer.

Agile modeling, RUP, and XP are the subjects of many books, articles and web sites. My point is not to provide a full description of these processes, but to make a case for them as useful alternatives for game development, which, I believe, is closely related to pure software engineering.

An argument against using RUP, XP, or agile modeling as alternatives to the current GWP might be that game development has a creative component that software engineering does not. Game developers will argue that artists feel constrained by "process" and cannot fully realize their potential in a highly structured environment.

My response is that iterative development processes are inherently *less constrained* than the waterfall process. They recognize that during the process of development new ideas will arise that need to be incorporated in the product. In a game, the creative feedback loop is a classic example of the need for frequent collaboration and iteration. (A slightly more parochial argument is that software engineering is also a creative process, it just lacks the visual expression of that creativity. Why should game development be any different?)

Changing Our Ways

After the experience we had with our first phase of development, the development groups proposed alternatives to the GWP—my game development group decided to try an agile iterative process. The content group and the software engineering group each researched the various processes and adopted various elements of these philosophies. I called our new process the *game unified process*, or GUP.

Each development group was given the latitude to adopt any of the interactive processes. Software engineering took a very RUP-like approach, creating use cases and following as best they could the dogma of RUP. The content group took more of an XP approach by working in small teams focusing on single games.

These changes significantly improved our predictability and output, but we were still not where I wanted the teams to be. The core problem was the entrenched nature of the GWP. Both development groups understood the new agile processes, but had a very hard time adjusting to them. Frequently, they would regress to the waterfall process.

The content group had an especially difficult problem with incorporating iterative minicycles and frequent cross-functional gameplay testing into the project. The software engineering group fell back on the waterfall process when the deadlines came closer and closer. They stopped collaborating cross-functionally and resorted to pure development without the frequent input of QA and product management. Ironically, this had the effect of jeopardizing product quality and the overall deliverables.

In retrospect, the adaptation of an agile iterative development process significantly helped improve our overall deliverable. However, old habits die hard, leading to the incomplete implementation of the new development process in our project.

I was convinced that these processes could be adapted to game development and would produce significant improvement. In our case, a partial implementation of agile processes showed promise over the traditional results from the waterfall approach. The content group did take a less structured approach to iterative development. However, the recognition of the natural tendency of game development to be iterative was an eye opener for the content developers.

We learned that, despite the faults in the traditional game process, development groups have a very difficult time making the transition to an organized iterative process. We also learned that content groups and software engineering groups could use the same agile processes with positive results.

We concluded that the establishment of a game unified process that combines the short cycle focus of XP with the longer cycle focus of RUP is the way to go for a multidimensional development group. We also recognized that getting everyone to fully understand and adopt the process is not easy. Educating everyone across organizational lines about the process is critical to the success of GUP.

From a management perspective, implementing GUP was worth the challenges. GUP changed the attitude of many developers and galvanized the entire organization. People involved in the managerial functions play a key role in the successful implementation of GUP. Managers need to make sure everyone involved in the development process understands GUP and is bought into the concept. If GUP is executed properly, product quality improves, upper management gets better visibility into the process, a documentation trail is created that others can refer to, and change can become a recognized and valuable aspect of the development process.

CHAPTER 18

MANAGING DIGITAL ASSETS IN GAME DEVELOPMENT

OTAMERE OMORUYI

Content management tools and techniques have existed in game design studios for decades. Since the introduction of personal computers, people have been creating, modifying, deleting, and filing digital media on floppy drives, disk drives, tape drives, and CDs. Heck, I still have all my 5.25 floppies of the games I wrote for the Commodore 64.

This article will outline a framework for evaluating a digital asset management (DAM) system and look at the process involved in reusing, repurposing, and hopefully turning digital asset into a digital product.

In today's game, it's not unusual to have hundreds of assets that make up the game—from wire meshes models, textures, storyboards, rough sketches, design documents, MO-CAP (motion capture) clips to various formats of the character. This raises the challenge of classifying and indexing material to allow individuals to search for and find digital content.

For many working in the media industry, the terms *media asset management* or *content management* are familiar. However, these terms are often used loosely to refer to various systems ranging from a few pieces of paper tacked to a wall to analog media content stored in a tape vault to a system consisting of complex programs and tools that manage huge archives of digital material in an online environment.

For the purpose of this article, I will refer to *digital product management* as the web-based process of digitizing, cataloguing, tracking, and managing digital media assets for reuse and repurpose from a single source.

There Be Dragons

About six years ago, I worked on a Macintosh game called *Shadow of the Dragon* (see Figure 18.1), which was a role-playing game in the same vein as *Myst*.

We had a great artist who was freelancing for us and working offsite most of the time. Being a creative guy, he would work all sorts of crazy hours, which made it hard for us to have regular creative meetings. So he would send us his designs, I'd review them and make suggestions like "make the beast look meaner" or "make the fog in the forest less dense," and so on and so forth. He'd go back, redesign them, and come up with four or five versions with different levels of fog densities.

Pretty soon, our assets were multiplying like Captain Kirk's Tribbles. We had the rendered versions, the BMP version, and GIF versions for the web site promo, and so on. Then our creative director would go through all the thumbnails, preview the finished work, and mark them as approved for use (see Figure 18.2). By that time we had eight or nine versions of orcs, forest scenes, monsters, footstep sound effects, water rushing effects, and so on.

Once we narrowed down all the characters, scenes, sound effects, and so forth, I'd start coding. A few months into coding and playing the game, I realized that the

Figure 18.1
Shadow of the Dragon: *the hero Blackwood and the Wizard*

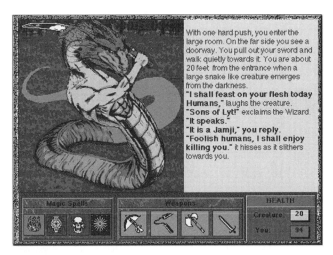

Figure 18.2
A scene for the game

first version of the forest with dense fog was probably better than the one we ended up picking. I kept thinking that it would have been great if we could have stored all the different versions of the forest so that we could go back and review them. It also became clear that we were not going to be able to use all the creatures that we had designed in this game (see Figure 18.3). But it would have

Figure 18.3
One creature that made it into the game

been nice to be able to use them in another game. That's where the beauty of an asset management system comes into play—things can be catalogued, searched, retrieved, and archived for future use.

The Asset Management System

One of the best DAM systems out there is Bulldog (www.documentum.com; see Figure 18.4). It'll handle any type of media, has a customizable web interface, and can be completely distributed geographically and across divisions.

Regardless of which content management system you decide on, there are a few key features to look for:

- **Keywords.** You should be able to assign one or many keywords to an asset so that you can quickly and easily find that asset again. Keyword systems can either be in a flat or tree structure. By tree of keywords, I mean only the way to present and organize large keyword lists. If assets get assigned a keyword from the leaf of the tree, it does not mean that the branch keywords will be assigned to the same asset.

- **Directory.** You should be able to see your file system organized by folders. Searches can be made in sub-trees to speed up the process.

Figure 18.4
The Bulldog web interface

- **Security/user settings**. The security model will reflect selected asset components so restrictions can be placed on asset, directory, keyword, media properties, media representation, versions, groups, etc.

- **Version control**. The media management system should automatically keep track of the versions. For example, if I have a picture of a dragon in my asset system and I "check it out," make changes to it, and "check it in" again, the DAM should automatically know that this is a different version that still has the same asset properties, but different media. Some version-specific information can be added per version, like a revision description label.

- **Association**. If you have a picture of an ogre that has been derived from other pictures, you should be able to create something like a "consists of" association. So my picture of the ogre is made up of three or four other pictures.

- **Group**. This is important. You should be able to organize your assets in groups that you can define. For example, you may want to organize the entire assets for a level into a group or all the weapons of a game into a group. You should then be able to apply security to that group so that only the guys working on the game can access them, for example.

- **Proxy**. This is just a way to have a preview or see a low-quality image for your high-quality image. This saves bandwidth if you've got really huge files that you're trying to view remotely.

- **Workflow**. This will probably vary among digital management systems, but at the very least, you should be able to update/change the asset's life stage to things like Scan, Design, Development, Retouch, Approved, and Production.

- **History/tracking**. When and how an asset was modified in the past and who made those changes.

- **Check in/check out/download.** This is how you get access to your asset. You should be able to check out an asset and check it in again after you've finished with it. Checking out an asset should "lock" it so that no one else can modify the asset while you are working on it. Downloading the asset should simply move the asset from the repository to the location that you want.

- **Report.** As you store metadata in a relational database, various off-the-shelf reporting tools can be used to produce custom reports. You may also want to see statistical information on your assets—what has been changed recently and which media asset is more frequently requested.

Also keep in mind that every asset has a life cycle, and your asset management system should be able to address all these stages:

- **Acquisition.** How easy is it to get assets into the system? The acquisition process involves the ingestion and digitization of the media content and all associated metadata (information that is used to track the asset within the system) into an asset management engine. The engine provides the mechanism for tracking both predefined and user-definable information about assets, as well as the ability to automatically index information about media properties, including format and size. The asset management engine serves as the repository for all content.

- **Editorial/production.** During the editorial process, digital media content is manipulated, resulting in changed content and changed metadata, possibly adding value to the asset. Effective digital product management involves controlling access to digital assets, enabling efficient searching and retrieval of those assets, and keeping accurate records of all transactions performed on them while they are being manipulated and prepared for final usage.

- **Distribution.** The distribution process involves the dissemination of changed content or products, accompanied by the supporting metadata, to various targeted divisions or departments.

- **Archiving.** The archiving process results in a comprehensive record of all digital assets, as well as all supporting metadata for each stored asset, regardless of whether the media resides online or has been migrated to offline storage.

The cooperation and interoperation of these processes results in an end-to-end enterprise solution that adds value to digital media products at every stage of their life cycle, from acquisition through to production and distribution.

Open Source

Getting an enterprise-wide DAM system up and running can be costly and time consuming. If you have more time than money, then you might want to go the open source approach.

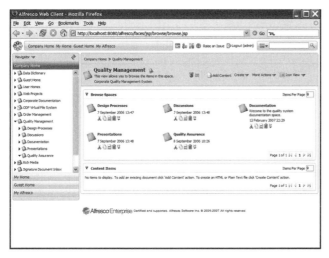

Figure 18.5
Alfresco interface

Open source software is ready for prime time and one of the best open source alternatives for enterprise content management is an application called *Alfresco* (see Figure 18.5).

If you decide to go with an open source framework for your digital asset management, here are some things to take into account:

- **Go with what you know.** There are competing open source applications, written in different languages, from Java to PHP to .Net. So go with a DAM that fits into your current environment. This will save you time in setting it up and in making tweaks or modifications. This ensures its longevity, innovation, and support.

- **Look at release history.** Look at the history of releases from the open source team. If a new version hasn't been released in years or there's not a lot of activity, then you should skip it and move on to the next one. Even if the license model allows you to modify the code, it's not worth it if you can't get help from fellow users.

- **Look for the wizard.** See who's "behind the curtains" of the open source project. Open source projects can gain a lot of innovation and speed if there are established software vendors leading or contributing to the projects.

- **Show me the money.** With open source asset management systems, there's almost always a basic edition (free) and enterprise edition with some associated license fees. Depending on your size and budget, you'll have to determine which option (and features) works best for you.

The Rewards

The implementation of a content management system once focused on setting up and maintaining an asset repository—ingesting, indexing, and storing media for reuse and repurposing. With the rich media demands of video games, this type of system no longer suffices; however, many vendors in this market have yet to reach beyond this point, so avoid them like the plague.

If you have chosen the right DAM system, you should be able to:

■ Protect the commercial value of media

■ Realize cost savings

■ Find what you are looking for easily

■ Facilitate a digital enterprise storage strategy

■ Facilitate digital collaboration

■ Enable reuse and repurposing of content

■ Facilitate proper distribution tracking

For a one- or two-person shop, a DAM may be overkill. But in any environment where you have to gather, track, and basically worry about a multitude of assets, the need for content management starts to become apparent.

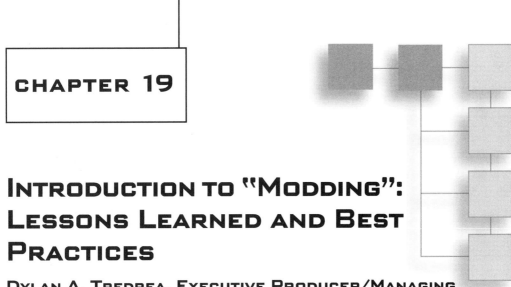

CHAPTER 19

INTRODUCTION TO "MODDING": LESSONS LEARNED AND BEST PRACTICES

DYLAN A. TREDREA, EXECUTIVE PRODUCER/MANAGING DIRECTOR, CREO LUDUS ENTERTAINMENT, LLC

My name is Dylan Tredrea, and I ran a series of mod projects to start the serious game company I now run, Creo Ludus Entertainment (www.creoludus.com). As there are already a number of great books and articles on game production that you should absolutely dive into for the nuts and bolts of project management, this article is written as a guide specific to mod development. I've tried to aggregate here what I've learned from the trials and tribulations of mod development on what I believe are the three most crucial ingredients for success: the team, the project, and the process.

Mods and Their Role in the Games Industry

So mods—what exactly are they for? Mods are not always endeavors with commercial goals, but a great deal are. Mod development has been proven again and again to successfully launch game careers and studios. *Frontlines: Fuel of War,* a cross-platform FPS from Kaos Studios/THQ was developed by the team behind *Desert Combat,* a mod for *Battlefield 1942.* Countless individuals have used mods to land their first job in the industry, by contributing to projects of all sizes from large well-known projects like *Counterstrike* to smaller and more niche creations. If you can deliver an engaging experience with a mod, then you have a good shot at getting someone to pay you for it the next time around.

In a sense, mods have evolved as the natural extension of one-man "garage projects" that led so much of the innovation in the early days of the games industry. Advances in technology and the resulting larger team sizes have reduced the options and payoff of one-man projects, though via mods the practice continues of amateurs developing something unique for professional and/or business development.

Mods play such a big part in the growth of the industry because, like every entertainment business, games are extremely difficult to break into. Any kid would love to spend a career making video games instead of scratching his way up a corporate ladder, but there are only so many jobs out there, and unproven hires are a risk many studios can rarely take. Hard skills can be learned in school and a formal education is certainly strongly recommended, but is not at all required. What is almost universally required, however, is experience making something (especially with a team), and this is where modding comes in.

There are immense opportunities for mod teams who deliver. Already huge, the interactive entertainment and training and simulation industries have an even bigger future. Ubisoft CEO Yves Guillemot recently said he expects the interactive entertainment industry to grow by an astounding 50% in the next four years.[1] In the bigger picture, investment bank Goldman Sachs predicts the combined productivity of BRICS (Brazil, Russia, India, and China) may surpass that of the United States, Japan, the UK, Germany, France, and Italy by 2039.[2] As the middle class in these and other developing nations grows, so will the global demand for interactive entertainment and training. While our grandparents may or may not come around to the Wii, it's safe to say nearly every person born worldwide into the middle class and above will be a gamer for life. This is demonstrated by the yearly creep of Entertainment Software Association's median gamer age[3] and probably any kid you've met in the past couple decades. Games have always been part of being human, and frankly, we're just all lucky enough to be alive when technology has advanced far enough to take games to such an exciting level.

Now, don't make the mistake of seeing this fantastic opportunity and thinking success is going to be easy. The big potential payoff is there for a reason—the ratio of launched to completed mods is likely far north of 99.99%. The trick to mod development, not unlike professional game development, of course, is actually getting a presentable product out the door.

---

[1] www.redherring.com/Home/22621
[2] "Dreaming with BRICs: The Path to 2050," by Dominic Wilson and Roopa Purushothaman, Goldman Sachs Global Economics Paper 99, October 2003.
[3] www.theesa.com/facts/index.asp

The Team

Bringing together an all-volunteer team, you're probably going to be operating in what I call Rumsfeld's reality—you go to work with the mod team you have, not the mod team you want. Still, there are a number of ways you can build a solid mod team from scratch.

Building the Team

1. **IGDA and GDC:** Join the IGDA and attend meetings religiously. Don't have a local IGDA chapter? Start one, even if it's only you and a buddy at first. Use IGDA and social networking resources to build it out. If at all possible, beg, borrow, and steal to attend GDC!

2. **School:** Find people into game development in like-minded classes and/or clubs. Feel free to skip out on formal involvement if there isn't anything interesting going on, but don't miss an opportunity to skim talent from their ranks!

3. **Open your mouth and ears:** Tell everyone you know what you're doing and what you're looking for and keep your ears to the ground for potential additions.

Note on "Virtual" Team Members

In general, I'd strongly recommend against starting with core team members no one knows in "real life"—*especially* if you've only known them for a short period of time. For external resources on finite tasks, such as music composition, art, and so on, fantastically talented people can be found online. Just make sure to start with small non-critical path tasks and add responsibility and involvement as they deliver. It's also good practice to solicit submissions from multiple resources to increase your chances of receiving something release-worthy.

These are people you are going to be relying on and investing your time and dreams in—so add to the team with discretion!

"Team Building"

Spend time together socially while starting off—"team building" as we used to call it in my internship days when we wanted the boss to pick up the bar tab. Get to know each other. In particular, everyone should be able to answer the following questions about everyone else on the team:

- What is their goal for the project: start a company or jump-start a career?

- What do they love doing with regard to game development? What do they hate? They may be a programmer now, but they may not want to be one tomorrow. At times, everyone is going to have to step up and occasionally take on work they're not excited about, but always try to have people doing what they enjoy!

- What are their current core competencies and which are they hoping to develop on this project? This is especially important when selecting the project.

- And of course, what kind of games do they like? In addition to learning about each other's interests, the team must come together and commit to a set of shared goals for the project. *Commit* is not a soft word here—this is a set of promises you are making to each other. At a minimum, they should include the following:

- Get it out the door.
- Hold each other accountable.
- Create opportunities for each other. Never, ever, ever, ever, miss an opportunity to talk up your team to anyone!
- Communicate honestly, professionally, and actionably:
  - Tell each other what you honestly think—it's the only way to work.
  - Speak professionally—not in a starched-shirt-big-word way, but communicate clearly (and concisely!!) what you have to say and how it affects your project and goals.
  - Be actionable. Don't just say something sucks. Roll up your sleeves, grab a cup of coffee/glass of beer with the appropriate people, and work it out. Most importantly, try adamantly to see the other person's point of view—they may just have a better approach, and you owe it to each other to take feedback seriously.

Team Structure

A good model for structuring your team isn't hard to find. It can, however, be difficult to implement. It's likely all or part of you are good friends, and it's not easy to see each other as superiors/subordinates—but to be successful, you'll have to.

Democracy Is for Government—Not for Development

This is a tremendous mistake I made working with a team of experienced professional developers. As always, pride came before the fall—and we believed the skills and experience of the team would allow us to work together democratically (making all the decisions as a group). This was quite possibly the biggest game development mistake I've ever made and has a good shot at keeping that title for a long time. If you attempt to run a project in this fashion—it will fail. The more "active" team members will soon realize they can sway decisions by lobbying less active team members, virtually guaranteeing politics fit for a teen prime-time drama. Every decision will require hours of debate, and in no time everyone will be burned out with little accomplished.

Leadership

Instead, pick a leader and a team willing to follow that leader. Use your own best judgment for selecting a leader, but everyone must understand the position means they'll have to deliver. For larger teams, select a lead artist, programmer, producer, and so on, as well. Give leads freedom to operate, but maintain high standards and truly demand they produce results. Jack Welch, former CEO of GE and extremely well-regarded management guru gave his managers free reign for every decision under $50 million, but he wasted no time in cutting someone who didn't deliver.

Of course, a mod project where everyone is learning and volunteering their time needs to be a bit more flexible than a professional studio. Hold people accountable, but don't make the mistake of setting an unattainable standard. Instead, focus on what led to the mistake and turn each misstep into a learning experience. If leadership makes a bad decision, look at how they are gathering information, weighing the options, and communicating the decision. If someone falls behind and isn't completing their tasks on time, scale back their responsibilities, pair them with stronger resources for mentoring/assistance, work with them to schedule tasks around their life, and maybe even shift their work to a different area. While it's important to cut someone loose who isn't delivering, mistakes happen, and how they're handled is what defines and drives the growth of a team.

On staffing, leads should be open to driven and determined green or inexperienced talent. Start them small and don't get your hopes up too much until they deliver; but even if it's only setting up an FTP, researching, or playtesting, give them a chance to show you they can produce. Of course, don't take on additional people arbitrarily. If someone is hanging off to the side too long, they'll lose interest and end up either underperforming or leaving the project of their own accord. The production person/team should take special care to ensure the workload can support the added resource.

Perhaps most importantly, good leads take ownership of the product and set a professional, presentable, and polished standard. You'll be judged only by what's released—so it's the mission of leadership to ensure that only the best possible work goes out the door.

Note

Don't skip over the word "possible." It's important (especially for the production lead) to make sure the scope of the project is achievable. If it's not possible to get there with a reasonable amount of time and effort, you're setting yourself up for disappointment.

Action! Drive Everything to Completion

As a team, probably the most crucial trait is the attitude to drive issues, tasks, and so forth, to completion. From top to bottom, a team is as strong as its individual and collective commitment to this. A team with this attitude will work around the seemingly endless issues that come up and make the forward progress that completes a project. Pay close attention to how your team handles issues, and you'll see the difference between the positive forces on the team and those who are holding the project back. Don't forget that everyone is learning and make the mistake of cutting "negative Nancy" right away. Always reach out and try to bring those who are out of sync with the team into the fold—set the standard fairly so that the team is just as honest and reasonably flexible when you inevitably slip up.

The Project

Selecting a project is easily one of the most fun parts of mod development. It's when everyone gets to sit back and dream up the awesome experience you guys are going to make happen.

When selecting the different parts of the project—from the core concept and platform to the tools—it's important to keep your original goals close in mind.

Often, this may be at odds with individual tastes, but for the project to be worth everyone's time and effort, it's important the end result serves the shared goals that brought them to the table.

Consider Your Audience

To address this, first ask the question, "For whose benefit are you using the mod to show your skills?" Are you a team hoping to start your own studio? Think about what a publisher and/or investor would like to see. It's not a bad idea to have a certain creative and/or technological direction. Targeting your mod projects gives you focus and carves out a little corner where your team can shine. Naturally, the more ubiquitous the technology, the better. And don't define your design focus too tight—as much as possible, let it evolve naturally in your work. Mods are low cost and low risk, so they're a great way to find out if a potential specialization fits.

For career development, select technology and tools based (in part) on what the studios you'd like to work at use. If you're a producer and they run projects on Microsoft Project, use this to manage your mod project. If mid-project you're applying to a studio using Hansoft, migrate to Hansoft—and certainly talk about your experience doing so in your interview(s). Also ask any questions you may have!

In general, I'd strongly recommend adopting widely used tools such as Unreal 3, MS Project, and so on, so that down the line your experience is more useful.

The Concept

When coming up with a concept for your mod, start with a good, honest, and deep evaluation of your team's capabilities. How innovative can you afford to be? What limits does this put on scope and available features on the platform(s) you're considering?

Note

In this phase, it can get depressing when you're forced to severely scale back your project. Remember, it's all about getting something professional and presentable out the door. Even if it's only you and a buddy designing levels from pre-existing assets, releasing something small yet professional and polished could be enough for a QA position. A finished presentable product on the shelf will also certainly make things easier when recruiting a team the next time around. Plus, there's nothing like the feeling of putting something out that you can be really proud of! So don't fret if the tools, team, and time aren't available to develop your dream project. Every step forward is, well, a step forward!

It's also wise to select for each project a single gameplay mechanic to focus on. If you are having trouble falling in love with something, spend some time perusing the forums of the game(s) you're considering to see what the fans are calling for. Make some quick prototypes to test out anything appealing, and iterate on the more promising ones to develop your own approach. Remember—stay focused on fun! While it may be interesting to build a level based on a giant scale model of your school's bathroom or something weird/cool like that, make sure gameplay benefits as well. Certainly, we can all think of games developed on the mistake of thinking a gimmick equals gameplay.

Due Diligence

Before diving in, do your due diligence and make sure the platform can handle what you're trying to do. One project I was particularly excited about focused on inter-vehicle battle. Thankfully, a chance conversation with one of the developers let me know in fact the game would crash with more than a few vehicles per map—rendering our concept essentially worthless. Before putting time and resources into an untested mechanic, make a quick prototype and see if the developer's community manager can offer any support. Just calling someone in the credits works well, too!

The Scope

Every developer, from the smallest mod team to the largest and most experienced studios, over-scope on occasion. The same way you stack your plate at a great buffet, expect and anticipate the desire to overload your development capabilities. To compensate, don't just plan conservatively—plan scalable. Prioritize the smallest amount of content and put your best people on it. Consistently make sure this core content is on track, and always be prepared to trim everything else. If game development is anything, it's working around issues and hold-ups; so starting from the earliest planning, always be at least mentally ready to go even smaller. The audience will never know what you left on the cutting room floor; they will, however, know if you put something out that wasn't in the oven long enough.

On the off chance anyone says your mod is awesome but small, tell them: "Of course! It's episodic."☺

The Process: Development

With the team in place, concept and scope set, and all possible due diligence and pre-production behind you—time to get to developing! Following are some key production processes for mod development:

- **Weekly meetings**. Have a weekly meeting, run by the producer, where everyone reports what they accomplished that week and what they plan to accomplish the following week. Ideally, have this meeting in person, or use Skype, AIM, or one of the many free conference call services if all/part of the team is working remotely. Keep these focused and brief—anything longer than 30 minutes and you'll lose people.

- **Playable iterations early and often**. Set up the development process so the team is playing through iterations of your core mechanic early and often. Getting everyone's eyes on the team's progress gives design gems and mistakes the time in the sun they need—often what you thought is a gem was a dud, and what you thought was a mistake turns out to be a gem.

- **Simple, professional, and updated web site**. At a minimum, have a simple, clean, professional, and updated web site. Include team bios, contact info, news, and some background on who you are and how you got started. Update the news section with everyone's accomplishments related or even semi-related to game development. Don't forget to post screenshots as your project moves forward!

- **Issue meetings**. Issues will continually come up requiring more than the usual discussions online. Set up a meeting to address issues either before, after, or at a separate time from weekly meetings (ideal if not all team members are needed). Make sure to keep the two separate to maintain the flow and focus of the weekly reports. Send out beforehand either a full agenda or a simple goal sheet and have the appropriate lead drive discussion to actionable conclusions.

- **Set deadlines for decisions**. There is this story of how Apple, Inc. got its name. Steve Jobs was so tired of endless debate on the subject, he grabbed an apple (his favorite fruit) off his desk and declared that unless someone came up with something better in five minutes, the company was going to be called Apple. Who knows if this story is true, but for the issue at hand, it was a great solution. The name is just not that important, so set a deadline, pick something, and move on. Not every issue is this simple, but once all the information is on the table, everything else is politics.

- **Keep a cost/benefit focus**. Would three amazing James Cameron–quality trailers take your project to the next level? Or would it just tie up talented resources when one trailer would do? Remember what you are trying to get out of the project, and if the work in question doesn't serve those goals, rein the project in.

- **Communication**. Keep everything as open source as possible. When leads make decisions, state clearly and definitively why the decision was made one way and not the other. Use a forum for e-discussions so all the information is in one place. Under no circumstances keep anything from anyone on the team. This isn't the film business—we're better than that.

- **Commit to improvement**. Take your work seriously and become a vacuum for the deluge of information available online. Furiously read anything you can find in and around your area of responsibility. Make reading sites like Gamasutra a habit, and pass on articles that your team may find helpful. (Forwarding articles related to your work, discussions, or shared interests with a person is also a great way to take your networking to the next level!) In addition, take advantage of the collective talent of your team. If someone is good at something you'd like to learn—pair up and absorb their wisdom sponge-like. Don't be shy to take notes! Ask questions, make suggestions, and repeat back core ideas. Don't underestimate the value of this sort of collaboration. Teaching is a natural way to coalesce your own knowledge and gain a deeper understanding of the subject matter.

- **Fall in love with Craigslist**. For external resources to broaden the experience you deliver (e.g., composers, voice actors, and sound engineers) make good use of Craigslist. Look for like-minded people wanting to work in the games industry. Be upfront that the position is unpaid but an established way to get game development work.

- **Don't just work—go out and have fun with each other!** It's important to unwind, so whether it's a Rock Band night or an all-nighter on the town—don't forget to forget about the project for a night and have fun with each other!

- **Cross promote your project, team, and contributors**. Never miss an opportunity to talk up your project and the people you are working with. If a composer does an awesome piece for you, place their info prominently on your web site and tell everyone how lucky you are to have them contribute. It's not just the right thing to do—it shows that you truly appreciate the people working hard for you and encourages everyone to return the favor.

Release

It's DONE! Wow, does that feel good. Bet you could use a break from the level editor, the forum, and maybe even each other. Don't just dump a zip file on your web site though—make sure you get credit for your hard work and do everything you can to get the right eyes on your content.

Release Checklist:

- **An installer**. Make it as *easy as possible* to play your work.

- **Tested**. Test it again, and again, and again.

- **A properly formatted press release on your web site**. Plenty of templates are available online. It doesn't have to be Hemmingway but cover the concept, core gameplay mechanic, team info, and where to download the mod.

- **A short gameplay-focused trailer**. Screen capture the best gameplay moments you can find and pair them with some music. If needed, use music so old that there aren't any license issues, but try to find a professional-quality resource to make something unique.

- **Promote, promote, promote!** You've worked hard, so make sure people know what you've done. Post on every forum you can. (If you're worried this isn't permitted, a personal e-mail to the admins can go a long way!) E-mail any and all contacts you have in and around the industry, fans of the game you know, and yes, even your mother! Show your friends why you've been busy, your family why you've been working for free, and your contacts in the industry what you can do.

- **Welcome—even seek out—constructive criticism!** A great way to network is by just asking for advice.

- **Remember, not everyone will play the game** so just having an awesome gameplay trailer may be enough to wow many o' people!

Conclusion

Your dream of a game development career and/or studio can happen, if you make it happen. Get some friends together, make something you can be proud of, and take advantage of this ideal time to jump into a growing industry and be a part of one of the most exciting advancements in what has been part of human culture since human culture existed—games!

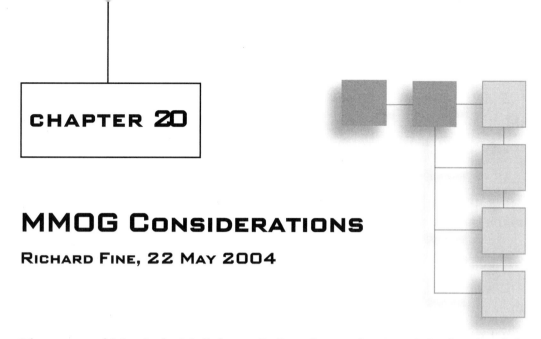

CHAPTER 20

MMOG CONSIDERATIONS

RICHARD FINE, 22 MAY 2004

The genre of Massively Muliplayer Online Games (or MMOGs for short) is relatively new, but increasingly popular, for game developers. Encouraged by games such as *Everquest, Star Wars Galaxies,* or *Ultima Online,* many new developers are inspired to create designs for huge online worlds with never-before-seen levels of interactivity and detail; professional developers may be more drawn by the constant stream of revenue such projects can provide after launch, in contrast to the usual once-in-a-blue-moon payment from the publisher. The market for MMO games is particularly strong in Asia.

But while such games are popular, they are also one of the most complex projects you will ever encounter. Leaving aside the game design issues—creating and balancing a virtual society that can accommodate thousands of players—the practical issues of developing and running an MMO game are extremely challenging to navigate.

This article seeks to provide an overview of some of the issues you should consider when thinking about an MMO project, to give you some of the questions you should be asking, as well as a few possible answers. It is not a how-to guide, or indeed intended to give you much in-depth guidance as to how you actually write an MMOG. It's simply intended to give you some degree of perspective, to help you understand just how many complex issues are involved in building and running an MMOG.

There's also some disagreement about how big a game needs to be before it's considered "massive." For the sake of this article, I'm taking massive to mean that the game aims to have at least 5,000 users concurrently online. Given that the names people often think of when considering MMOGs—names such as *Ever Quest*, *Ultima Online*, or *Lineage*—have hundreds of times that many; in fact, it's probably a generous lower limit. Many of the issues here still apply to smaller games, but they're not *massively* multiplayer (perhaps *largely* multiplayer?) and so they may have different concerns.

Servers, Sniffers, Systems, and Suits

The issues I will cover can be broken down roughly into four categories, though there is some overlap:

- **Connection issues:** All issues regarding the actual transfer of data between the client and server—security, stability, speed, protocols, and so on.

- **Operating platform issues:** All issues regarding the architecture of your server platform—things like load balancing, backups/redundancy, clustering, and so on. Much of this category is common to standard Internet applications and is not game-specific, but it is still of the utmost importance.

- **Technology issues:** All issues regarding the architecture of the system you run on the server. This may seem similar to the previous category, but focuses more on game-specific issues, such as cheat-proofing and dynamic updates.

- **Business issues:** All issues regarding the business side of running an MMO game. Hobbyist developers may be tempted to skip this section, reasoning that it's not relevant to them; but in fact, the costs and business details are what most frequently cause hobbyist MMO projects to fail.

One category that you may have expected to show up—client issues—is something that I do not feel I need to cover, as the issues inherent in writing a client for an MMO game are pretty similar to those for any other type of network game.

Connection Issues

In any networked game, you need a system for sending data between nodes in the network. Given that we're talking about MMO games—and all major MMO games use a client/server model of communication (as opposed to peer-to-peer, which would suffer major security and management issues)—you can assume that we're talking specifically about the connection between the client and the server. What do you need to be aware of when designing this part of the system?

Security

In general, you do not want third parties to be able to screw around with the data that you're sending over the wire. Interception of packets could lead to a victim's game account details—such as the username and password they use to log in to the game—being hijacked. A more worrying scenario is the interception of credit card details, in the case of a game that lets players pay their subscription fees from within the game or supports micro transactions.

Encrypting every packet you send is probably impractical, not to mention largely unnecessary—intercepting a packet that gives a player's current position in the game world may help someone cheat, but the effort required to obtain such a small piece of information makes it unlikely that people would bother with it. Still, it is likely that you would want the facility to transmit data securely, even if you do not make use of it all the time. So how will you provide that? Which pieces of information will be encrypted and which won't?

Authentication

How can you ensure that the packets you're receiving are really from your client software? How will you prevent someone from hacking together their own client software, which allows them to do things you don't want them to? How can you be sure the source IP address is "safe"?

Stability

Players will not be happy if their connection to your server is cutting off every few minutes. Whatever technology you use to connect your servers to the Internet should be very stable; protection against things like Denial of Service attacks is also something you may want to invest in. Running your MMO server on, for example, a home broadband connection that disconnects for five minutes every few hours is not advised.

Bandwidth

The connection will be handling packets from potentially hundreds of thousands of clients; the realtime nature of most games means that each player will be sending and receiving many packets per unit of time, compared to non-realtime services like web sites. You need to have a connection that, as a whole, can handle this much data; several gigabytes per hour is not an unreasonable expectation. It's unlikely that you'll be handling everything through a single pipe.

Latency

Sadly, it's not yet possible to send information to the average client through quantum entanglement; so, the time it takes for your packets to go from server to client is significant. When sending packets across the Internet, your data will be potentially handled by a pretty large range of devices, each of which is running under different loads and imbued with different levels of power. The time taken by a packet to reach its destination will vary, and it may not be small. How will you attempt to minimize latency, at least within the parts of the connection you control? How will you deal with packets that take a long time to reach their destination and packets that arrive out of order?

Failure Response

What will you do, both at the client and server ends, if the connection drops or packets are lost? This has implications in your game design—particularly dealing with players who conveniently "drop" from the game just as they're about to be killed violently—but it bears thinking about on the technical end as well. Should the client try and reconnect, or should it wait for the player to instruct it to do so? Should the server give the player a grace period of a few seconds to reconnect, perhaps based on their ping time, or should it treat the disconnection as a proper one immediately? When it comes to the per-packet level, when will you use guaranteed delivery (which causes all lost packets to be automatically resent, but requires extra packets to be sent back to the server for every packet that is received by the client), and when will you use non-guaranteed delivery?

Protocol

What conventions will you use in your networking protocol? (By "protocol" here, I do not mean TCP or UDP; rather, I mean the custom protocol that you build on top.) An example would be strings: You could go with C-style null terminated strings, or you could go with Pascal-style strings where the length is prepended to the string. Will you stick to network byte order (big-endian) for your data?

Operating Platform Issues

Your operating platform—server-side, at least—is the entire server system. It may well be spread over multiple machines, multiple processes and applications, and even multiple continents. What do you need to think about when designing the operating platform for your server?

Load

How many players do you expect a given element in the operating platform to have to handle at any one time? How much spare capacity do you want to build into the system? Expecting and thus designing for 10,000 players in the beginning is fine, but if later on you want to expand your market share and thus attract new players, you're going to need to either have the capacity to handle them in the beginning or come up with a concrete plan for extending the platform at a later point in time. (By a "concrete plan," I do mean something pretty specific; "buy another server" is not very good, while a detailed breakdown of what you will need, step-by-step instructions for integration into the platform, and how much you expect it to increase capacity by is better.) Also, be aware of the difference between total players and concurrent players—even if you have 25,000 total subscribers to your game, you may only have 3,000 players online at any one time. That may not affect the requirements for some parts of the system, but it can heavily affect others.

Distribution

How are you going to spread the load over multiple servers? Will you have one server per subsystem, or will all servers run all subsystems for some part of the game? (For example, will you have one server dedicated to physics processing and another dedicated to AI, or will both servers run physics and AI for separate parts of the world?) How will load distribution be controlled—will you use a single, central depot server, or will individual servers pass off excess work to each other?

Security

You have to provide a way for the outside world to connect to your servers; otherwise, none of your clients could ever log in. But you must be careful—every open port is another potential avenue of attack on your platform. Take the utmost caution when dealing with data from the client; your aim is to make it impossible for someone to crash your servers by sending in a carefully crafted packet. What measures will you take to verify the integrity of the data you're getting or to protect routines that work with that data? Also, you need to protect your internal services—things like database servers. How will you architect your network to allow the necessary machines to communicate with them without providing a route to them from the outside world?

Redundancy

Say you have a hardware failure, a power cut, or your security fails and someone manages to crash your servers. How will you go about restoring the world to a state as close as possible to before the problem? You can go for backups. Dumping the entire world database to a tape drive every day may be enough for your purposes. (And besides, there may be reasons beyond technology failures for keeping backups, such as responding to endemic cheating.) How precisely will that be achieved? Which parts of the system will be backed up?

Another thing to consider, as well as backups, might be something like RAID. It means a higher initial cost (instead of buying one 120GB disk for the server, you're buying two or three plus a RAID controller), but it means you can respond to a couple of disks failing without your server dying entirely. (If one disk fails, you can respond in a controlled way to replace it while the game continues to run, though you don't want to hang around because the other disks could go, too.) If you do go with a RAID array, how many disks should you invest in? Which RAID level do you want? What's your plan of action when the RAID controller reports that one of the disks has failed (given that you usually can't hot-swap disks around)? How will you cope if the entire RAID array fails (the controller blows out)? Even if you do include a RAID system, it will only account for what's on disk and not what's in memory; so how will you restore what was in memory? If you're not even going to try, how will you minimize the data being kept in memory at any given time and ensure that it gets written to the disk as often as possible without slowing down?

Synchronization

When you've got a system composed of multiple processes communicating with each other, you're bound to run into synchronization issues at some time or another. It's particularly a problem for the database servers—what if two machines are accessing the same record at the same time? Do you implement a locking system so that the first one there gets it and the others have to wait or drop out with an error? Perhaps you go for atomic operations? Or just allow it to happen and to hell with the consequences? The last approach might be perfectly valid if you don't think the chances are high of a given record being used by multiple other processes.

Technology Issues

In this section, I'll discuss some of the MMOG-specific technology issues, covering both client and server applications (the "server application" being the collection of programs you run on the server-side operating platform).

Caching

Caching is the practice of storing resources that you're more likely to need in a place that's faster to get to than the regular data storage. In MMO gaming, the client programs will pretty much always be caching data—that's because the "regular data storage" is all the way over the network at the server, so accessing it is likely to be very slow. So, we're talking about data that the client will need for the very next frame—models, textures, sounds, and other assets for the player's current status and location would be an example. A key concept with caching is *temporal coherence*, the idea that something is the same from one frame to the next. If something is temporally coherent, there's no point reloading the data from the server, so you cache it. Beyond that, though, what do you want to cache? How much of that content needs to be picked up dynamically (from the servers) and how much can be included in the client software (i.e., on the CD)? The rule of thumb is, cache anything you might need in a hurry, especially if you can't predict when you'll need it. Graphics for an in-game menu would be an example—you have no way of knowing when the player will bring up the in-game menu, and you *definitely* don't have time to sit around downloading the graphic from the server. Given that they're unlikely to change, they'd be prime candidates for including in the client software.

At the server end, you'll probably find advantages to caching things as well. You might want to cache things like level geometry around spawn points so that it can be sent more quickly to players joining the game, rather than having to pull it out of hard storage; or maybe you'll cache information about a specific item that people keep asking for. The best way to find out what to cache is to monitor the requests and see which ones come up the most frequently; a truly rock-solid caching system will do exactly that and has the advantage that it can adjust over time (i.e., if people hardly ever use a given spawn point, it can detect that and stop caching it).

You'll also want individual servers to cache information within the operating platform. Say you're processing collision detection for a bunch of entities; you'll get a good performance boost from fetching them all into the cache and testing them there, rather than fetching them one by one, testing, and then dropping them so that you have to get them from the database again next time.

Also, at both ends of the wire, how large will caches be? Client-side, you'll probably be limited by both the amount of system memory and the amount of hard disk space you can reasonably use; server-side, though, you've got more control. You should definitely take cache sizes into account when designing your operating platform.

Dynamic Updates

The ability to dynamically update the game—adding new content, removing existing content, or changing content—is crucial. New content keeps the game from getting boring and thus keeps the players playing; there may also be bugs or gameplay balance issues that haven't emerged until several thousand players are present in the game (the latter is especially common). What's your procedure for updating the server application? How about the clients? Will you just stop all the servers completely, make the changes, and relaunch it? Perhaps you'll take down servers one by one (after moving their load off to other machines), update them, and then bring them back into an operational state? This means that until you've done all the machines, some parts of your network will be running the old version and some the new—how will you deal with that? Or perhaps you'll avoid bringing the machines down at all, providing a mechanism for the server application to assimilate changes while it's still running?

The effects of content updates can be extremely extensive. Say you want to create a brand-new building in a specific place—will you just sit there and wait until the space you want becomes clear of players? If you're placing the building in a town, that could be quite a wait. So perhaps you'd go for some system that lets you mark the space as about-to-be-built-upon, turning it into a no-entry zone for players until you're done building? The addition of a brand-new chunk of geometry to the world would force players in the vicinity to download it from the server into their caches—how would you give the clients advance warning so that they could pick up the mesh before it's needed to prevent an awkward pause when you place it?

Then, say you want to remove that building a few months later. What do you do with players (or NPCs, for that matter) who are currently inside it? Just drop them on the floor outside with no warning? Would you tell clients that the assets for the building no longer need to be cached, and if so, how?

The most difficult type of update is usually a code update, where you're changing the actual software running either client-side or server-side. You may well want players to refrain from playing until they've installed the client-side update (for example, if it closes an exploit that some players were using to cheat with)—how will you enforce that? Will it be done from within the game, or will players have to exit and visit your game's web site to get the update?

Security

It's probably been said that computer security is all about being openly paranoid about your users; if it hasn't, then I'm saying it, because it's true. Any user is a potential cheater, cracker, or malicious script kiddie aiming to take down your servers or generally ruin the game for other people. As such, you should never trust any information coming from the user, even if you have authentication measures in place to try and ensure that data from the user really is from your client app. Say that your client app is repeatedly sending the position of the player to the server, and the server is simply copying this position into the database as holy writ. An enterprising cracker could modify the client application to send a position value of his choice, and, presto, he's granted himself the ability to "teleport." Even if your authentication system prevents modifications to the client software, there are still ways of modifying packets on the fly. If someone finds a way around your authentication, then it's as good as non-existent. So look at things from that point of view, of the position of having no client authentication.

The most secure situation would be to send data to the server purely as a stream of input commands, and then have the server do the actual processing of those commands to move the player around and so forth. Even then, a cheater could still take advantage of you; he could record a stream of keypresses and send them all to the server in quick succession, allowing him to "press keys" faster than a real human actually could. So you'd still need some kind of "sanity checker" to watch the user input streams, just to check that what it's seeing is reasonable input for a human player. Of course, this whole approach isn't used because of the processing power it requires; you'd effectively be moving the load from *all* of your clients (who may number in the hundreds of thousands) onto the server, which is a pretty hefty load. The MMO client-server setup represents a significant distributed computing platform, but you have to be careful about what the clients are actually doing.

As such, it never hurts to keep things fairly tightly locked down on the client side; server-side security systems are all very well, but it's nicer if you don't have to use them. Pirating an MMOG client is usually pointless (you still need to pay a subscription fee), so copy-protection schemes are generally unnecessary; instead, the client should be watching out for modified data files (perhaps through a checksumming mechanism), unsavoury-looking programs in memory (particularly so-called "trainers" that attempt to alter the client's memory while it's running), and debuggers. All three could be signs of someone trying to cheat the game.

Synchronization

Here it is again, though in more of a gaming context—you need to keep all your clients, and all your servers, synchronized (or as close to it as possible). That doesn't just mean that they need to all display the same game clock time; they all need to be working with the same set of data. A player shooting at an enemy will be less than impressed if that enemy actually moved away several minutes ago and they're shooting a ghost (but couldn't tell because the server isn't keeping them up to date).

This issue is particularly prominent in MMO games where different servers are handling different regions of the world. When the player travels from one region to the other and hits a server boundary (i.e., reaches the edge of the area controlled by the current server), he must transfer to a different server. If the two servers are out of sync, it could cause major problems. For example, standing in one server, the player sees a tank rolling in his direction but still far off; when he switches servers, he discovers that the tank is actually right on top of him. Even to an observer it can look very strange—an entity can be seen to skip boundaries as an out-of-sync position is suddenly updated to a correct one.

Business Issues

By now I've shown you that MMO projects are pretty complex beasts to plan. Combine the work required to create a stable server application with the cost of the hardware for a strong operating platform, and it adds up to a simple truth: *MMO games are expensive.* Even with that in mind, you may still have the resources and/or backing to go ahead with the project; in this case, I salute you and present the following issues for your consideration.

Business Structure

Once you've developed the MMO game, are you going to run it yourself, or are you going to set up a separate company to do that? It's like a franchise; the new firm is purely dedicated to running the game that you have developed. It's not hard to find ways to flow money from the new firm back into the old—royalty payments would be the obvious choice—and control can be kept by simply owning the new firm. The advantage is that the finances of the game and of the developer are kept separate; if the game is making losses, it doesn't eat into the developer's own finances, only the game runner's.

Maintenance Costs

It won't surprise you to know that if you're going to run a load of servers, you need to supply them with electricity, keep them in a building somewhere, and probably keep that building secure. You'll probably also need to employ a few people to keep them running and deal with crashes and crises. Of course, that means you'll need to heat the building, too (though the heat from 30 servers may be enough, if you can persuade your staff to huddle together a bit). So purely to keep the game running in the same state as it was at launch, you're already running a small office. If you're lucky, your publisher will handle things like subscription payments for you, but you should consider the scenario in which you have to handle that sort of thing yourself. You'd try and automate the actual payment process as much as possible, hopefully to the extent that a problem-free signup requires no human interaction at all; but you'll still need a staff of people on support to deal with the more severe payment and connection problems.

Content Development

As noted previously, games that aren't continually revised and updated tend to lose player interest. So how will you go about developing new content for the game? You could keep the team who wrote it in the first place as the people behind the project, but that does keep them from moving on to other projects. You could subcontract. You could hire a permanent development team to keep adding to the game. If you've opted for the franchise approach I suggested earlier, this may be the most attractive option—hire a game designer and crew of artists and programmers to "grow" the game from its initial launch state.

One option that doesn't seem to be as common is that of using the player base for content. It's quite possible that there are talented artists or designers in the community; perhaps it would be worth setting up a mechanism whereby they can contribute content they'd like to see in the game?

Revenue Stream

It's something of a foregone conclusion that you will want to generate a constant stream of revenue from the game *somehow*—at the very least to pay for maintenance costs, assuming no new content is being developed. How exactly will you do it? Purely through subscription fees? Will you charge for the initial client portion of the game (the retailed, boxed copy)? How will the subscriptions work—will it be one-fee-fits-all, or different subscription levels for people playing the game to different levels? Will there be unlockable content for players paying more?

There are a few other options to consider. One of the biggest is advertising—is it plausible to try and sell product placements in the game? *Unreal Tournament 2004* did this with a fair amount of success. The fantasy setting of many MMO games often makes product placement difficult, but it's still something to be considered. Beyond actual in-game ads, perhaps there are places within the game's user interface where ads can be integrated, such as in menu screens.

Middleware

There's already middleware out there aimed specifically at MMO games— Butterfly.net's *Butterfly Grid* is one example. Such middleware aims to provide both an operating platform and server application framework upon which you can build your own game without needing to deal with many of the issues raised in this article. There is a certain loss of control, and of course it isn't free, but it's another option that should definitely be considered.

Conclusion

This article has just been a taster of some of the issues facing a developer who wants to enter a project into the MMO market. I've more or less sidestepped the game design issues inherent in such games—and yes, there are many further decisions to be made in that area. It is quite telling to note that of all the MMO games out there, only eight or so have more than 50,000 subscribers (www.mmogchart.com).

Still, while it may be tough work, the MMO genre *does* provide some very unique opportunities for game designs, most of which have not yet been explored. As the proliferation of broadband technologies continues across the world, the size of the target market increases, and MMO gaming looks like it's going to stick around for quite a while.

INDEX

mod development, 237
press release, 239
updating with current information, 69
Welch, Jack, 233
Westward, 195
what you like doing, 98
where people get product, 38
Wikipedia, 25
will to make it happen, 150
window displaying stats, 135
Windows, 126
WIPO, 73
work-for-hire, 91, 93–94, 184

workflow, 66–67, 225
working virtually, 102
workstations, 61
wrapping up, 68

X

XP approach, 217–219

Z

zlib, 29